GREAT TOM

GREAT TOM

Notes Towards the Definition

of T. S. Eliot

T. S. MATTHEWS

1817

HARPER & ROW, PUBLISHERS

New York, Evanston, San Francisco
London

Portions of this book have previously appeared in *The Atlantic Monthly* and *Vogue Magazine*.

GREAT TOM: NOTES TOWARDS THE DEFINITION OF T. S. ELIOT. Copyright © 1973, 1974 by T. S. Matthews. All rights reserved. Printed in the United States of America. No part of this book may be used or reproduced in any manner whatsoever without written permission except in the case of brief quotations embodied in critical articles and reviews. For information address Harper & Row, Publishers, Inc., 10 East 53rd Street, New York, N.Y. 10022. Published simultaneously in Canada by Fitzhenry & Whiteside Limited, Toronto.

FIRST EDITION

Designed by Sidney Feinberg

Library of Congress Cataloging in Publication Data

Matthews, Thomas Stanley, 1901–
  Great Tom: notes towards the definition of T. S. Eliot.
  Bibliography: p.
  1. Eliot, Thomas Stearns, 1888–1965—Biography.
I. Title.
PS3509.L43Z737   821'.9'12 [B]   73–14068
ISBN 0–06–012838–0

To Frances Lindley, whose idea it was

Contents

Illustrations

TSE, John Hayward, Christopher Sykes. *Courtesy Christopher Sykes.*

TSE, age sixty-seven. *Courtesy James F. Coyne, Black Star.*

TSE in Nassau in 1959. *Copyright © Slim Aarons.*

Acknowledgments

It is now a common practice among biographers to acknowledge their gratitude to all those who have helped them in any way. I too am happy to have such a list. I might also have made some less usual acknowledgments: to those who did not answer my letters, or who denied me access to various unpublished papers, or who refused to see me. (To some of these I owe thanks for their courtesy in writing to tell me why. And perhaps I should name the chief of these: Valerie Eliot, T. S. Eliot's widow and sole executrix, who felt herself bound —at least for seven years after his death—to carry out her husband's expressed wish that no biography of him should be written. Although she has now changed her mind, and will choose an official biographer, the reversal comes too late to affect the writing of this book.)

My thanks are due to William S. Dix, Librarian of Princeton University Library, for access to the unrestricted T. S. Eliot letters there; to Mrs. Holly Hall, head of the Manuscript Division of the Washington University Libraries, for access to various Eliot papers; to Professor George H. Healey, Curator of Rare Books, Cornell University Library, for access to some Eliot letters; to Dr. A. N. L. Munby, the Librarian of King's College, Cambridge, for access to those parts of the late John Hayward's Eliot collection not reserved under Hayward's will or under the college's arrangement with T. S. Eliot's Literary Executrix; to D. Pepys-Whiteley, Deputy Keeper of the Old Library at Magdalene College, Cambridge, for access to the Eliot collection there; to Dr. Stuart C. Sherman, John Hay Librarian at

Brown University, for access to the manuscripts and books of the Eliot collection there; to Dr. Robert Shackleton, Bodley's Librarian, for access to the Vivienne Eliot papers.

I am also grateful for help from the late Conrad Aiken, Mrs. B. J. L. Ainsworth, Professor William Arrowsmith, George Aschman, the Rt. Hon. the Earl of Avon, Thomas Barbour, Mrs. Ellwood Beatty, Jr., Mrs. Sybille Bedford, Mrs. Wilbur Bender, John F. Benton, Sir Isaiah Berlin, Blair F. Bigelow, George Bijur, Mrs. Cecil Binney, Noel Blakiston, Mervin Block, Professor George Boas, Mrs. Fredson Bowers, Christopher Bradby, Miss Jeanne Broberg, Cleanth Brooks, the Rev. D. H. Bryant, Mrs. Alden Taylor Bryan, Baroness Moura Budberg, the Rev. Bernard G. Buley, D. M. Burt, J. Douglas Bush, the Rev. John V. Butler, Roger Butterfield, Mr. and Mrs. John Cahill, the Rev. Henry T. Callan, S.J., J. W. Carter, William Clary, Marquis Childs, Nevill Coghill, Mrs. Gordon Chalmers, Mrs. George Davol, Peter Davison, F. W. Deakin, Mrs. Jean Raphael Demos, Lady Mary Dunn, Mrs. David du Vivier, Mather G. Eliot, Dr. Thomas H. Eliot, Osborn Elliott, Professor Richard Ellmann, Mrs. Dorothy O. Elsmith, J. E. S. Fawcett, James A. Fechheimer, Professor John Finley, Miss Joan Fitzgerald, Maxwell E. Foster, William Frankel, Joseph E. Garland, Vernon Goslin, Mrs. Maurice A. Glasser, Professor William S. Gray, Thomas Griffith, D. J. Hawkings, Professor George H. Healey, Professor Peter Heath, Miss Jeanne Heaton, Sir Nicholas and Lady Henderson, P. O. Hereward, Mrs. Alan Hodge, Harley P. Holden, Philip Hofer, Mrs. George F. Howe, Professor Charles Kaplan, Mrs. A. Kerr, Mrs. Wendell Kerr, Mrs. Wyncie King, Dr. Russell Kirk, Professor J. G. Keogh, Quentin Keynes, Robert Lasch, Mr. and Mrs. Laurie Lee, the late C. Day Lewis, Professor Harry Levin, O. S. L. Low, Professor William S. Livingston, Philip Mairet, Mr. and Mrs. Raymond J. Mitnik, Jack H. Mooney, Professor Marston Morse, Frank Morley, the Rev. George E. Mullard, John Nicoll, Charles Norman, Eric Norris, Dr. Patrick O'Brien, Colin Oliver, Mrs. A. R. Orage, the Rev. Lionel Ostler, Mrs. Lola Paulsen, Ph.D., Moish Pearlman, Mrs. Virginia W. Powel, Sir Alec Randall, Professor Lindsay Rogers, Professor Edouard Roditi, Mrs. Robert N. Roth, Mrs. Vera Russell, Norman Saunders, Henry Eliot Scott, Sir Sacheverell Sitwell, Dr. James Brainerd Smith, T. Spera, John Stanley, the Rev. Victor Stanley, Mrs. Harold Steinberg, Richard Stern, Noel Stock, Miss Mary H. Tolman, Professor John C. Thirlwall, Professor Willard Thorp, Mrs. Bayard Turnbull, Mrs. Igor Vinogradoff, John David Watkins, the late Edmund Wilson, Mrs. Henry Weddle, Jr., Mr. and Mrs. Richardson Wood.

More particularly, I wish to thank Mrs. Antony Tyley for all the chores done and errands run with cheerful efficiency in pursuit of her snarklike assignments; and to Mrs. J. H. Bennett for her devoted care in typing and retyping the manuscript of this book; to Mrs. Roland Oakeley for invaluable information about her brother, John Hayward; and to Maurice Haigh-Wood for his memories of his sister, Vivienne Eliot. I owe especial thanks to Mrs. Robert Gibney for the time and energy she spent in tracking down the surviving friends of Miss Emily Hale. To Dr. Donald C. Gallup, of Yale University, bibliographer of Eliot and Joyce, I wish to express my thanks for lending me a patient ear and giving me generous amounts of his time. I am deeply indebted to Miss Joyce Weiner and her sister Margery: to the first for much-needed encouragement and for valuable suggestions and for many useful practical hints and criticisms; to the second for her gallant attempt to bring order into the chaos of my files. I am most grateful to Christopher Sykes for reading the typescript and for saving me from several gaffes.

I owe the book itself to Mrs. Frances Lindley, my editor, whose idea it was. I owe my thanks to her not only for that but for her unfaltering encouragement and help as well. And, finally, I wish to thank my wife, who read the whole manuscript at least twice and in its varying stages and endured my Eliot-centered conversation for three whole years.

T. S. M.

Cavendish, Suffolk

Foreword

When the New York publishers of this book asked me to write a life of T. S. Eliot, I was curious to know why they had thought of me. The reasons seemed to be—apart from the coincidence of my sharing Eliot's initials and first name—the general similarity of our upbringing and background. Both of us were born and brought up in the American Middle West, the sons of formidable fathers. As children, we were both impressed with a sense of hierarchy, a reverence for proper authority. We began our education in the same kind of Eastern school and university, moved to England, the country from which in the seventeenth century our forbears had emigrated, became Anglo-Catholics and married Englishwomen. Both of us were hypochondriacs, but did not like to be told so. We both stopped smoking when we were sixty-eight. Both lived longer in London than anywhere else, and belonged to two of the same London clubs.

There the likenesses ceased. There was as little probability of my becoming a British subject as of my winning the Nobel Prize for Literature; and, far from being a great poet, a powerful critic and a brilliantly unsuccessful playwright, I was a writer who went astray and became a not altogether repentant journalist.

I had met T. S. Eliot on widely spaced occasions over some twenty-five years, and he had treated me with the same tender but formal solicitude he showed in all such encounters. Mine was an outsider's acquaintance: we could not be called friends. When we met, however, he remembered or almost remembered who I was. I think I could be listed among his not quite anonymous admirers.* I would have given a great deal to have him read some verses I had written, but never nerved myself to ask him.

My first reply to the publisher's proposal was a question: What would Mrs. Eliot's attitude be, and would she be willing to put her late husband's papers at my disposal? In due course the publisher sent me Mrs. Eliot's answer. She could not give the slightest encouragement or help to any biography of her husband, because he had forbidden such a thing in a memorandum left with his will. Some day his biography must be written, of course, but she could not assist in any such project. In spite of this flat refusal her tone was friendly (we had met, two or three times, while her husband was alive).

For reasons which I still fail to understand, the publisher found this letter encouraging. I did not; but by this time the idea of writing Eliot's biography had begun to appeal to me strongly. I signed a contract for the book. Was this a mistake? Some people have said so; and if they read this book perhaps they may see no reason to change their minds. Those who would put unauthorized biography on a level with graverobbing might call it an offense rather than a mistake. But not many, I hope, will take so extreme a view.

For seven years after his death in 1965, Valerie Eliot conscientiously carried out her husband's injunction. No one who was suspected of planning to write a life of Eliot was permitted to see any of his unpublished papers. She also enlisted the support of the Eliot family, and many of his surviving friends.

As late as 1956, when he was sixty-eight, Eliot had not yet hardened his heart against biographers. He said then: "I do not suggest that the personality and the private life of a dead poet constitute sacred ground on which the psychologist must not tread. The scientist must be at liberty to study such material as his curiosity leads him to investigate, as long as the victim is dead and the laws of libel cannot be invoked to stop him. Nor is there any reason why biographies of poets should not be written. They are very useful. Any critic seriously concerned with a man's work should be expected to know something about the man's life."

---

*A friend of mine, on being introduced to Eliot, could think of nothing to say except that she knew me, whereupon Eliot replied, "Oh, I could never measure up to Tom Matthews's idea of me!" This is a remark I should like to believe.

This public statement of Eliot's, hedged about though it is with "if and perhaps and but" and embellished with his characteristic donnish jokiness, is clearly at odds with the memorandum he later attached to his will. What was it, or who was it, that changed his mind? This is one of the awkward questions that are bound to be asked as long as the Eliot papers are kept locked up like a guilty secret. And perhaps the answer will not be found among his papers.

Seven years after Eliot's death, Valerie Eliot admitted that her husband's veto would have to be disregarded. The circumstances that forced her hand were of two kinds: the publication of four books about Eliot, two of them memoirs, the other two supposedly studies of his work but containing a good deal of biographical material; and the growth of scandalous rumors and gossip about him. In order to scotch these rumors and correct the record, Valerie Eliot felt obliged to start looking for a biographer. In an interview in *The Observer* (February 20, 1972) she was reported as saying: "The right person will not be easy to find. He must have a real understanding of the American background, in addition to knowing England and Europe. Ideally he should be able to sympathize with my husband's religious outlook, and, above all, he must have empathy."

In short, there is to be, after all, an authorized biography of Eliot. The official biographer will have to please the family or a committee, may have to smooth over some rough facts, perhaps even suppress others. A good many private papers will still not be available, even to him. Such a biography is not likely to be definitive (if indeed there can be such a thing). And no matter how empathetic with Eliot the chosen biographer may be, his point of view as a biographer will differ, in Richard Ellmann's phrase, "from that mixture of self-recrimination and self-justification which the great writer, like lesser men and women, has made the subject of his lifelong conversation with himself."

All biographies, whether they are official, definitive or, like this one, intermediate, must be to some extent guesswork. "Hints and guesses, hints followed by guesses." As Professor Ellmann says, "Biographies will continue to be archival, but the best ones will offer speculative conjectures, hypotheses . . . the effort to know another person as well as we know a character in fiction, and better than we know ourselves, is not frivolous. It may even be, for reader as for writer, an essential part of experience." Of the awkward questions a biographer is obliged to ask, many must be unanswerable. The evidence on which we base our knowledge of a man's life is, in essence, circumstantial. "Some circumstantial evidence is very strong, as when you find a trout in the milk." Yes, but our Anglo-Saxon law has assayed the value of circumstantial evidence by declaring that no one charged with a capital crime shall be convicted on such evidence alone.

Although for our knowledge of a man's life we must still depend primarily on the archivist, on the known record, on what and on whom does the archivist depend? On eyewitness evidence, on documents, on hearsay. Called to the witness box himself, the defendant may find it difficult or impossible to answer certain questions with complete candor. Eyewitnesses, as we know, cannot always be wholly trusted: they contradict one another, they misremember or fail to see; sometimes they lie. Documents are simply eyewitnesses at one or more remove. A sleazy newspaper report, perhaps with some of its facts wrong or with their emphasis askew, ripens in time into "an invaluable firsthand account." In the case of such an elusive character as T. S. Eliot a biographer should be happy if, in the course of his struggles against failure, he can now and again strike bedrock, if only a glancing blow. As the reader may have noticed, the subtitle of this book is "Notes Towards the Definition of T. S. Eliot." The phrase suggested itself not merely as a bantering echo of Eliot's *Notes Towards the Definition of Culture* but also as an acknowledgment, like his, that this will not be the last word on the subject.

An authoritative biography of Eliot is needed, and some day will certainly be written; and the longer such a biography is postponed, the more secondhand it must be, for the survivors among those who knew Eliot at firsthand are fast dwindling and will soon be gone.

With all the jealously guarded secrets (or, at any rate, the jealously guarded bits of paper) buried at Harvard, at King's College, Cambridge, at the University of Texas, at Princeton, not to be disclosed until all who saw him plain are safely dead, no biographer could claim full knowledge of all the facts of Eliot's life. But we have enough to be going on with. We have everything Eliot published during his lifetime (and since his death perhaps a bit more than he would have liked us to see); we know the main facts of his life; there are still a few survivors who knew him, whether or not they knew who he was.

(There is no substitute for the man who has actually been there, even if he hardly knows where he has been.) There are also, I am told, more than a thousand books in the British Museum about Eliot and his work. I have not counted them or even read them all.

In the pages that follow, some awkward questions will have to be asked, whether or not they can be satisfactorily answered. These are some of them: Who *was* T. S. Eliot? Why did he want to keep his private life a secret? ("After such knowledge, what forgiveness?" Is that what he thought?) Is there less, or more, in his poetry than meets the eye? To what extent does his poetry depend on plagiarism and parody? Did he have a "tin ear"? Was he a phony scholar? A phony saint? What sort of American was he? Was he a Christian? Why did he take Ezra Pound's editing of *The Waste Land* so meekly? Did Pound create Eliot? Were his plays any good? Why was Eliot's first marriage so unhappy? Was he a homosexual? Did Bertrand Russell seduce Vivienne Eliot? Why was *Ode* published once and then dropped? Why did Eliot abandon his first wife? Because she was mad? *Was* she mad? Should he have abandoned her, in any case? How deep did Eliot's affectations go? Was he a great poet—or a monstrous clever fellow? Did late happiness rescue him from horror but turn him into a dullard?

And was Mrs. Eliot wrong, was she letting the Persians through the pass, in abandoning the defense of her husband's Spartan position? Should Eliot's wishes not be respected, after all? The short answer is, under the circumstances, No. The more that human beings can learn about other human beings, this side of nausea, the better. There is more to learn than we can take in, and not much time in which to learn it. And from whom should we learn but from those who—no matter what they think of themselves—act, ponder, speak, or write in ways we can all admire but which few of us can hope to emulate? T. S. Eliot was of that kidney.

With all these foregoing considerations in mind, a biography of sorts can now be written. This is a biography, of sorts.

Great Tom is cast,
And Christ Church bells
Ring one-two-three-four-five-six
And Tom comes last.

—Seventeenth-century round

ONE

▄▄

A Strong Brown God

(1 8 8 8 – 1 9 0 4)

1

THE CITY of St. Louis has always roused in its inhabitants a fierce love and a protective pride. One of its few flaws that they will admit is the climate. Winter is likely to be rawly inclement, summer steamy with prickly heat; the region is visited by violent storms, floods, sometimes by tornadoes, even by an occasional slight earthquake. These facts are admitted, with a shrug; the compensations are considered to be overwhelming. The nature of the city itself, its personality, in the eyes of St. Louisans, is unique: friendly, comfortable, *gemütlich*— qualities not always perceptible to the outlander, and untranslatable. To the outside world the city is brought to mind by two popular songs, one now quite outmoded, commemorating a long-past World's Fair ("Meet me in St. Louis, Louis, meet me at the Fair"); the other an American classic, "St. Louis Blues." A poem entitled *The Dry Salvages*, which celebrates the river and some domestic scenes in St. Louis, is not sufficiently well known to enhance the city's name.

St. Louis is disjointed, ugly, and amiable, a frump with an agreeable personality and some attractive physical features, like a woman whose plainness is redeemed or at least considerably reduced by good hands or a pair of "fine eyes." To those Americans—and they are not a negligible number—whom New York horrifies by its polyglot sharpness, murderous morals, and heartless manners, or who are

1

repelled by the strident crassness of Chicago, St. Louis can appear as wholehearted as home.

The hopefulness of St. Louis had in it, and perhaps still has, something fresher and more innocent than the blowhard optimism common to most American towns. St. Louis's ambition to better itself included the desire to become more civilized as well as bigger and richer. The Germans, who started coming in the 1830s and who came in increasing numbers after 1848, Europe's *annus terribilis,* so that in 1860 "more than half of St. Louis's population of 186,000 had been born abroad," brought with them a tradition of music, liberalism, and earnest scholarship, which has infused the civic life of the city.

The vulgarity of St. Louis, more parochial and lesser-scale than New York's or Chicago's, does not reach for imperial magnificence but yearns toward civilized comfort. One of its chief manifestations was the residential enclosures in the west end, enclaves of large stone or brick houses fenced off from the public streets, with massive gateways emblazoned with their exclusive names—often a title from the Waverley novels. In 1892 they overawed Theodore Dreiser, the Indiana bumpkin who had come from Chicago to work as a reporter on the *Globe-Democrat,* but his inimitably ungainly prose was a perfect match for them: "The first time I saw one of these *places* I was staggered by its exclusive air and the beauty and even grandeur of some of the great houses in it—newly manufactured exclusiveness. Here were great gray or white or brownstone affairs, bright, almost gaudy, with great verandas, astonishing doorways, flights of stone steps, heavily and richly draped windows, immense carriage-houses, parked and flowered lawns."

The city has a better claim to architectural fame. In 1890 the great Louis Sullivan, not yet recognized as great, had designed in the Wainwright Building a structure which Frank Lloyd Wright called "the master key to the skyscraper as Architecture the world over"; and in 1892 a competition among outstanding architects resulted in the Union Station, which is still something to see although it is no longer of much use.

When St. Louisans attempt to describe their town they are apt to cite singular items: the Arch, Shaw's Garden, the Milles fountain, the Art Museum, Washington University, Forest Park, the Zoo. They are so accustomed to the city's face that they no longer see it. It is an ugly face—if indeed it can be thought of as a face; it is really more like a two-headed monster. Downtown St. Louis, strung out along the western bank of the Mississippi, is miles away from the residential district, and these two areas are connected, or separated, by half-deserted and decaying slums.

From its eighteenth-century beginnings as a French trading post, a smear of dwellings along the greasy bank of the Mississippi, the development of St. Louis has been rapid. British soldiers ousted the French traders, German immigrants followed; the railways came, first supplementing, then superseding the river steamers. Until Chicago sprinted from behind to win the race, St. Louis was the railway center of the United States, and had high hopes of becoming the chief city of mid-America.

In 1834, when the Reverend William Greenleaf Eliot arrived from Boston to save St. Louis's soul, or to give it one, the town was only a small town. Dr. Eliot was a small man, "short of stature and of delicate frame," whose energy was relentless. " 'If I could have had Dr. Eliot for a partner,' said an able man of business once, 'we should have made most of the money west of the Alleghenies.' " This was just the kind of Midwestern thinking Dr. Eliot wanted to change. He thought of himself as a spiritual leader, a son of Mary, but he was driven and consumed by incessant ambition. The ambition was to excel in doing good, and his kind of good demanded visible results —money collected, buildings raised, laws passed, decisions carried out, the sick nursed, the hungry fed. He was primarily a man of action, a natural son of Martha. He regarded his fellow men as raw material for good works. What he really wanted to do to St. Louis was not to convert it but to civilize it. Though he misread his own nature, he had a keen sense of his worth: ". . . on one occasion being present at a gathering where there were many large men, he was asked how he felt. 'Like a silver shilling among copper pennies,' he quickly answered."

He was a Unitarian, as all proper Eliots were.* One of his great-

---

*The Unitarians are a Protestant sect which apparently originated in Poland and Hungary in the seventeenth century, appeared in England in the eighteenth century, were so called because they reacted against the Trinitarian view of God and believed in His single personality: Christ being only His Son and the Holy Ghost nowhere.

grandfathers, the Reverend Andrew Eliot, was pastor of the Old North Church in Boston; he was offered the presidency of Harvard College and refused it. His father had been a shipowner whose fortunes were ruined by the War of 1812, whereupon his cousin, John Adams, second President of the United States, got him a job in the civil service in Washington.

In St. Louis Dr. Eliot founded the Unitarian Church of the Messiah. After three years, when he felt that he could safely leave it for a few months, he went east to fetch his chosen bride, Abby Cranch, daughter of a district court judge in Washington, D.C. The journey in 1837 was not one to be lightly undertaken.

Mr. Eliot and she went from Washington to Philadelphia in the steam-cars, which had been running only a few weeks, and they were "nearly shaken to pieces." They sailed to New York by steamer, and thence by the Erie Canal to Buffalo, and across Lake Erie to Cleveland. They started from Cleveland to Columbus, Ohio, on a canal-boat, but a broken lock necessitated their transference to an old broken-down stage-coach, driven by a colored man equally ancient and historic. After riding all night they reached Cincinnati in time for the St. Louis steamer. As the river was low and full of sand-bars, its usual condition when not inundating the country, they were two weeks in reaching their destination, and nearly ran out of provisions . . . in St. Louis . . . the smoke and mud [were] even worse than she had imagined.

Education was the field that most powerfully attracted William Eliot, and he helped to found Washington University (originally Eliot Seminary, changed at his request to Washington Institute). Shortly afterward came Smith Academy, a boys' school affiliated with the university and now defunct; a few years later Mary Institute, a school for girls, still flourishing. Dr. Eliot wanted a literate citizenry but not mass education. "To educate one man thoroughly, to make him one of those that stand first. . . . One best was more than many good."

Unitarianism became the most etherealized and most intellectual of New England's sects, clustering around Harvard in the early nineteenth century and making King's Chapel, Boston, its headquarters. Its two best-known preachers were William Ellery Channing and Edward Everett Hale. Ralph Waldo Emerson began as a Unitarian minister but went up higher and became a Transcendentalist (with Henry Thoreau, Bronson Alcott, Orestes Brownson, and Margaret Fuller).

Unitarians believe in good works but their good works are apt to be cultural, not to say bookish. To reduce them to English terms, they form a kind of Fabian Society among the Protestant churches.

The inescapable politics of his day forced him into another unpopular position. Missouri was a slave state. Dr. Eliot abhorred slavery and foresaw its finish if Missouri could be kept in the Union. Like Lincoln, he believed that the only sure way of abolishing slavery was to keep the Union intact. This attitude drew furious attacks from the abolitionists, who demanded that all slaves be freed forthwith, let states' rights and the Union itself fall where they might. "The mere fact of a minister's continued residence in a slave State was considered by some of the 'extreme friends of freedom' as an unpardonable offense, implying approval of an obnoxious system." Nevertheless, the Fabian tactics of Dr. Eliot and his party prevailed: the Union was preserved and slavery was abolished. Unlike Lincoln, who could only hope that he was on God's side, William Eliot had no doubts that God was with him; he was sure that the Civil War was "a struggle whose moral grandeur has never been equalled . . . the war of barbarism against civilization, of slavery against freedom . . . the great event of the nineteenth century."

War not only brings out the best (sometimes the unsuspected best) in some people; it may also introduce them to their right job. It was the Civil War that gave Dr. Eliot full scope for his managerial powers. The Western Sanitary Commission, which had nothing to do with cleaning streets and everything to do with military hospitals, became his second career. By May 1, 1862, there were fifteen military hospitals in and near St. Louis, accommodating six thousand patients; when Memphis was captured and the Mississippi opened as far south as Vicksburg, three more hospitals were set up in Tennessee and Arkansas. When money was needed, Dr. Eliot was sent east to advertise the Commission and raise the money. He did both.

With the war won, the Union preserved, and slavery abolished, at least in principle, Dr. Eliot returned to the paths of peace. He had never relinquished his ministry at the Church of the Messiah; he now added to his duties there the stern pursuit of civic virtue. He severely arraigned the grand jury in St. Louis for recommending that prostitution be regulated (hence condoned): "I am sorry to be again at this work, but the Devil shall not win if I can help it." And he was a mighty advocate of "temperance"—meaning the prohibition of liquor, not only in Missouri but throughout the United States.

One of his fellow laborers in the vineyard was a hunchback

preacher named Henry Giles. Mr. Giles was invited by Dr. Eliot to come to St. Louis and deliver some temperance lectures. On the way, Mr. Giles stopped to make a speech in Chicago, where he fell among friends and appeared on the platform "in a state of undue exhilaration." When he reached St. Louis the news of his lapse had preceded him. Dr. Eliot forgave him, however, and told him he wanted him to lecture the following week and preach for him on Sunday. "But," said Dr. Eliot, "on this condition, that you are not to stop at the hotel. I have provided entertainment for you at a friend's house." It was once suggested, perhaps seriously, that Dr. Eliot should be appointed police commissioner of St. Louis.

His work in the educational field took up more and more of his time. In 1870 he accepted the chancellorship of Washington University and resigned from the Church of the Messiah. He remained chancellor until his death in 1887. The political scene continued to attract and distress him almost equally. At one point he urged his friend, General William T. Sherman, to offer himself for the presidency, and drew one of the most judgmatical replies that shrewd soldier ever made:

The office of President of the United States has never had the least attraction to me. It was my fortune to be somewhat behind the curtain in Taylor's administration. I witnessed the fearful agonies and throes of that good and great man Lincoln, and saw General Grant, who never swerved in war, bend and twist and writhe under the appeals and intrigues from which there was no escape, so that I look upon the office as one beyond human endurance, each year being worse and worse. . . . I do not expect to live long, and will not disturb the peace of the small remainder of my life by such hopes, fears and disappointments. The country is full of men of average ability who seek the office. Our salvation and hope as a nation must depend on the system, not the goodness or badness of the agent. In Hayes's position I would likely do pretty much as he does—certainly no better. The country is full of his equals, and I propose to leave the office to them. In no event, and under no combination of circumstances, will I allow the use of my name in that connection.

Dr. Eliot celebrated his seventy-sixth birthday, August 5, 1886, by writing a poem entitled *Nunc Dimittis:*

> Fain would I breathe that gracious word,
> Now lettest thou thy servant, Lord,
>   Depart in peace.
> When may I humbly claim that kind award,

And cares and labor cease?
With anxious heart I watch at heaven's gate—
    Answer to hear;
With failing strength I feel the increasing weight
    Of every passing year.
Hath not the time yet fully come, dear Lord,
    Thy servant to release?

Be still, my heart! In silence God doth speak,
Here is thy place; here, not at heaven's gate;
Thy task is not yet finished; frail and weak,
Doing or suffering, steadfast in thy faith,
Thy service is accepted, small or great;
His time is thine—or soon or late,
If daylight fades, work while the twilight lasts.

Except for this uncharacteristic indulgence, when he wrote it was always to get something done; he evolved a functional prose style that was easy, lambent, and lucid.

Alas for reformers! Only sixteen years after his death, St. Louis had sunk into such political corruption that it attracted the attention of S. S. McClure, who singled it out for investigation and exposure in *McClure's Magazine.* Lincoln Steffens wrote two articles on St. Louis in 1902 and 1903 for McClure's famous muckraking series, *The Shame of the Cities.*

Steffens described St. Louis as

... the government of the people, by the rascals, for the rich. ... Everything the city owned was for sale by the officers elected by the people. ... In St. Louis the regularly organized thieves who rule have sold $50,000,000 worth of franchises and other valuable municipal assets. This is the estimate made for me by a banker. ...

Go to St. Louis and you will find the habit of civic pride in them; they still boast. The visitor is told of the wealth of the residents, of the financial strength of the banks, and of the growing importance of the industries, yet he sees poorly paved, refuse-burdened streets, and dusty or mud-covered alleys; he passes a ramshackle fire-trap crowded with the sick, and learns that it is the City Hospital; he enters the "Four Courts," and his nostrils are greeted by the odor of formaldehyde used as a disinfectant, and insect powder spread to destroy vermin; he calls at the new City Hall, and finds half the entrance boarded with pine planks to cover up the unfinished interior. Finally, he turns a tap in the hotel, to see liquid mud flow into wash-basin or bath-tub. ...

As there was a scale [of bribes] for favorable legislation, so there was one for defeating bills. It made a difference in the price if there was opposition, and it made a difference whether the privilege asked was legitimate or not. But nothing was passed free of charge. . . .

Irate citizens complained to the mayor because some street lights were out and nothing was done to replace them. His reply became locally famous: "You have the moon yet—ain't it?"

2

The Eliots were not strong on discussion. The family motto was *Tace et fac* ("Shut up and get on with it"). And there were some matters that surely did not require discussion. Should not a father have the right to expect his sons to follow in his footsteps? Dr. William Greenleaf Eliot felt that he, at any rate, had the right to expect it. Yet only two of his four sons followed him into the Unitarian ministry. His second son, Henry, after graduation from his father's Washington University, simply went into business; he became a St. Louis businessman. Why? All he would ever say was, "Too much pudding choked the dog." When he broke the news to his father that he wanted to go into business, the old man said sharply, "Then your education is wasted!" He collected himself and added, "Except that it has made a man of you."

In declining the gambit—which his father did not so much offer to him as indicate, did not so much indicate as simply expect him to see for himself—Henry Eliot in effect was abdicating, or taking the first irrevocable step toward abdicating, from that leading role in American life that the Eliots and their peers had filled since the country's colonial beginnings. These first families had traditionally supplied the leading men of their communities: the divines, the scholars, the judges, the commanding officers—in short, the shepherds of the common herd.

Henry Eliot, although he withdrew from the civic traditions of his caste, remained a Unitarian, a teetotaler, a nonsmoker, a model citizen. But it would have been difficult to equate the Hydraulic-Press Brick Company, of which he became president, with the Lord's work. Though he was most certainly an upright man, in his father's eyes he had not chosen the better part.

Like his father, Henry married an Easterner. Charlotte Stearns was a teacher in the Normal School of St. Louis, but she was New England-born, and one of her forbears had been a judge in the Salem witch trials in the seventeenth century. (Andrew Eliot, her husband's ancestor, an English immigrant from East Coker, Somerset, was a juror in the same trials; he afterward recanted publicly.) When Charlotte had completed her primary duty of bearing children, in her mid-forties, she was free to crusade for the juvenile court and other remedies for delinquency. She wrote a life of her father-in-law, William Greenleaf Eliot, but her lifelong ambition was to write poetry. Her *Savonarola, a dramatic poem,* was in fact not a long poem but a series of short verses, tied together by prose passages; not bad enough to be funny, but deadly serious enough to be a bore. Her rhymes betray the fact that her Eastern accent never succumbed to the Midwestern slur: *morn* and *dawn, saw* and *pour, gone* and *torn, cross* and *source,* etc., etc.

Charlotte Eliot appears to have been one of those admirable women who have strict standards of conduct and no intimate friends, and who are admired, disliked, and feared by all who know them. Her handwriting was uncompromisingly ugly. When she made a mistake it seemed more glaring than it might have if she had not been so unbending a person. Her seventh and last child, Thomas Stearns Eliot, was born on September 26, 1888. She was then forty-five, her husband forty-seven. The sixth child, Theodora, had died in infancy, leaving a gap of nine years between little Tom and his elder brother, Henry Ware, Jr. Between Tom and his oldest sister, Ada, there was a difference of nineteen years.

William Greenleaf Eliot, his grandfather, had died the year before. In Hailey, Idaho, Ezra Loomis Pound was already two years old. In New Zealand and in England two girls were born in 1888 whose lives would intersect T. S. Eliot's, one of them critically: Katherine Mansfield and Vivienne Haigh-Wood. Edward Lear and Matthew Arnold died, each leaving Eliot a legacy which he would later collect.

For once history had no great war, pestilence, famine, or other disaster to record. Wilhelm II succeeded his father as German Emperor. The British Empire was still expanding: a protectorate was established that year over North Borneo, Brunei, and Sarawak; a royal charter was granted to the East Africa Company; Cecil Rhodes got a concession from Lobengula to mine Matabeleland for gold.

The arts too were seeing placid days, with the usual exceptions. Rodin produced his *Burghers of Calais*. William Wordsworth, although he had died thirty-eight years before, had a poem published: *The Recluse*. The only notable new poetry was George Meredith's *A Reading of Earth*. W. B. Yeats's contribution to the year was in prose, *Irish Fairy and Folk Tales*. Other literary events were J. M. Barrie's *Auld Licht Idylls*, Lord Bryce's *American Commonwealth*, C. M. Doughty's *Travels in Arabia Deserta*, and Rudyard Kipling's *Soldiers Three* and *Plain Tales from the Hills*.

To the small soul emitting his first wails in his father's house in St. Louis, not one of these names, nor any other in English poetry's stately procession of apple carts, meant a thing. For the next sixteen years, the whole long life of childhood, he would be absorbing impressions from the family life around him, getting his bearings in a perplexing world. Forty years on, he would describe this painful progress in the first part of *Animula:*

> Moving between the legs of tables and of chairs,
> Rising or falling, grasping at kisses and toys,
> Advancing boldly, sudden to take alarm,
> Retreating to the corner of arm and knee,
> . . .
>
> Confounds the actual and the fanciful,
> Content with playing-cards and kings and queens,
> What the fairies do and what the servants say.
> The heavy burden of the growing soul
> Perplexes and offends more, day by day;
> Week by week, offends and perplexes more
> With the imperatives of "is and seems"
> And may and may not, desire and control.
> The pain of living and the drug of dreams
> Curl up the small soul in the window seat
> Behind the *Encyclopaedia Britannica* . . .

He also liked looking at the pictures in "The Donkey Book," his father's name for the fat edition of *Don Quixote* with Gustave Doré illustrations. At Christmas and Thanksgiving dinners, when he was first allowed to come to the family table, he sat on this book, as his sisters and elder brother had done before him.

His father's house, in which he was born and where he lived all his St. Louis years, was a large, two-story frame house, with a wide porch, its eaves garnished with Victorian "gingerbread," across the front and around two sides; there were some shade trees in the yard. The house stood on part of a large piece of land which had belonged to William Greenleaf Eliot. Old Mrs. Eliot still lived around the corner, at 2660 Washington Avenue. Next door to the Henry Eliot house stood Mary Institute, the girls' school Dr. Eliot had founded; a wall shut off the Eliots' back garden from the school grounds. There was a door in the wall which was never opened; behind it little Tom often heard the hidden laughter of children.

On hot summer mornings, at first light, when the risk of a night prowler was no longer a dangerous possibility, the mistress of the house or one of the maids would open wide all the ground-floor windows to let in the cool dawn air. Before the sun rose high enough to collect its strength the windows were shut again and the blinds lowered. This primitive form of air conditioning was fairly effective: all day the ground-floor rooms, at least, kept their shaded coolness.

The house was lit by gas jets, and the fixtures were of two kinds: the old-fashioned sort, now largely confined to back passages, the kitchen and servants' bedrooms, from which issued a flat, pentecostal leaf of flame; and the much more sophisticated Welsbach burner, a fragile cylinder that looked as if it were made of white ashes, which when lit leapt into incandescence and emitted a slight hissing sound.

3

The Eliot house was long ago demolished, and Mary Institute, now an independent girls' school, moved to another site. Even in Tom Eliot's childhood the only "good address" was in the west end of town, far from the river. It would never have occurred to an Eliot to live, or to think of living, in one of the vulgar residential "places." The Eliots of St. Louis, known as "the St. Louis branch" of the family, lived in St. Louis but did not consider themselves St. Louisans, at least in the ordinary sense: they were Eliots. Superior people? Yes, of course, but not showy. There was no smoking in the Eliot house, and no drinking either; to buy candy for oneself was considered selfish indulgence. The atmosphere was cool, orderly, civic-minded New England. Moral passion (Shut up) and business efficiency (Get on with it) combined. On cold winter mornings a maid would come to little Tom's room to light the fire under a kettle of water and pull a tin tub from under the bed. His childhood God was Unitarian, authoritarian, absolute, grandfatherly.

Expatriation was in the Eliot blood. The early Eliots were expatriates from England; the later ones from Massachusetts. William Greenleaf Eliot revisited whenever he could the capitol of his soul. In his later years it was his habit to take his family for a summer holiday to the New England coast; his son Henry followed his example. It was not a popular example. Plain people in St. Louis suspected and disliked the East. "When the long, sultry, summer days come, and all fashionable St. Louis have betaken themselves to far-away sweat-boxes, called summer resorts, at Newport, Rye Beach, Long Branch, Saratoga, and Niagara, the residue of the people, which constitute by far the most numerous, and infinitely the most respectable elements of the inhabitants, remain at home, and seek recreation and enjoyments in their own way, in the suburban groves of the city. . . . The well-to-do and sensible go to the lakes of Wisconsin and Minnesota, or to the mountains of Colorado and Utah; or perchance to the ancient seats of arts and culture in Europe. . . ."

The Eliots were not aristocrats (*pace* the resentful St. Louis vulgarians) in the European or even the Virginian sense, but bluestocking bourgeois. All the same, they felt superior to St. Louis.

Being by far the youngest, little Tom naturally came in for a great deal of attention. Was he spoiled? He was pampered in some ways, put-upon in others. Like clucking, protective, apprehensive, and possessive hens, his mother and sisters sat on him and brooded over him. His father, almost stone deaf, middle-aged, and remote, yet managed some small, awkward gestures of conciliation toward his perplexing offspring. He would draw faces on their boiled eggs (he was also renowned for his drawings of cats), and he made a point of calling nasturtiums "nestertians," hoping that one of them would correct him. No one in the entire Eliot connection could beat him at chess; and his handwriting was un-Americanly tidy and legible. His son Tom copied it, to good effect. Was it from his deaf, dry father's bearded lips that he first heard the saying: "The Eliots have to put on their climbing irons to get up a molehill"?

His mother did not like children. She never said so; she bore seven and did her maternal duty by them, but none of them needed to be told how she felt. To her intimates she signed herself "Lottie," and she referred to her husband as "Hal"; this impression of easy informality was misleading. Little Tom's precocious reading was not exactly censored, but there were certain books—vulgar stuff—he was not allowed to read. *Tom Sawyer* and *Huckleberry Finn** were two of them. There was no objection to the *Encyclopaedia Britannica.*

Tom had his treats, and remembered them: the zoo in Forest Park, where he was allowed to photograph the "rather mangy buffalo"; being taken to the Eads Bridge, one of the glories of nineteenth-century St. Louis, to see the Mississippi in flood;

> . . . the river with its cargo of dead Negroes, cows and
>   chicken coops,

expeditions along the high limestone bluffs above the river, searching for fossil shellfish; the steamboats "blowing in" New Year's Day. Certain smells and sights haunted his memory years later:

> In the rank ailanthus of the April dooryard,
> In the smell of grapes on the autumn table,
> And the evening circle in the winter gaslight.

A portrait of him by his sister Charlotte, painted when he was about ten, shows him in profile, in a hard chair, dressed in the formal suit and laced boots prescribed for well-brought-up little boys in those days, large-browed and languid-eyed, downcast on the open book in his left hand. A touching picture; also, in hindsight, a formidable one. Here is a small boy; here is the poet in chrysalis. A photograph of him with his nurse, taken a few years earlier, is more to the general taste. He looks sturdy and mischievous, an engaging rascal; his beguiling dimpled smile and straight gaze are charms that will be with him all his life. His Irish nursemaid, Annie Dunne, the very spit of Mary Poppins, leans possessively alongside, one arm akimbo, lips pursed ("Mind you, I said nothing!"), backed by the grimy stone and

---

*Forbidden also to his brother Henry, who read it anyway. T. S. Eliot later lamented, "If only I had read it when I was young. Now I read it as a critic does."

brick wall of a city house. All this pictorial evidence shows that he was bright (very bright), thoughtful, reserved, and mischievous—as mischievous, that is to say, as his overwhelming family would allow him to be.

It has been said that children are savages, and crave authority—a sweeping statement that generates some dust but does seem to clear the ground. The savage in little Tom rarely showed more than the glint of an eyeball, glimpsed for a doubtful second between the waving fronds and the underbrush; even in later life he kept under cover, and only the whiz of the dart from his blowgun betrayed his presence in the thicket. The pitiless, lurking, savage hunter and the circumspect, rigidly conformist Puritan—these two mutually hostile sides of his nature must have begun their lifelong warfare in his childhood. But the craving for authority was plainly there, in the unquestioning obedience he rendered to the hierarchy that lorded it over his world: his mother, his father, his teachers, God. It was a trait that was to stay with him all his life. Years later he acknowledged: "I think it is a very good beginning for any child, to be brought up to reverence such institutions [the church, the state, the university] and to be taught that personal and selfish aims should be subordinated to the general good which they represent."

Who can tell what is going on in a small boy's head? The only witness, the child himself, is less witness than observer, most of the time enthralled, some of the time in flight (either from fear or from what he will later call boredom), and never capable of reporting his observations in any form that his elders can understand. He is seldom even interested in trying except when something has gone terribly wrong, and then he is tongue-tied with terror or indignation, or bawling his head off—in any case quite unable to find words to fit his condition. His elders look at him, absently noting that they must really do something about that boy one of these days, or wondering to themselves what in the world is going on inside him. They see that he is more alive to the events within him than to the world outside. The best comment they can manage is like a grown-up sigh of resignation:

A boy's will is the wind's will,
And the thoughts of youth are long, long thoughts.

They are begging the whole question: *What is going on in that boy's head?* Yet the question itself must have occurred sometimes to young Tom Eliot's middle-aged parents, or at any rate to his mother. Did she see the twinkle in his eye, the cunning little rascal? Did she muse, watching his faraway look, "Now what on earth do you suppose—"? It is fairly safe to assume that she had no tiniest inkling of the fact, which would have been a most alarming fact, that within this small boy's brain, "the word within a word, unable to speak a word," some infinitely gentle, infinitely suffering thing was readying itself to set a tiger among the pigeons.

4

Annie Dunne was the first exciting woman in Tom Eliot's life. His mother, omnipresent as the climate, was cool or chilly weather; his sisters were sisters—no excitement there. He remembered Annie as "the earliest personal influence" on him, besides his parents. She laughed at him as a small oddity: he tickled her Irish humor. When she took him with her to the little Catholic Church on the corner of Jefferson Avenue and Locust Street, did he notice and file for future reference the liturgical order and richness of the Mass and compare it with the bloodless prolixities of Unitarian prayer meetings at the Church of the Messiah?

He was a delicate child, or thought to be, which amounted to the same thing. The home remedies, the lotions and standard antiseptics, tonics, and germicides of the day were familiar to the Eliot household and particularly to little Tom: peroxide, antiphlogistene, *baume analgésique,* Listerine, camphor ice, malt extract, Castoria. Parental anxiety about his health may explain why he was not sent to his first school until he was seven or eight. Miss Lockwood's was a primary school, "a little way out beyond Vandeventer Place." Here his precocity first began to shine before outsiders. One of the other little boys, Tom McKittrick, always remembered his puzzling and exasperating failure to learn his lessons as fast and as well as Tom Eliot did. By the time Tom was old enough for Smith Academy he was tall and skinny, and had outgrown his strength. He did not play on any Academy team; his light weight put him out of the running. And he must have had a hernia even then. By later diagnosis he had congenital hernia, a chronic condition that might have been cured in infancy by surgery, and which made him unfit for active service in 1918, and persisted until an operation in middle age.

In the classroom, however, Tom Eliot swept the boards. Or almost. He and another boy were the best pupils in school. To keep from wasting their efforts (years later, he maintained that he had had a practical, labor-saving mind even in childhood), they agreed that one would take the Greek prize and the other the Latin. English was his best subject. His English teacher was Roger Conant Hatch, Harvard 1900, a muscular athlete of heroic stature in small boys' eyes. Young Tom was soon writing stories and verse for the school paper, *The Smith Academy Record*. It was precocious, clever boy's stuff, not unusually promising, strongly reminiscent of *The Ingoldsby Legends*, with dashes of Edward Lear—and no wonder, for Lear and Barham were two of his favorite versifiers. Before that, he had written "a number of very gloomy atheistical and despairing quatrains" in the style of Edward Fitzgerald's *Rubaiyat of Omar Khayyam*, but never showed them to anybody and apparently destroyed them. The best of his artificial productions was an imitation of Ben Jonson ("If Time and Space, as sages say"); a revised version of this poem was later published in the Harvard *Advocate*, and eventually, with some other juvenilia from his school days, was included in his *Complete Poems*. It is inconceivable that Eliot himself would have wanted them there, but the pious gesture was made over his dead body, as many pious gestures are.

His brother Henry seemed of a different generation when they were young; later the gap between them narrowed rapidly and they became friends. Even now, when Tom was a small boy, his older brother's attitude toward him was one of protective benevolence. Henry's chums did not always share his sympathetic view. To them young Tom was sometimes a pain in the neck, and always an incomprehensible highbrow. They would see him folded up in a chair in his father's library, reading some sort of heavy stuff. He always seemed to have money in his pocket, but would he part with any of it, even just a small temporary loan? Not a chance! And who let the cat out of the bag about Henry's having been in a place where his father had strictly forbidden him to go? And this? Yesterday, when one of them had telephoned Henry, young Tom answered the phone, put the receiver down, off the hook, and went back to his reading, never troubling to let Henry know he was wanted.

To his doting sisters, Tom was perfect, or on the way to being, but there were times when even they felt that he overdid it, a little. One summer, when he was thirteen, a word game was briefly all the rage in the family; it went like this:

Q. Mr. and Mrs. Keeto?

A. And little Moss Keeto.

Tom was extraordinarily skillful in fabricating far-fetched and ingenious puns for this game. His sisters tired of it long before he did. At last Marian said, "Tom, don't you think that vein of humor has petered out?" Like a flash Tom retorted, "Mr. and Mrs. Dout and Peter Dout?" Screams of anguish from his sisters; exit Tom in triumph.

In the 1890s the train trip from St. Louis to the East was nothing like as hazardous, uncomfortable, and lengthy as the journey had been fifty years before, when William Greenleaf Eliot had brought his bride to Missouri. When his son Henry took his family east in June, they traveled by Pullman, in gas-lit grandeur, in a stateroom and two sections: uppers and lowers. But sometimes floods interrupted train service from St. Louis; and then they had to go by steamboat from the levee to Alton up the river, on the Illinois shore, and there take the train. To eke out the uncertain presence of a dining car, they usually carried food hampers: the staple was deviled ham, in tins.

Young Tom was an apprehensive traveler, visited by various fears —that the train would leave without them, that his father would be left behind. Once an unforeseen disaster befell him. Waiting for the train to start, he was leaning out of the carriage window. He was wearing his favorite article of dress, a Civil War kepi, with crossed sabers. The train started, he hastily drew back his head, the kepi fell out of the window and was lost forever. He was inconsolable.

When he was considered old enough to sleep by himself in an upper berth, he was proud, but doubtless found something more to worry about. Watching the Negro porter unlock the upper berth, like a shiny trunk lid on its side, letting it down with a rattle and clunk as the chain at each end, rather like a bicycle chain, drew taut with the weight of the berth, he must have wondered whether those two not very impressive supports were enough to hold up the heavy berth and its mattress and all those bedclothes which the porter, standing on his stepladder, was now expertly unfolding and piecing and smoothing together; or whether one of the chains would break and dump him and his bed down into the aisle. And if the berth was easy to open, it was also easy to shut. Supposing they forgot he was in it, and just came along and pushed it shut. He would smother!

He became familiar with the noises and smells—he was particularly sensitive to smells—of train travel: the choking stink of coal smoke, the strong, sour smell of morning coffee, the astringent, faintly urinary flavor of steam leaking up from under the cars, the horrible whiffs from the long lines of shiny brass spittoons, awash with tobacco juice and floating cigar butts, in the parlor car; the panting of the great locomotive at rest, and the whuff-whuff-*whuff*-*whuff*-WHUFF as the engine blew steam and the drive-wheels spun before they settled down to pull the train away; the scary and at the same time sad sound of the train whistle moaning through the night. It was exciting to follow his father or his brother Henry in a swaying, staggering progress from one car to another, through the clashing vestibules. When he had lived down his fears of being catapulted out of his upper berth, or of being smothered in it, he liked it better than sleeping in a lower berth: it was snug up there; he felt secure. In a lower, with the window open just a crack, you were much more exposed; in the morning, in spite of the fine-meshed copper screen, there would be a ridge of soot along the windowsill, a drift of coal dust on the sheet and the pillow beside you.

Every summer for fourteen years (from 1896 to 1909), the Eliots left the steamy swelter of St. Louis for the pines, fog, and granite islands of the Massachusetts coast. In 1890 Henry Eliot bought two acres of land outside Gloucester that overlooked the whole of Eastern Point. Five years later he began to build a summer house there, which he called "The Downs": a large, hip-roofed, shingled, cottage-style house, with a pillared porch around three sides. The house is still there, and from the outside looks much the same as when it was built. It is characteristic of the seaside summer houses of the North Atlantic coast, from Massachusetts to Maine; simpler and more modest than the Victorian Gothic villas of Newport, Henry James vintage (secluded in trees and gardens, out of sight of the sea), but resembling a smaller version of the early twentieth-century "cottages," shingled and gray, along Newport's Ocean Drive. There were no trees near the Eliot house, only coarse grass, muscular bushes, and great outcroppings of gray rock.

One of the many books young Tom read and enjoyed was Kipling's *Captains Courageous.* He also delighted in the discovery that Gloucester fishermen who had also read it complained that Kipling sometimes got things wrong: at times, for example, he mixed up the way they talked with the dialect of Cape Cod, all of ninety miles to the south.

At Gloucester, as in St. Louis, he was wrapped in the cotton batting of female apprehensiveness. When he went sailing with the man who was hired to teach him how to sail his mother went too, and usually a corporal's guard of sisters as well. "Whatever happened, the boy must not get his feet wet, or get too much sun, or get cold, or overheated, or too tired." He was left alone, however, when he was reading.

Shall I Part My Hair Behind?

(1 9 0 5 – 1 9 1 4)

1

LIKE ALL THE REST OF US, T. S. Eliot was born in blood, sweat, and tears; unlike most of us, he was born in St. Louis. This is the first open secret about him, the first well-known but almost forgotten fact of his life: that he was born and brought up (but in a special way, peculiar to his family traditions) a Midwestern American.

At sixteen he went east to school, with the traces of a Missouri accent, a quiet but unshakable sense of his own and his family's superiority to almost all his countrymen, and a deep feeling of homelessness that only a native American can know. To be an Eliot was to remember always who you are ("a silver shilling among copper pennies"); to do one's Unitarian best to civilize the moral wilderness in which all Americans live but which only the Eliots and their kind fully recognize; to be kind to one's inferiors; to work harder than your competitors.

The Missouri accent of which Eliot was so conscious may well have been quite inaudible to other ears. There are St. Louisans, and the Eliots were certainly among them, who speak like educated people. The generality of Americans mumble a dialect which has been well dubbed Slurvian, and whose monotonous sound pours out as if from cleft palates or from roofless mouths. The Eliots and their dwindling sort in the Middle West, where Slurvian is rifest, react consciously against this sloppy talk and have developed an anti-dialect which seems to their resentful fellow countrymen exaggerated, prissy, and false.

The year 1905 marked the end of T. S. Eliot's life in St. Louis. In June he finished his schooling at Smith Academy in fairly high style. He won the Latin prize and as class poet wrote and recited a lengthy ode of fourteen stanzas, unexceptionably "poetic," stuffed with the wide-eyed clichés of adolescence, sentimental, echolaliac, not worth preserving.* His mother was proud of him: this was just the kind of poetry she herself tried to write.

Young Tom was being sent east to school for good and sufficient worldly reasons. At the age of not quite seventeen (his birthday did not come till late September) he was considered too young for Harvard. It would have been a handicap for him to enter the freshman class direct from a St. Louis day school, whereas the stamp of Milton Academy, traditionally a training school for Harvard, would give him a good start, socially and academically. The fact that Milton would accept him for so short a time as one year seems to indicate the pressure of Eliot influence, and its efficacy.

In the ten months they were together, Milton Academy and T. S. Eliot apparently left no marks on each other. We do know of two friends he made there: Howard Morris, his roommate later at Harvard, and Schofield Thayer, afterward publisher of *The Dial.*

In late June 1906 he passed his entrance examinations for Harvard: French, Greek, Elementary Physics, History, and English. Of his interior life we have no record, but we know it existed and suspect that it was his home address. Also he was an adolescent, and we know, or can partly remember, what that was like.

Did he masturbate? Of course. And was he ashamed of it? Unspeakably. For an adolescent boy of his sort, as for a monk, "purity" had one overriding sense: refraining from masturbation. The relief of a wet dream, although a sin, was by far the lesser sin. He had one other equivocal recourse, partly pornographic, partly purgative: he could write about it.

> Then he knew that he had been a fish
> With slippery white belly held tight in his own fingers,

---

*Nevertheless, it has been preserved, with other *Poems Written in Early Youth,* in *The Complete Poems and Plays of T. S. Eliot.*

Writhing in his own clutch, his ancient beauty
Caught fast in the pink tips of his new beauty.

It had been incumbent on his father to tell him, to warn him, about these murky "facts of life." When? Ah, there was the rub: to hit on exactly the right moment. Too soon might shock the tender young mind; too late would find its petals browned and withering in corruption. (They really thought in such terms.) Henry Eliot was a man who knew his duty and did it. He may have considered it no dereliction to prepare the way by first giving his thirteen-year-old son a book to read, as the general practice was in those days among such fathers and sons: *What Every Young Boy Should Know.* This book pretended to impart, in solemn and admonitory tones, all that an adolescent boy needed to know about sex. In fact, its only intelligible message was that masturbation results in impotence, madness, and often an early death.

Crushed by this printed (and therefore incontrovertible) proof that all his fears and guilt were more than justified, the boy would have listened with half an ear to his father's cautious roundabouts, the customary euphemisms about birds and bees. Had he not been half stunned with fear and horror he might have been able to notice that his father was hesitant, uncertain, almost apologetic—a lost soul like himself. But hearing only the words, he would have mis-heard the tone. His father's voice overwhelmed him with the weight of Sinai, and he crept from the presence knowing in his heart that all was lost.

Sex and sin were the same thing: that much he learned at an early age, and never altogether shook off this puritanical *reductio ad absurdum.* But why, surrounded by women as he was, should his feelings about them have been so faint-hearted? Because his mother and his sisters were ladylike women, terrified of sex and disgusted by it, and ashamed of their female bodies. By precept and example, they encouraged his own shame. In the male society of Harvard he began to shake off some of his preoccupation with his own guilt, and in his bawdy verses (never published) about King Bolo and his big black queen, "whose bum was as big as a soup tureen," to assert a new confidence and carelessness. But the foundations were flimsy: they covered but could not stifle his deep horror of women. He was fascinated by women and preoccupied by sex, yet in all his poetry Eliot never once managed to convey what Yeats did a hundred times: the feeling of desire for a woman, the sense that a woman is desirable. Eliot's Grishkin may be nice and pneumatic, but she *smells.*

> The sleek Brazilian jaguar
> Does not in its arboreal gloom
> Distil so rank a feline smell
> As Grishkin in a drawing-room.

Smells haunted Eliot: some (only a few) pleasantly nostalgic,

> Is it perfume from a dress . . .

> . . . the smell of hyacinths across the garden . . .

some merely neutral,

> With smell of steaks in passageways . . .

> That smells of dust and eau de Cologne . . .

more of them strongly unpleasant:

> And female smells in shuttered rooms . . .

> La sueur aestivale, et une forte odeur de chienne . . .

Appropriately, Tom Eliot's nose was his most prominent feature: large, slightly hooked, with flaring nostrils. As the Irish say, "he had a good handle to his face." His ears, also somewhat outsize, jutted out from the side of his head. In spite of these asymmetrical features and his thin and gangling body, he was a good-looking boy, whose face beamed with intelligence. He was indeed almost too good-looking. His Harvard friend Conrad Aiken remembered him as "fabulously beautiful and sibylline," with a mind that was "best of all." He had read so much more and so much more widely than other boys of his age that he could (and did) correct their misquotations, and tell them what they meant to say.

But he was neither an aesthete nor a bookish prig: he was a conservative conformist. He was careful to dress correctly, according to the canons of his social class, and to obey the conservative conventions of his school and college set. He parted his hair in the middle. His suits, waistcoats, ties, and shirts were inconspicuous, neutral, and moderate. He carried two handkerchiefs, a "shower" and a "blower":

a corner of the "shower" peeping modestly from the breast pocket of his jacket. To all outward appearances he was no sort of bohemian or rebel. His rooms in freshman year were at 52 Mount Auburn Street, on the "Gold Coast," an enclave too expensive and too exclusive for the common run of university students. In his second year, at 22 Russell Hall, he roomed with Howard Morris, his schoolmate from Milton Academy, a large, heavy, pleasure-loving boy who was a complete philistine.*

Their room was a perfect model of the collegiate room of 1910. It was well lighted: in the middle of the ceiling hung a chandelier, fitted for both gas and electricity; two wall brackets, each with gas and electric fixtures; on a small table by the fireplace a "student lamp," with a green glass *art nouveau* shade. On the table, cluttered with tobacco tins and a small pile of books, was a copy of the *Saturday Evening Post* (that would be Morris's); on the other side of the fireplace a small bookcase, shaped like a truncated pyramid, filled with an encyclopedia and a set of "the classics" (that would be Eliot's). A sizable oriental rug covered most of the floor. A chafing dish stood on top of the bookcase; a tea set was on another small table. The space under two of the three bay windows was filled by a divan, spread with pillows and rugs. There were two Morris chairs, with flat wooden arms and frame and leather-covered cushions; a third chair, uncompromisingly hard.

Over the fireplace and above the mantelpiece a large rectangular crimson banner, bearing the legend HARVARD 1910, was tacked to the wall; the 1910 was partly obscured by two photographs of football teams. Between the photographs stood a beer stein; on the second mantel shelf were four more, flanked by two silverplated trophy cups (Morris's). In the center of the shelf were a dozen books (common property). Just over the fireplace hung a pipe rack, a line of trolls' heads in plaster; at the side, a German peasant's pipe depended from a hook. The andirons in the fireplace were piled with short birch logs.

*After leaving college Morris became a Wall Street broker, with a summer house at East Hampton. When he married, he took a copy of *The Waste Land* on his honeymoon, tried to read it, pronounced it "junk" and threw it out the train window. He and Eliot kept in touch until shortly before Morris's death in 1954. Eliot's letters to him exhibit the forced joviality of a man talking down to someone of whom he is fond but whose divergent path has taken him almost out of earshot.

The framed pictures that covered the walls were mostly photographs: family groups, classical buildings and statues, a framed diploma.

2

Such were the physical surroundings, the integument of this seedling poet, this larva-writer, who only ten years from now would turn the world of poetry upside down. No one of his instructors, contemporaries, friends, or family had the remotest suspicion that this shy, reticent, watchful, conformist undergraduate was headed in *that* direction. Did he know it, or suspect it, himself? No, not yet, although he knew he could write verse, and intended to write more and better. But he had not yet encountered his first guide, a recently dead French poet named Jules Laforgue.

This is not to say that the acquaintances he made, a few of whom ripened into friends, were not congenial or convivial. One of them was Conrad Aiken, a small, freckled, sandy-haired boy whose earliest recollection of Eliot was of "a singularly attractive, tall, and rather dapper young man, with a somewhat lamian smile, who reeled out of the door of the Lampoon on a spring evening and, catching sight of me, threw his arms about me—from the open windows above came the unmistakable uproar of a punch in progress."

Another friend, the first of his classmates to be taken on the board of the *Advocate,* Harvard's literary magazine, was William Tinckom-Fernandez. "Tinck" was seven years older than Eliot, the son of an English-Portuguese father and a Hindu mother; he had been born in Quetta, on India's northwest frontier. Cutting classes was his dangerous habit and at last his undoing. In his third year he was expelled from college, to his tearful dismay.

The *Advocate* rooms were then under the eaves of the Harvard Union. Then, as now, the editorial function was marked by informality; but in Eliot's day, at least, that casualness had a cutting edge. He described the process later. "Everyone threw his poems into a basket, and then they held a round robin to see who could say the most sarcastic thing about the other man's work."

Tom's brother Henry, who had preceded him at Harvard, had

been a great diner-out and party-goer in Boston. Samuel Eliot Morison, a distant cousin of the Eliots, who later became a well-known naval historian, describes one of the entr'actes: "Sunday afternoon was the time for Harvard upperclassmen to make their party calls. One could see them, resplendent in frock coat, fancy waistcoat and high hat, carrying a cane, walking up and down Commonwealth Avenue to call on the mamas who had invited them to dine or dance. And woe betide them if they failed to turn up within a week or two —they were struck off 'the list.' "

Tom Eliot did his social duty, but no more than the necessary. He paid his respects to Mrs. Jack Gardner, the Boston monument. He called on Adeline Moffat (and pinned her on the wall in *Portrait of a Lady*); he took tea with "Cousin Nancy Ellicott" and "Cousin Harriet," and dined with his rich aunt, "Miss Helen Slingsby" (such were the pseudonyms he gave them in his early poems). But these were older women. Were there no girls in his life at Harvard? What about

> . . . that woman
> Who hesitates toward you in the light of the door
> Which opens on her like a grin.
> You see the border of her dress
> Is torn and stained with sand,
> And you see the corner of her eye
> Twists like a crooked pin.

How close did he get to *her?* Not within touching distance. Or did he, almost—once? Why "stained with *sand*"? Had he seen her, or even been with her one evening, on Revere Beach? His occasional nights out took him sometimes to cocktails at Locke-Ober's—a heady variety known as a "Ward 8"—dinner at the Hotel Thorndyke (now defunct), with much bawdy wit and spur-of-the-minute dirty limericks, then on to a burlesque show at the Old Howard or a melodrama at the Grand Opera House. But that was as far as his libertinism went.

If Tom Eliot's undergraduate pleasures were mainly cerebral, that is not to say that they were exclusively highbrow, but only that gross and fleshly adventures were not among them. He enjoyed playing poker at the Southern Club; he accepted election to the Digamma, the Stylus Club, and the Signet Society. These last two clubs contained most of the editors and the aspirants to the editorial board of the *Advocate,* and among these Eliot made his closest college acquaintances. With Morris he pretended a heartiness he never felt. Like his mother, he had no intimate friends, then or later. Conrad Aiken came as close as any, but only by dint of dogged and devoted pertinacity: he was a *fidus Achates* whom Eliot patronized, mocked, sometimes treated brutally. Tinckom-Fernandez cultivated Eliot assiduously, running him to earth in his room, visiting him at the Eliots' summer home in Gloucester. Yet after college they never met again, although Tinckom-Fernandez was in London at the time of the Armistice, and worked there later as a newspaper correspondent for more than a year, and knew that Eliot was living in London. Another friend and fellow *Advocate* editor was Frederic Schenk, a boy from Groton who became a Rhodes Scholar and eventually a professor of English at Harvard.

As Eliot began to develop he did not expand, he contracted. Sometime during his second year at Harvard he decided to finish his undergraduate course in three years and take a master's degree. This was not an uncommon thing to do, but it required concentration and hard work; and it left him no time for anything else. Although he remained an editor of the *Advocate,* he no longer came to meetings of the board, or read and criticized manuscripts, or wrote much for the magazine himself. In his seven years at Harvard, the *Advocate* published only eight of his poems. *The Literary Digest,* the most popular middlebrow magazine of the day, made a survey of American undergraduate verse, and the *Advocate,* asked to submit samples, naturally included some of Eliot's—none of which was chosen by the *Digest.*

Though Eliot retired from extracurricular fun and games, he never became a grind or a complete recluse: he was generally available for a talk, in which he did more listening than talking. "He was always the commentator, never the gusty talker," says Tinckom-Fernandez, "and seemed to cultivate even then a scholarly detachment." For exercise he occasionally went sculling on the Charles.

The Harvard course of study in Eliot's time was almost completely elective: i.e., within certain limits, an undergraduate could choose the courses he wanted to take. In freshman year Eliot took English Literature, Elementary German, Constitutional Government, Greek Literature, Medieval History. In his second year he chose History of Ancient Art, French Prose and Poetry, Greek Prose

Composition, Greek Literature (Aristophanes, Thucydides, Aeschylus, Sophocles), History of Ancient Philosophy, History of Modern Philosophy. In his third year: Literary History of England (to Elizabeth), Literary History of England and its relation to that of the Continent, Tendencies of European Literature in the Renaissance, English Composition, General View of Latin Poetry, the Roman Novel.

At the end of his third year Eliot had qualified for his A.B. (bachelor of arts) degree, with an overall average of 2.70 (four A's, three B's, two C's, one D). In the fall of 1909 he started his first year in graduate school, with these courses: Studies in the History of Allegory, Chaucer, Drama in England, Poets of the Romantic Period, Literary Criticism in France, Philosophy of History. His academic average for this year was 3.75.

There were famous teachers at Eliot's Harvard, and he had his share of them: Le Baron Briggs, Barrett Wendell, George Lyman Kittredge, George Pierce Baker, George Santayana, Charles Townsend Copeland, William James, Josiah Royce, Ralph Barton Perry, Irving Babbitt, Bertrand Russell—but only the last two, whom he did not meet until he was a graduate student, really impressed and influenced him. Of Russell Eliot said that his mind would have been considered first-rate even in the thirteenth century. A compliment which he afterward balanced by writing that "it is a public misfortune that Mr. Bertrand Russell did not have a classical education." But Eliot despised the ultrapopular "Copey" (Professor Copeland), who taught English composition, for admiring and teaching his pupils to admire the second-rate. Eliot was not alone in disliking Copeland, but he was emphatically in the minority. One of Copeland's idols was Kipling. For this very reason, when Eliot took his course, in his third year, he wrote a paper attacking Kipling. In his criticism of the paper, Copey gave as good as he got. On the "theme" signed Thomas Eliot he wrote, ". . . you must now be on your guard against becoming pompous, orotund, and voluminous." There was no love lost between them, and no common ground. Eliot said afterward: "I could not learn to write English according to the methods by which Copeland taught it."

He objected to Copeland because he felt that Copeland was wasting his time and interfering with his education. Though Eliot could not yet formulate his wants, he knew what they were. When he was sixteen he was infatuated by Byron; but by the time he was an undergraduate the poets of his own day and those of the 1890s had nothing to say to him, and the lightning flash from France had not yet lit up his sky. Cheerfulness, optimism, and hopefulness, the Browning quality of the nineteenth century, he hated, but as yet he had nothing to put in its place. Then he discovered Dante, and learned by reading him that "genuine poetry can communicate before it is understood." He puzzled out *The Divine Comedy* by himself, from an edition with an English prose translation alongside the Italian, memorizing his favorite passages and reciting them to himself when he was lying in bed or on a railway journey. "Heaven knows what it would have sounded like, had I recited it aloud; but it was by this means that I steeped myself in Dante's poetry."

3

One day in the Harvard Union library, in the same building that sheltered the *Advocate* under its eaves, Eliot came across a small book by Arthur Symons, *The Symbolist Movement in Literature*, published in London less than ten years before. Eliot found it absorbing. It was full of lucid, tantalizing sentences like these:

... there are certain natures (great or small, Shakespeare or Rimbaud, it makes no difference) to whom the work is nothing, the act of working, everything. . . .

[Verlaine] knows that words are suspicious, not without their malice, and that they resist mere force with the impalpable resistance of fire or water. They are to be caught only with guile or with trust. Verlaine has both, and words become Ariel to him. . . .

No long poem was ever written; the finest long poem in the world being but a series of short poems linked together by prose. . . .

Only very young people want to be happy. What we all want is to be quite sure that there is something which makes it worth while to go on living, in what seems to us our best way, at our finest intensity.

How can undergraduates recognize, among the shining crowd of their sophomore years, the few, the very few, who will excel? They can't and they don't. So Leon Little, secretary of the class of 1910, can speak for them all. "Everybody liked Tom," he said, "but except for his extraordinary brain power, he seemed rather ordinary." There were others in the class who showed more promise or who performed with more notoriety. Some of their names are still familiar, or seem as though they should be: Walter Lippmann, the newspaper sage; John Reed (of *Ten Days That Shook the World*), duped by the Russian Revolution, buried in the Kremlin wall; Heywood Broun, lazy, laughing liberal columnist; Stuart Chase, frowning, doom-singing muckraker; Hamilton Fish, rock-ribbed football player, rock-ribbed Republican Congressman. The class even boasted two declared poets. One of them, Alan Seeger ("I have a rendezvous with death"), looked and acted the part; the other, Edward Eyre Hunt, being more presentable, was elected class poet. Tom Eliot was not even a candidate for that position. But when it came to choosing the class odist, whose job it was to turn out an impeccably ordinary bit of traditional light verse, capable of being sung to the tune of "Fair Harvard," Eliot was the logical choice.*

The teacher who most influenced Eliot at Harvard was a professor of French Literature named Irving Babbitt. Babbitt was a fiercely energetic man who had sold newspapers in New York, worked on a farm in Ohio, as a cowboy in Wyoming, where (according to Herbert Howarth) he had pulled a rattlesnake out of a hole by its tail and been scarred by an eagle whose nest he was rifling. Paul Elmer More had been his fellow student at Harvard, and became his friend. By the time Eliot came to the university, Babbitt had been a professor in the French Department for twelve years.

Babbitt called himself a humanist, as did Paul Elmer More; but More got religion and Babbitt never did. Both were upholders of something they called classicism, and savage critics of something they called romanticism. Babbitt himself was an appealingly romantic figure who liked to take solitary walks, shouting poetry as he strode. His tone, in his lectures and published essays, was assured, authoritarian, flat-footedly omniscient: a series of declarative statements which came thumping out like a schoolmaster's ferule, rap-

---

*The resultant piece of nothing is piously enshrined in *The Complete Poems and Plays of T. S. Eliot*, from which his other *Ode*, a savage memorial to his first marriage, published in *Ara Vos Prec* (1920), was primly excluded.

ping the knuckles of the balky or inattentive student. Here are some samples that obviously impressed a pupil named Eliot:

. . . a writer is great, not only by what he says, but by what he omits saying.

It is well to open one's mind, but only as a preliminary to closing it, only as a preparation, in short, for the supreme act of judgment and selection. . . .

[In Rousseau's notion] the generations of man can no more link with one another than the flies of summer. They are disconnected into the dust and powder of individuality.

. . . the purpose of the college . . . must be in a quantitative age to produce men of quality.

[The Terror] lends color to the assertion that has been made that the last stage of sentimentalism is homicidal mania.

. . . the notion that wisdom resides in a popular majority at any particular moment should be the most completely exploded of all fallacies.

. . . it may be said some day of us that, as the result of a series of outbursts of idealism, we changed from a federal republic to a highly centralized and bureaucratic empire.

Eliot pondered all these things in his heart, and in due time echoed many of them in his own manner. Babbitt certainly put more than one bee in his bonnet; he was, however, not responsible for Eliot's discovery of Laforgue. Babbitt pointed him in the general direction of "classical" French writers; the rest was Eliot's doing.

It was Arthur Symons who led him to Jules Laforgue, who had died at the age of twenty-seven, the year before Eliot was born. Eliot was tremendously taken by him, not only by his verse but by everything he could learn about the man himself: his reticence, his protective disguise of a clergyman's sad-colored costume, his umbrella, his pose of aloof politeness. Laforgue had written only three volumes; Eliot ordered them all. As far as he knew, he was the first American to own them, and the first to read them. He tried writing verse in Laforgue's manner, imitating—not very well—his dry tone of voice and sardonic matter-of-factness.

But Laforgue was only the half of it. The Elizabethan playwrights (but not Shakespeare) were the other half. Fifty years later Eliot said, "The form in which I began to write, in 1908 or 1909, was directly drawn from the study of Laforgue together with the later Elizabethan drama; and I do not know anyone who started from exactly that point."

Do any two people (but he had in mind "poets") start from exactly the same point? What Eliot meant was that he was an original, and knew it. But the fact that he knew where he started from did not mean that he knew where he was going. As yet he had as little idea, or as many ideas, about what he might do as undergraduates of his age usually have.

After his first year of graduate work he was still pointing in several directions. Philosophy was one, French literature was another. Poetry was only a secret possibility. The four poems he published in the *Advocate* that fall and winter were practice canters in the hoofprints of Laforgue, and gave nothing away about his serious intentions. In the spring of 1910 he wrote to order two poems of occasion: one for the annual dinner of his "final" club, Fox, the other the class ode. Neither showed the slightest sign of originality or was worth preserving.

4

In June 1910 Eliot was supposed to take his master's degree when most of his class were taking their bachelor's, but he came down with scarlet fever, and had to proceed M.A. *in absentia*. He had already decided to spend his next academic year in Paris. This dismayed his mother, who disliked and distrusted the French. His father did not cotton to the idea either, but finally agreed. So Tom Eliot had the most romantic year of his life, "on the old man's money," in Paris.

The cloud of odoriferous impressions in which Paris first presented itself to a young American of Eliot's day was a mingling of smells and colors, *caporals* and garlic, grayness and *grisettes*, haunted by the ceaseless awareness of femininity. This was a lure, in Eliot's case as in others of his sort, that led him not to bed but to a book. The book was *Bubu de Montparnasse*, by Charles-Louis Philippe—a tough-guy story about tough bohemians. Twenty-two years later Eliot wrote the preface to an English translation of it, confessing that the book had always been for him a symbol of the Paris he first

saw in 1910, and adding a breast-beat that only an Eliot—or a Calvinist with a Catholic turn of mind—could have struck himself with:
"Even the most virtuous, in reading it, may feel: I have sinned ex-
ceedingly in thought, word and deed."

The romanticness of his romantic year was general, not particular. Eliot was too thoroughly inhibited to be bewitched by a model
or rescued by a golden-hearted tart; of Baudelaire's drugs, suffering
was the only one he shared; it was Paris itself that bowled him over,
its smells and sounds, its evenings, mornings, afternoons, its book-
stalls and its books. And, that first summer, he had college friends
with him to share his fervors and to spur them on: Conrad Aiken and
Frederic Schenk. Talk was their stimulant. Champagne or strong
drink was more than they desired or could afford: all they wanted
were *pâtisseries* and syrupy soda-water. Eliot lived in a Left Bank
pension, rue St. Jacques, went to hear Bergson lecture at the Collège
de France (an experience which, according to his mother, made him
decide to change his Harvard doctorate in literature to a doctorate
in philosophy) and had the good luck to have Alain-Fournier* as his
friend and tutor in French. Alain-Fournier got him to read Paul
Claudel, André Gide, and Dostoevsky, and introduced him to his
brother-in-law, Jacques Rivière, who wrote for the *Nouvelle Revue
Française* and whose generous enthusiasm had a warming effect on
Eliot's inherent coolness.

Another friendship that Eliot made in Paris was with a French
medical student, Jean Verdenal, who lived in the same *pension.* All
we know about Jean Verdenal is that he and Eliot once met in the
Luxembourg Gardens, and that Verdenal was waving a branch of
lilac; that he died (we don't know how and neither did Eliot) at the
Dardanelles in 1915; and that Eliot dedicated to him his first published book, *Prufrock and Other Observations,* adding an epigraph
from Dante's *Purgatory:* "Now can you understand the quantity of
love that warms me towards you, so that I forget our vanity, and treat
the shadows like the solid thing." What are we to make of these facts?
Not much, beyond inferring that a friendship between young men
can be warm and may stir the blood without firing it; and that there

*Henri Alain-Fournier, who wrote one magical book, *Le Grand Meaulnes* (trans-
lated into English as *The Wanderer*) before he was killed in action in 1914.

may well have been some exaggeration in Eliot's melancholy remembrance of this foreign friend.

It was a cold winter in Paris that year, and a late spring; all the better for that. Except for Alain-Fournier, Rivière, and Verdenal, Eliot knew no one. But he was reading hungrily (Julien Benda, Charles Maurras, Jules Romains, André Salmon, Baudelaire, Anatole France, Remy de Gourmont) and breathing in the sights and sounds of Paris, never to be forgotten. One slight instance of something he must have seen and may have stored up for use later: in the Tuileries Gardens he often passed a pair of vividly horrifying nineteenth-century statues by Auguste-Nicolas Cain which flank the gateway opposite rue Castiglione: one was of a wild boar beset by a leopard, the other of a rhinoceros goring a prostrate lion. More than forty years later, when Eliot was writing his play, *The Confidential Clerk,* he has scatterbrained Lady Elizabeth explain what happened to her old lover: "He was run over. By a rhinoceros. In Tanganyika."

The temptation into which Eliot was chiefly led in Paris was to stay on there, scraping a living somehow, and gradually learning to write in French, as his compatriot, the novelist Julian Green did, a few years later. Luckily for him and for us, he resisted the temptation, and returned to Harvard after his romantic year to study philosophy. As a gesture partly of youthful defiance, partly from that instinct for protective disguise which was already well developed in him, he sported a malacca cane, "exotic Left Bank clothing" (his friend Conrad Aiken reports this, without going into details) and with his hair parted behind. It gave his Harvard acquaintances something to talk about.

His three years as a graduate student were far more exhilarating and productive than his undergraduate three. For one thing, he encountered the two professors whose minds and opinions he could respect: Irving Babbitt and Bertrand Russell. With Babbitt this respect developed into something close to friendship, and with Russell (after they met again in England) into an intense father-and-son relationship; both these friendships cooled off eventually into near-hostility. Babbitt felt that Eliot had betrayed him, and Eliot must have felt (though he never gave a hint of it) that Russell had betrayed *him.*

In the Harvard days when they first met, however, it was the perfectly balanced give-and-take of the first-rate teacher, avid to impart, and the first-rate student, hungry to learn. The precise statement of ideas fascinated Eliot, but the thought that drew him even more was the possibility of expressing the inexpressible:

> I will show you fear in a handful of dust.

It was not Russell's mathematical logic nor Babbitt's French classics that nourished this tendency, but two years' study of Sanskrit. That nearly made a Buddhist of him; it left him in "a state of enlightened mystification"; it gave him the red rock and the thunder of *The Waste Land.* And in the sutras of Patanjali he discovered that only essential words are necessary, and that a complete sentence structure is not always needed.

One of Eliot's fellow students was a Greek, Raphael Demos, who introduced him to his native food at a restaurant called the Parthenon, on Kneeland Street, and to another, Jacob Wirth's, which specialized in fish. Both Eliot and Demos were members of the postgraduate class of twelve who met for tea every week at Russell's apartment on Craigie Street. Eliot stuck in Russell's memory because he was "extraordinarily silent and only once made a remark which struck me. I was praising Heraclitus, and he observed: 'Yes, he always reminds me of Villon.' I thought this remark so good that I always wished he would make another."

One day one of them asked Russell who he considered was the greatest living philosopher. Russell said that reminded him of the story of the Athenian generals, assembled to elect a commander-in-chief on the eve of the Battle of Marathon. Each general voted for himself but all agreed on Miltiades as second choice. Then whom would Russell vote for as second? F. H. Bradley, of Oxford. Demos regarded Eliot, who was then president of the Harvard Philosophical Club, as "the best philosopher among us." Later he was shocked by Eliot's poetry, which struck him as an aberration, and his private epitaph on Eliot was: "It is a pity that he abandoned philosophy. He would have been a good philosopher." He was at any rate a good student. His record for three years of graduate work at Harvard: one B, all the rest A's.

He was learning, and on several levels at once. But it was to take years of patient practice before his protective camouflage fitted him without a wrinkle, like a second skin. At this stage he still showed an occasional waspishness (that was the word his friend Aiken used). "Shelley was a fool!" he would say, or, dismissing Chekhov, "I prefer my Ibsen straight." In Josiah Royce's seminar in philosophy, Eliot wrote a paper on the interpretation of primitive religions. Full of his reading in F. H. Bradley, he said that no simple statement was absolutely true. Someone interrupted to ask if he thought that last statement true? The argument grew, warm words were exchanged; at last Eliot said, "You can't understand me. To understand my point of view, you have to believe it first."

Another friend who dated from these days was George Boas, from Brown University, who had come to Harvard for a year of graduate work. Together with Conrad Aiken they patronized a Levantine restaurant in Boston, where they chose their dinner by invading the kitchen to see what was being cooked. Boas, two years behind Eliot and less well versed in French literature, looked up to him with near-veneration and was also very fond of him. After Harvard their paths diverged, but they were to meet again.

Was it about this time that Eliot met Sweeney, his famous anti-hero? In South Boston he frequented a gymnasium, smelling of arnica and stale sweat, where he took boxing lessons from an Irish ex-prizefighter, and learned "how to swarm with passion up a rope." He once returned from his lesson with a beautiful black eye, having thus been reproved for the mistake of inadvertently hitting his instructor a little too hard. He also took part in a play: he had the part of Lord Bantock in an undergraduate production of *Fanny and the Servant Problem*. (E. E. Cummings, another poet-in-progress, played the second footman.)

The level on which he was living most intensely was hidden: he was writing poetry in secret. In two years, 1910 to 1912, he had written the four poems that were to make his reputation, five years later. Conrad Aiken had read them; perhaps one or two others. When Aiken went to London in the summer of 1913, he took with him copies of *The Love Song of J. Alfred Prufrock* (title from Kipling, "hero's" name from a St. Louis sign, epigraph from Dante) and *La Figlia che Piange* to try to sell them to some London editor: nothing doing. So there they were, in his desk drawer, waiting, with *Portrait of a Lady, Preludes,* and *Rhapsody on a Windy Night.* In another drawer, well hidden, was the unfinished, never-to-be-finished bawdy ballad, *King Bolo and His Big Black Queen:*

> that airy fairy hairy 'un,
> who led the dance on Golders Green
> with Cardinal Bessarion.

—

THREE

"They Called Me the Hyacinth Girl"

(1915-1920)

1

IN JULY 1914, with only a year or so left before he would start writing the dissertation for his Ph.D. degree, Eliot was given a traveling fellowship by Harvard, and set off for Germany, to do his final year's reading at the University of Marburg. It was not a good year to be in Europe, as he soon discovered. On August 4 the First World War began; three weeks later he managed to get to England and to be accepted for a year's residence at Merton. On September 22, a few weeks before the Oxford term began, he went to London and called on Ezra Pound. Conrad Aiken was the go-between.

Pound was an American poet and literary missionary of stupendous energy and tactlessness. He had then been in England for almost three years—long enough to annoy or alienate everyone in the British literary establishment except such heretics or nonmembers as Ford Madox Ford, Wyndham Lewis, and Harriet Weaver, the saintly, long-suffering literary nanny who kept James Joyce in the bankrupt affluence to which he was accustomed, and who would support the first tentative steps of the young T. S. Eliot.

It might be too much to say that Eliot and Pound took to each other on sight. Pound, at any rate, took to Eliot, even before seeing anything he had written. When Eliot sent him *Prufrock* Pound snapped it up and dispatched it to Harriet Monroe, editor of the Chicago magazine *Poetry* (whose agent in England he was), announcing it as "the best poem I have yet had or seen from an American. PRAY GOD IT BE NOT A SINGLE AND UNIQUE SUCCESS." He described Eliot as "the only American I know of who has made what I can call adequate preparation for writing. He has actually trained himself *and* modernized himself *on his own.*"

Pound's encouragement revived Eliot, who had written no poetry for three years. During his months at Oxford he wrote *The Boston Evening Transcript, Hysteria,* and *Aunt Helen.* Pound also gave him an introduction to the Arnold Dolmetsch family, makers of archaic musical instruments and enhancers of life in general. In their company Eliot "passed one of the most delightful afternoons I have ever spent, in one of the most delightful households I have ever visited. . . . I made friends with the extraordinary children in no time and am wild to see them again. As for the dancing, they all danced (except the head of the family) for about an hour, I think, while I sat rapt."

Merton was the Oxford college where Eliot's admired F. H. Bradley was a Fellow, but Eliot apparently made no attempt to get Bradley as his tutor and there is no record of their ever meeting, which may have been just as well. According to Raphael Demos, who came to Oxford a few years after Eliot, Bradley "was a difficult person," and "could not stand the sight of a student." Eliot made Bradley's philosophy the subject of his dissertation: "Experience and the Objects of Knowledge in the Philosophy of F. H. Bradley."

He and his tutor, a Fellow of Merton named Harold Joachim, hit it off very well. A year later Joachim wrote him a warm letter of recommendation, praising Eliot's ability and conscientious habit of hard work, and enthusiastically endorsing his pupil as a prospective teacher.

At this point Eliot was far from being an Anglophile, and Oxford particularly left him cold. People who could actually *like* the disgusting food the British ate could not be called civilized. He wrote to Conrad Aiken: "Come, let us desert our wives and fly to a land where there are no Medici prints, nothing but concubinage and conversation. Oxford is very pretty, but I don't like to be dead."

Nevertheless, he worked hard. He read, marked, and learned like the conscientious student he was, and took a gingerly part in the wartime-diminished life of Oxford, winning a pewter mug for stroking a college four "at a time when the real oarsmen were fighting for England and France." But when the Philosophy Department at Harvard offered him another year at Oxford, he declined. He told Aiken that he would prefer London to Oxford, with its archaic notions about poetry, its frozen traditions of discomfort and academic high life, its pregnant wives and untidy children. He supposed he could work at the British Museum, even though he thought he would never get to like England. But if Oxford did not enthrall him, he dreaded returning to Harvard and the college bell and all the people who would be against everything he believed in but who would manage to waste his time for their own ends.

It was in this dissatisfied and vulnerable state of mind that Eliot met the girl who was to plow up, harrow, and strip his life to the bone.

2

What did Dante's Beatrice look like? No one knows. We cannot even be sure we have the right name of the Dark Lady of Shakespeare's sonnets. But of the maenad-madonna who was T. S. Eliot's muse, we know enough to sketch a likeness.

Her name was Vivienne Haigh-Wood, and she was born in 1888, four months before her future husband, into a family whose place in the English social order would then have been described as middle class. Her birthplace was Bury, Lancashire, an old Saxon town near Manchester. She was the elder of two children. Her brother, Maurice, eight years younger, grew up to be the very model of a British soldier: tall, lean, quiet-spoken, patient, completely dependable. He was an infantry officer fresh from school, in the First World War, and was badly wounded; in the 1939–1945 war he served in Intelligence. Their father, Charles Haigh Haigh-Wood, was a portrait painter who became fashionably well known but who stopped painting when he inherited enough money to bring him a comfortable income.

Vivienne was in every way a contrast to her quiet brother. She was small, dark, and lively, with darkish brown hair and blue-gray eyes, mercurial, flirtatious, moody, given to outbursts of anger or despair. Her fitful health was the increasingly somber background against which her lifelong struggle to keep calm, to keep rational, was thrown into nightmare relief. When she was seven or eight she had an operation for tuberculosis of the hand, and her mother took her to Margate for a lengthy convalescence. By then her nerves were so on edge and her hearing so sensitive that any loud noise was painful to her. If she thought someone near her was about to laugh, she would say sharply, "Don't let him laugh!"

The Haigh-Woods' house was in Compayne Gardens, a dull part of Hampstead, and is now converted into flats. Vivienne went to the King Alfred School in Hampstead until she was about fourteen, then to a boarding school at Eastbourne. She had a darting intelligence, intermittently lit by an irreverent imagination. Like Zelda Fitzgerald, she loved dancing and was an accomplished ballroom dancer. Her taste in people, as in clothes, was uncertain. Less than a year before she met Tom Eliot she had gone through an intense, off-again on-again affair in London with a young man she called "B" in her diary. The affair had ended with a whimpery kind of bang when "B" was called up in September 1914 and went off to war. A butterfly of a girl, you might say, but a butterfly who could stamp, and also sting. She was attractive to boys and had many beaux. One man whom she refused to marry was so cut up that he walked all night, from one end of London to the other.

We do not know, as yet, exactly when the first meeting between Vivienne and Eliot took place. Sacheverell Sitwell, who saw a good deal of Eliot when he first came to England, says that Eliot met Vivienne on the river (presumably at Oxford), and that she was playing a phonograph in a punt alongside his. We do know that they met at Oxford, in Schofield Thayer's rooms at Magdalen—whether or not that was their first sight of one another. Thayer's cousin Lucy was a close friend of Vivienne's. The Haigh-Woods and the Thayers had been at Sierre, in Switzerland, at Christmas 1908, and saw each other frequently thereafter.

During the spring of 1915 there were other meetings between Vivienne and Tom Eliot, sometimes at parties, sometimes only the two of them. And then—the news must have come like a thunderclap to the Eliots in America—on June 26, in the Hampstead Registry Office, Thomas Stearns Eliot, Bachelor, twenty-six, and Vivienne Haigh Haigh-Wood, Spinster, just twenty-seven, were married. No other member of either family was present; the witnesses were Lucy Thayer and Lillia Symes. Apparently the Haigh-Woods were soon reconciled to the marriage; obviously the Eliots were not. Mrs. Eliot did not meet her daughter-in-law until five years later; Mr. Eliot died without ever setting eyes on her.

In June 1915, the month he and Vivienne were married, T. S. Eliot's first paid poem was published. *The Love Song of J. Alfred Prufrock* at last appeared in *Poetry*. Harriet Monroe had been reluctant to accept this odd poem and was apprehensive about printing it, but Pound kept beating at her until she did. She paid Eliot eight guineas. The annual *Poetry* prize of $200 went to Vachel Lindsay for *The Chinese Nightingale*.

Shortly after the wedding Tom Eliot was summoned home to give an account of himself and his sudden marriage. He went alone; Vivienne absolutely refused, then and later, to brave the submarine-infested Atlantic. What took place at the meeting between Tom Eliot and his parents we can only surmise. The scene, presumably, was the family summer home at Gloucester. In accordance with the family motto, no voices would be raised and no long speeches would be made, though some almost surreptitious tears might be shed. An agreement would be arrived at, one of its terms being that Tom should finish his dissertation on Bradley and submit it to the Harvard Philosophy Department (a proviso which would seem to show a parental hope that all was not yet lost, that he might still be recalled to his senses and return to the academic life at Cambridge); another, that his father would continue Tom's small but vital allowance. When Henry Eliot died, four years later, this subsidy died with him.

The family conclave over, Tom returned to the foster-country he had not yet adopted and which he still half-disliked, to the alien bride of whom he was uncertain, and to his doubtful future. In his father's view there was no doubt about it: his youngest son, now at the ripening age of twenty-seven, when a proper man should be settling into a proper career, had already made a mess of his life. What hope could there be for this prodigal son who would not accept his father's qualified forgiveness but insisted on returning to the far country and the swine-husks that must be the inevitable reward of riotous living? (In Mr. Eliot's Unitarian ethic, ideas running riot were no less damnable than radicals throwing bombs or bohemians making free with love; and Tom's ideas, although so cautiously expressed in his father's presence as to be inaudible, nevertheless were felt by Mr. Eliot as immediately as the odor of a rose; and he felt them to be subversive, or at least potentially dangerous.)

3

If he did not like the country or the people or even the food they ate, what was it that drew Eliot so powerfully to England, estranging him from his native land and straining the ties that bound him to his family? The complex of feelings that decided him may have been something like this—"these naked thoughts that roam about and loudly knock to have their passage out" may stand a better chance of being received in England than in my own country; the atmosphere and the manner of life in England, alien though they are, might allow me more scope and give me firmer support than I could find at home; if I am to make a living and write my poetry too, England may make me, America might break me; for better or worse I am committed to Vivienne, and she will not live anywhere but England. Had he said or even tried to say something of this sort to his parents, during that family conference? It seems possible but not very likely, in view of his father's conviction about his son's precocious failure, and of his mother's distrust of foreign parts and her lack of faith in his "vers libre."

The attraction which England had for him was in large part Vivienne herself. Englishmen who do not share the American romantic feeling about women find such a thing hard to credit. Cyril Connolly, for example, throwing "a small grenade," has said that Logan Pearsall Smith told *him* that Eliot's sudden and almost clandestine marriage could be explained only by Eliot's New England conscience: "Eliot had compromised Miss Haigh-Wood (a schoolteacher from Southampton,* according to Leonard Woolf) and then felt obliged as an American gentleman, the New England code being stricter than ours, to propose to her. This would account for the furtive nature of

---

*She was not.

the ceremony, and for his subsequent recoiling from his conjugal privileges."

> By Richmond I raised my knees
> Supine on the floor of a narrow canoe.

The whole affair with Vivienne was a mistake, almost instantly recognized and repented? Is that how it was? A seduction in which Eliot played the part of "the young man carbuncular" of *The Waste Land*, and Vivienne the indifferent typist? If we consider Eliot's nature and upbringing (not to speak of Vivienne's), this will be difficult, if not impossible, to credit.

Connolly had in mind, perhaps, the evidence of Eliot's poem, *Ode*, which appeared in his 1920 book of verse, *Ara Vos Prec*, and was then suppressed. (Edmund Wilson said that when Eliot was asked why he omitted *Ode* from all further collections, he replied, "An oversight"; obviously untrue, said Wilson.)

Professor Donald Gallup, the authority on Eliot's bibliography, if not on Eliot's psychology, says that the typescript of *Ode* is headed "Ode on Independence Day, July 4th, 1918," so that the poem, written three years after the wedding, cannot possibly refer to their wedding night. Wilson was just as positive that it did. Strong emotions can surely be recollected after a lapse of three years, or even longer. In spite of its elaborate obscurity, *Ode* does indeed appear to be based on personal experience of an excruciating kind. From these few lines, the reader may judge for himself:

> . . . Tortured.
> When the bridegroom smoothed his hair
> There was blood upon the bed.
> Morning was already late.
> Children singing in the orchard
> (Io Hymen, Hymenaee)
> Succuba eviscerate. . . .

The epigraph to the poem is ambiguous, as Eliot's epigraphs are often intended to be. It is a quotation, or a partial misquotation, of two lines from *Coriolanus* (Act IV, Scene 5), Eliot's favorite Shakespeare play. The original read:

> To thee particularly, and to all the Volscii . . .

Eliot has changed it to read:

> To you particularly, and to all the Volscians
> Great hurt and mischief.

He has also converted *thee* to *you*, and *Volscii* to *Volscians*, presumably to give the fragment a more contemporary flavor. Quoted thus, out of context, the two lines have an ominous, almost a comminatory ring. But those who are familiar with the play (or who look up the lines) will know that the speaker, Coriolanus, is frankly disclosing himself to his great enemy, the commander of the Volscians. Coriolanus is confessing who he is, surrendering himself, and turning traitor all in one. Guilt, and the acknowledgment of guilt, is the note. But as Eliot uses the words, the deep, soft undertone is a curse.

Was there resentment as well as guilt on Eliot's side, and did the resentment add to his sense of guilt? Was it partly that he did not fully return her love—or wholly that he did not really love her at all? Did he feel that he had sacrificed another human being and jeopardized both their lives by "the awful daring of a moment's surrender"—a surrender which he soon regretted? Whatever the situation may have been, it was certainly not a simple one. The Eliots' marriage was unhappy, as everyone within miles of it was aware. But how to define the unhappiness of this particular unhappy marriage? The least—and perhaps the most—we can do is to tell, as far as we know, some of the things that happened.

4

Eliot's first job was schoolteaching: it lasted one term (thirteen weeks) at Wycombe Grammar School in the dreary town of High Wycombe, where in the autumn of 1915 he taught small boys French, mathematics, history, drawing, and swimming. He was paid at the rate of £140 a year, with free dinner. At Christmas he found a better berth at the Highgate Junior School, in Hampstead, where he got £160 a year, with dinner and tea. Sir John Betjeman, who was then a small boy at the school, remembers Eliot as "a tall, quiet usher there whom we called 'The American Master.'" Little Betjeman presented him with a manuscript entitled "The Best Poems of Betjeman," which Eliot returned without comment.

For some months the Eliots lived with Vivienne's parents in Hampstead. Then Bertrand Russell, who at Harvard had wished Eliot would speak up more, and was grinned at, with an admiring grin, as "Mr. Apollinax," encountered his well-remembered pupil one day in Oxford Street. Renewed acquaintance warmed to cordiality, and led to introductions: to Lady Ottoline Morrell (Russell's current mistress) and all the Comus crew that battened on her at Garsington Manor for well-fed weekends—Leonard and Virginia Woolf, Katherine Mansfield, Middleton Murry, Aldous and Maria Huxley, Vanessa and Clive Bell, Duncan Grant, Lytton Strachey, and lesser lights. It led also to a *ménage à trois*.

Bertrand Russell had a first-rate mind, humane aspirations, and the sexual morals of an alley cat. Although he strongly resembled Tenniel's illustration of the Mad Hatter, he was apparently attractive to some women; and many women helplessly attracted *him*. He now invited the impoverished Tom Eliots to come live with him in his small London flat. Only a very innocent or a very sophisticated couple would have accepted the offer. The Eliots were not sophisticated.

Russell had first met Vivienne only a few weeks after she married Tom, and wrote about her to Lady Ottoline Morrell: "Friday evening I dined with my Harvard pupil, Eliot, and his bride. I expected her to be terrible, from his mysteriousness, but she was not so bad. She is light, a little vulgar,* adventurous, full of life; an artist, I think he said, but I should have thought her an actress. He is exquisite and listless. She says she married him to stimulate him, but finds she can't do it. Obviously, he married in order to be stimulated. I think she will soon be tired of him. She refuses to go to America to see his people, for fear of submarines. He is ashamed of his marriage, and very grateful if one is kind to her."

Four months later Russell wrote to Lady Ottoline: "It is quite funny how I have come to love him, as if he were my son. He is becoming much more of a man. He has a profound and quite unselfish devotion to his wife, and she is really very fond of him, but has

---

*Aldous Huxley used the same word in describing her: "I rather like her; she is such a genuine person, vulgar, but with no attempt to conceal her vulgarity, with no snobbery of the kind that makes people say they like things, such as Bach or Cézanne, when they don't." Sacheverell Sitwell did not agree that she was vulgar.

impulses of cruelty from time to time. It is a Dostoievsky kind of cruelty, not a straightforward, everyday kind. I am every day getting things more right between them, but I can't let them alone at present, and of course I, myself, get very much interested. She is a person who lives on a knife edge, and will end as a criminal or a saint; I don't know which yet. She has a perfect capacity for both."

Russell was indeed "very much interested." In January 1916 Eliot wrote him an effusively grateful letter: "Dear Bertie, This is wonderfully kind of you; really the last straw, so to speak, of generosity. I am very sorry you have to come back, and Vivienne says you have been an angel to her. . . . I am sure you have done *everything* possible, and handled her in the very best way; better than I. I often wonder how things would have turned out but for you. I believe we shall owe her life to you, even."

Russell explains this letter, or partly explains it, in a deadpan footnote that may or may not reveal more than he intends: "Mrs. Eliot was ill and needed a holiday. Eliot, at first, could not leave London, so I went first with her to Torquay, and Eliot replaced me after a few days." Did Russell seduce Vivienne; and was Eliot, at least for a time, unaware of the fact? The probable answer to both questions, in the light of the circumstantial evidence and of the characters concerned, is Yes. How could Vivienne, married only a few months and supposedly much in love with her husband, have taken part in so cruel an adultery? One possible answer is that she was a flirt, and flirts sometimes go too far, sometimes get themselves into situations they can't get out of; sometimes a determined seducer is one too many for them.

5

Bertie's angelic handling of Vivienne was not the only reason for Eliot's gratitude. Russell's conscience, which was sleepy only in sexual affairs, troubled him about some debentures he held, with a face value of £3,000, in an engineering firm that was making munitions: Russell was a pacifist at the time, so he handed over the debentures to Eliot. The small but steady income from them was a great help. (Eliot kept the debentures for some years and finally returned them.)

The year 1916, halfway through the war, though it was neither so terrible nor so rewarding for Eliot as other years would be, set the pattern for those to come. Two ever-present problems dominated that time, as they would continue to dominate his life for the next sixteen years: earning a living and Vivienne's ill health. Of these two desperate problems, the first proved to be soluble; the second was not.

From the start of their life together (and before that) Vivienne suffered from blinding, excruciatingly painful migraines and from some internal ailment to which the doctors of that day gave the name of intestinal catarrh. She had always been painfully sensitive to noise: her nerves were too close to the surface, as they say, and often bad. ("My nerves are bad tonight. Yes, bad. Stay with me.") She was under frequent and eventually constant medical treatment. The treatment included drugs; this fact, added to her uncertain and occasionally violent behavior, gave rise to the rumor that she "took drugs," and, more specifically, that she was "an ether-drinker." Aldous Huxley's wife, Maria, was one of those who launched this stinging fly in the echoing Pandora's box of Garsington Manor. Vivienne's brother, Maurice, calls these rumors malicious nonsense. He says she took the drugs that were prescribed for her by her doctors but never became addicted to them.

The effect of Vivienne's ill health on her husband can only be imagined. Here again some significant facts are available, even if we cannot always be quite certain of their significance. When visitors came, Vivienne would sometimes be indisposed and in bed. They would stay too long, and talk too much, and the sound would drive her into a sick rage. Eliot sometimes went on weekends without her. Some of his friends thought her alarming and alarmed. Hope Mirrlees said of her: "She gave the impression of absolute terror, of a person who's seen a hideous ghost, a goblin ghost, and who was always seeing a goblin in front of her. Her face was all drawn and white, with wild, frightened, angry eyes. An overintensity over nothing, you see. Supposing you would say to her, 'Oh, will you have some more cake?' she'd say, 'What's that? What do you mean? What do you say that for?' She was terrifying. At the end of an hour I was absolutely exhausted, sucked dry. And I said to myself: Poor Tom, this is enough! But she was his muse all the same." For long periods, sometimes for months, she stayed by herself in a country cottage, where the air and the quiet were thought to be more salubrious than London, but where Tom could join her only for weekends. Her constant and increasing ill health not only sickened their marriage but was also a heavy drain on Eliot's pocket, thus sharpening the tooth of his other plaguy problem: how to make ends meet.

They were poor, and ailing, but they were young, and they had each other. Besides being utterly miserable, were they ever happy? It is not a word that lives comfortably with either of them, but at this point in their marriage they must have had days, hours, or moments of happiness, or how could Tom write to his old friend Conrad Aiken as he did in January 1916—that Vivienne has been very ill, that his friend Jean Verdenal has been killed at the Dardanelles, that the *Catholic Anthology* (not a religious book but a collection edited by Ezra Pound and published in New York the previous November), in which five of Eliot's poems appeared, has not been a success, in spite of Yeats's presence in it; that he is worried about money and about Vivienne; and that he has written nothing lately—"but I am having a wonderful time nevertheless. I have *lived* through material for a score of long poems in the last six months." They were the first six months of his married life.

Eliot himself was deeply dissatisfied with the kind of verse he was now trying to write, and told his friend Aiken as much. He thought it "strained and intellectual." He knew that this was not the sort of thing he wanted to write: he knew, or thought he knew, what that kind was. But he felt that he could not force his own hand, that he would have to wait until he was ready.

By April 1, 1916, he had somehow found time to finish his dissertation on Bradley and had bought his ticket to sail that day for the United States to deliver it to Harvard and present himself for the final stages of his doctorate in philosophy. At the last moment the sailing was canceled. That sign from heaven decided him: forthwith he gave up the completion of his degree, even though he sent his dissertation to Harvard, where it was accepted.

He also found time, in order to eke out his schoolmaster's pittance, to write some wretchedly paid literary journalism. The *Monist* and the *International Journal of Ethics* were not noted for the size of their book-reviewing fees. The *New Statesman*, the *Manchester*

Guardian and the *Westminster Gazette*, to all of which he contributed, paid slightly better. He never really stopped working, but that summer he and Vivienne managed to take a seaside holiday at Bosham, near Portsmouth, a place the Eliots thought charming because it alternated between mud and water, the tide being either very high or very low.

The only ways he knew of making money were writing and teaching, and he found teaching the more onerous of the two. In September he began a series of two-hour lectures on Modern Literature which were to spread over three years: the first series, on modern French literature, was given at Southall, under the auspices of Oxford's Extramural Department. The sum total of his earnings from the three-year series was £45.16.9.

Yet Richard Aldington gave him high marks as a lecturer, comparing him, much in his favor, with Ezra Pound. "Unlike most poets, Eliot is not only a competent but a brilliant lecturer. Pound, on the other hand, relies chiefly on a faulty memory, an almost nonexistent power of improvisation and a cough."

6

The war of 1914–1918 is now ancient history. We tend to forget that London was subject to air raids and that consequently a nightly blackout was enforced, just as it was in the war of 1939–1945. On October 2, 1916, Eliot got a summons for showing too much light through his curtains.

By December he had had enough of schoolteaching. At Christmas he resigned from his job at the Highgate Junior School, and until the following March he tried to support Vivienne and himself by freelance literary journalism, mainly book reviewing. The pay then for reviewing fiction was 2/6d a novel; the sale of the review copy brought another 1/6d, making a total of 4/- a book. Eliot figured that if he could review six a day he could make a living from reviewing novels. Try as he might, he could manage no more than four.

The first two months of 1917 were a nightmare of ends not meeting. Then the Haigh-Woods came to the rescue. They had a friend high in the banking world, L. E. Thomas, chief general manager of the National Provincial Bank. This gentleman was kind enough to give Tom Eliot an introduction to the Colonial and Foreign Department of Lloyds Bank, at 20 King William Street, in the heart of the City of London. There on March 17 Eliot was given a job, at £2.10.0 a week, tabulating the balance sheets of foreign banks. He liked this job, which he found less fatiguing than teaching; furthermore, at five o'clock each afternoon he was free to go home to his own work.

The bank manager was impressed by Eliot's knowledge of languages. His Italian had indeed been fluent but, as he told Stravinsky many years later, it was an Italian of Dante's vintage, not exactly suitable for business letters. He also knew a little Rumanian and modern Greek, and this not only impressed the bank manager but somehow led him to believe that Eliot knew Polish to boot. Though Eliot assured him that this was not so, he seemed to think it illogical that a man who knew Rumanian and Greek should not know Polish as well.*

Eliot got a bit of help on his modern Greek from Raphael Demos, his old friend in the Harvard Graduate School, who had followed him to Merton and came up to London frequently. Once Demos and his wife had dinner with Eliot at I. A. Richards's flat. Mrs. Demos asked Eliot a question about modern poetry. His answer: "You know, I don't read contemporary poetry enough to say. If the poet is doing more or less what I am doing, it is—er—confusing. If he is doing something quite different, it is—er—er—irrelevant."

Others besides the Haigh-Woods had an anxiously benign eye on him. One was Ezra Pound, who now introduced Eliot to Harriet Shaw Weaver, that extraordinary woman who resembled a strait-laced governess but who, by a series of accidents, as editor of the fortnightly *Egoist,* found herself marshaling the extreme advance guard of modern English writers, and became one of the lonely saints of literature. When Richard Aldington, her assistant editor, joined the British Army in June, Pound saw to it that Eliot got his job, which carried with it a salary of £36 a year—more than half of it secretly contributed by Pound.

*Spanish was not one of Eliot's languages, as may be seen in this line from *Animula* (1929): "Pray for Guiterriez, avid of speed and power." No one with any feeling for Iberian words would have spelled the name that way. It should have been *Gutierrez,* a well-known Spanish name.

Eliot earned his pay. He carried out his editorial duties conscientiously and wrote brilliant criticism for the paper. At year's end, when contributions were skimpy and an issue threatened to run short, he filled the breach by writing five undetectably deadpan letters to the editor. Here is a sample:

> ... The philosophical articles interest me enormously; though they make me reflect that much water has flowed under many bridges since the days of my dear old Oxford tutor, Thomas Hill Green. And I am accustomed to more documentation; I like to know where writers get their ideas from.
>
> CHARLES AUGUSTUS CONYBEARE
>
> The Carlton Club, Liverpool.

No one guessed how much this sedulous aping cost him, nor why he did it. Some of it, like these imitation-suburbanite letters, was pure fun and games; but the whole thing was deadly serious. He had dedicated himself to "the intolerable wrestle with words." The kind of English he wanted to write must be purified, classical, combed free of Americanisms, of fashionable, perishable, quick-decaying phrases or idioms. And it *was* a struggle. After living in England for three years he could still write such stilted American as this: "Dear Mrs. Woolf, Please pardon me for not having responded to your note immediately." A far cry from the rhymed letters he would soon be inditing her, mannered but more pleasantly so, and a nation easier. "The Woolves" took him up, had him (and sometimes Vivienne) for weekends at Rodmell, and in 1919 published his *Poems.*

Virginia, who succeeded in feeling superior to most people, tried to laugh at him but found it harder and harder. It was she who called him, behind his back, "Great Tom." She used to tease him about his religious beliefs and try to make him talk about them, "but from such assaults," says her nephew, Quentin Bell, "he would retire, smiling, unruffled but unwilling to engage." She also (according to Elizabeth Bowen) said to him once, " 'It's such a pity, Tom, that you started being a poet instead of remaining in a bank. By now you might have been the Manager of the Bank of England.' He looked rather taken aback, but on the whole pleased. He purred like a very serious cat." And what did *he* think of *them?* He never said, in public; but he took none of them very seriously and was wary of them all.* Conrad Aiken

---

*The popular idols Bernard Shaw and H. G. Wells, being in his opinion fossils, were of no interest to him.

remembered his warning from those days—"that he should never, under any circumstances, in English literary society, discuss his 'first-rate' ideas, lest they be stolen, and rushed into print at once, by those jackdaws, those magpies: one should restrict oneself to one's 'second-rate' ideas, as the loss of these wouldn't so much matter."

Vivienne, in her staggering-butterfly way, tried to help the family finances. Without Tom's knowledge and against his wishes, she applied for a job in a government office, and was much surprised to learn that because she was married to an American citizen she was disqualified. She meant to be a model wife, but her bad health and her temperament combined to prevent her. She was determined to keep tabs on every penny they spent, and for a time her account books were a model; then somehow she got in a muddle, and Tom had to step in and straighten things out. Tom was always having to step in. These rescue jobs, added to other domestic chores which he had to take over in an emergency, with the time he had to give to his literary journalism, after office hours, built up to a working day with no time off. With this strain piled on top of the worry and stresses of his life with Vivienne, some sort of crack-up was inevitable. Aldous Huxley described him at the time as "haggard and ill-looking as usual."

But in these early days, when Vivienne still enjoyed bouts of good health and high spirits, they could occasionally afford to take an evening off, or a Sunday afternoon. They rolled up the rug, put a record on the gramophone, and danced. Tom was not a natural dancer, as she was, but under her intense tutelage he became "adequate." Ten years later, when Eliot was guest of honor at a literary society dinner in Cambridge, he was heard explaining to the High Table that because of the Negro influence in American music, no American could waltz properly and no Englishman could really fox-trot.

Hard up as they were, they could still afford a part-time "general." Her name was Ellen Kelland, and her scatteration of Cockney idiom a fair treat. Vivienne used some of Ellen's sayings in the stories she was later to write for the *Criterion,* and others are embalmed in *The Waste Land.*

> Well, that Sunday Albert was home, they had a hot gammon,
> And they asked me in to dinner, to get the beauty of it hot—

Another part-time retainer, dating from their early married days, was a gruff, mustachioed ex-policeman named Janes, who was handy at doing odd jobs and not above washing Polly, their Yorkshire terrier.

On a Sunday afternoon they sometimes went to a dance hall in Queensway with Brigit Patmore—a pretty girl-about-Parnassus who thought Tom's "slow way of speaking in a slightly booming monotone, without emphasis, was quite beguiling," and who later went off with Richard Aldington (she might have preferred to go off with Tom Eliot). Now and then Vivienne would leave Tom at home and go dancing with someone else. Of one such occasion she noted in her diary: "Picked up by 3 Canadian flying men. All exquisite dancers. I danced as I never have since before the war." Brigit Patmore tells of Vivienne, Eliot, and herself coming away from a dance hall and stopping at a chemist's shop for aspirin. "Vivienne was talking about a ballet and said, 'I think I can do what Karsavina does at that moment.' And she held on to the counter with one hand, rose on her toes and held out the other hand which Tom took in his right hand, watching Vivienne's feet with ardent interest whilst he supported her with real tenderness . . . most husbands would have said, 'Not here, for Heaven's sake!' "

When Miss Harriet Weaver thought it necessary, the *Egoist* became a publishing house. In June the Egoist Press published five hundred copies of the most arresting of Eliot's early poems, which has since been called "the best known English poem since the Rubaiyat": *The Love Song of J. Alfred Prufrock*. As G. S. Fraser says: "Nearly every important innovation in the English verse of the last thirty years is implicit in this poem . . . *Prufrock* is a beginner's poem, and it has lessons for all of us in the art of how to begin . . . poets must share the general admiration of the public for enormous talent, for enormous learning, and for a steady, sad and noble vision of the world . . . they have also . . . this special gratitude to him, as a craftsman who has provided them with new, sharp tools . . ."

In certain quarters—and they were quarters that counted—the impact of *Prufrock* was immediate and sensational. At a weekend at Lady Ottoline's at Garsington, with the flower of Bloomsbury strewn amid the trees, Clive Bell excitedly passed around a dozen copies, and Katherine Mansfield read the poem aloud. Would T. S. Eliot have picked that audience and chosen that reader? The Bloomsbury circle and many of his first admirers praised him ignorantly, and for the wrong reasons. The day would come when they would repudiate him, saying that he had turned his back on them and on his early self —two quite separate things which they found easy to confuse.

Ottoline Morrell's only daughter, Julian, was nine when she first met the Eliots, at her mother's house, and they made a lasting impression on her. She remembered him as tall, friendly, strikingly handsome, kind, like a man stooping courteously to those of smaller stature; Vivienne as coy, actressy, flirtatious, amusing. His poetry attracted her tremendously: when she was ten she had the whole of *Prufrock* by heart, and her mother got her to recite it to Virginia Woolf. Julian found his critical writing uninteresting ("too difficult") but loved all his poetry, whether she understood it or not.

Clive Bell, the complacent ninny who was the husband of Virginia Woolf's sister Vanessa, implied that he had launched Eliot (by distributing those copies of *Prufrock* at Garsington!) and later undertook to lecture him on the error of his ways in an article in *The Nation*. Eliot, who despised Bell, thought the article "disgusting and filthy" but said nothing ("the sort of thing one can only receive in silence").

He was well away in his clamber up the Acropolis of English letters; nothing could stop him now or divert him from reaching the top. In five years (1917–1921) he "carried out what must be the most arduous, the most concentrated critical labor of which detailed record exists . . . a re-thinking of the traditional heritage of English letters." At the time, Eliot was "a virtually anonymous foreigner aged about thirty."

7

As writers Eliot and Pound were so closely related, and their careers were so interwoven, that our opinion of one must affect our opinion of the other. They were in some ways complementary, in others antithetical.

Pound was silly, bumptious, extravagantly generous, annoying, exhibitionistic; Eliot was sensible, cautious, retiring, soothing, shy.

Though Pound wrote some brilliant passages, on the whole he was a failure as a poet (sometimes even in his own estimation); Eliot went from success to success, and is still quoted—and misquoted—by thousands of people who have never read him. Both men were expatriates by choice, but Eliot renounced his American citizenship and did his best to become assimilated with his fellow British subjects, while Pound always remained an American in exile.

At the University of Pennsylvania Pound schooled himself so thoroughly in Latin that he could read it easily the rest of his life; he was less well acquainted with Greek. Basil Bunting said of him, "He was learned in a large, careless, inaccurate way." His intensity either annoyed or impressed the recipient. "Miss Adele Polk remembered one day at the Pound home when Ezra . . . methodically pulled out the tail of his shirt as he talked, carefully tore off a square of material, with gravity placed the square on his knee, and tapped it during the rest of the conversation. She could not fathom his purpose but she was impressed."

Ford Madox Ford reacted differently. At his first meeting with Pound, when he read Pound's latest book, *Canzoni,* he was so horrified by the artificial language that he rolled on the floor. This time it was Pound's turn to be impressed. "That roll on the floor," he said, "saved me at least two years, perhaps more. It sent me back to my own proper effort . . ."

All his life, but particularly when he was young (generally the most self-regarding time of a man's life) Pound was generous to the point of recklessness. He was "as much concerned with the encouragement and improvement of the work of unknown writers in whom he discerned talent, as with his own creative work." He "formulated, for a generation of poets, the principles of good writing most needful for their time"; he "saw that their writings were published; saw that they were reviewed somewhere by critics who could appreciate them; organized or supported little magazines in which their work could appear—and incidentally, liked to give a good dinner to those he thought could not afford it, and sometimes even supplied the more needy with articles of clothing out of his own meagre store."

As a writer, Pound must have been one of the most unselfish men who ever lived. In a profession notorious for backbiting, bitchiness, and barracuda-like egotism he was justly famous for the time, trouble, and money he spent on furthering the careers of other writers. As a man he made frightful mistakes and paid terribly for them; but as an instigator and encourager of other writers' work he came near being the kind of literary saint that Harriet Weaver was.

Eliot was careful; he hoarded his lines (and the lines of others he wanted to use) as he saved his money. He was the ant to Pound's grasshopper. Pound enraged many and stepped on many toes; Eliot sometimes slipped in a stiletto but always studied to give no offense. It was with an unerring sense of their different natures that Pound once wrote to him: "You let *me* throw the bricks through the front window; you go in at the back door and take out the swag."

When we say that a man's character is complex, we mean that he has certain traits that do not jibe with other traits, that he is capable of behavior that seems to be at variance with what we know about him; in short, we mean that we simply do not understand him. It may be that a great many human beings are complex in this sense. Pound and Eliot most certainly were. Here is some of the evidence on Pound, from people who knew him well. This is from William Carlos Williams, on Pound as a fellow undergraduate at the University of Pennsylvania (1904): "If he ever does get blue nobody knows it . . . But not one person in a thousand likes him, and a great many people detest him and why? Because he is so darned full of conceits and affectation. He is really a brilliant talker and thinker but delights in making himself just exactly what he is not: a laughing boor. . . . It is too bad, for he loves to be liked, but there is some quality in him which makes him too proud to try to please people."

Iris Barry on Pound in London about 1910: "Into the restaurant with his clothes always seeming to fly round him, letting his ebony stick clatter to the floor, came Pound himself with the greenish cat-eyes, clearing his throat, making strange sounds and cries in his talking, but otherwise always quite formal and extremely polite." Ford Madox Ford: "Ezra had a forked red beard, luxuriant hair, an aggressive lank figure; one long blue single stone earring dangled on his jawbone. He wore a purple hat, a green shirt, a black velvet coat, vermilion socks . . . sandals . . . and trousers of green billiard cloth . . . an immense flowing tie . . . hand-painted by a Japanese Futurist poet."

Pound developed the habit of writing letters in his own kind of tough baby talk. Sometimes, as in this letter to Amy Lowell, it was funny and had a childlike acumen: "Auw shucks! dearie, aint you the hell-roarer, aint you the kuss." Or, to William Carlos Williams: "My Dear Old Sawbukk von Grump: How are your adenoids?"* But it got to be too much of a muchness: "Waal, I heerd the *Murder in the Cafedrawl* on the radio lass' night. Oh them cawkney woices, My Krissz, them cawkney woices. Mzzr Shakzpeer *still* retains his posishun. I stuck it fer a while, wot wiff the weepin and wailin . . .

"My Krrize them cawkney voyces!"

When you have read enough of Ezra Pound's irritable and irritating prattle (and the saturation point comes inevitably) you are thankful for Eliot's boring but unfailing good manners. Herbert Read, about eight years later: "Apart from [Pound's] exotic appearance, he rattled off his elliptic sentences with a harsh nasal twang, twitched incessantly, and prowled round the room like a caged panther." Though Wyndham Lewis thought Pound "a sort of revolutionary simpleton," he also said, "He has really walked with Sophocles beside the Aegean; he has *seen* the Florence of Cavalcanti; there is almost nowhere in the Past that he has not visited." Hemingway, in his patronizing way, was grateful to him: "It was from Pound that he had learnt more about 'how to write and how not to write' than from any son of a bitch alive and had always said so. . . . Ezra was the most generous writer I have ever known and the most disinterested."

Of his own great work what are we to say? The *Cantos* are in the same category as Joyce's *Finnegans Wake*, and the same question must be asked about both. Is this a *magnum opus* or an *ignis fatuus?* Both were labors of lonely love, stubbornly pursued year after year, in the face of skepticism, indifference, or incomprehension. And even of self-doubt (in Pound's case, at any rate). Is it possible that these two literary monuments were in fact a monumental waste of time, and that they are unread and uncomprehended because they are unreadable and incomprehensible? Alas, alas, it is possible.

Why should the same dusty answer not apply to *The Waste Land?* For one thing, because that poem is very much shorter; for another, because, for all its obliquities and obscurities, it is not completely

---

*And as late as 1955 he was addressing a letter to "T. S. Elyfunt Eliot Esq. O.M. Lld."

opaque. *The Waste Land* is like a cave to whose dim light our eyes gradually accustom themselves, and whose acoustics are well suited to the resonance of musical echoes. Eliot is eminently quotable; Pound is more quoted than he is given credit for, but in the *Penguin Dictionary of Quotations* (an inexact but representative yardstick) he is given half a column, Eliot four and a half.

As a critic Eliot makes the right sounds and comes out even. Where Pound was braggadociously insecure, Eliot was quietly sure of himself. But Eliot as critic is also Eliot at his least satisfactory and least likable—a know-it-all who puts us in our place and keeps us there; a martinet of a teacher who demands our silent assent but whose omniscient authority we privately take leave to doubt. His besetting phrase, as recurrent as the plain man's stuttering "y'know," is the intellectual's maddening "of course. . . ." Unlike Edmund Wilson's critical writing, which is as appetizing and reviving as whiffs of oxygen, Eliot's critical utterances breathe out a cold carbon dioxide. One fellow intellectual, Aldous Huxley, thought the whole thing impressive but bogus: "A great operation that is never performed; powerful lights are brought into focus, anaesthetists and assistants are posted, the instruments are prepared. Finally the surgeon arrives and opens his bag—but closes it again and goes off." Literary criticism in general indulges in violent and greedy words *(profound, indissoluble, incredibly);* perhaps Eliot's awareness of this tendency may partly account for the primness and dryness of much of his own criticism.

Pound takes a good deal of explaining. In some ways he must be allowed to have had a subtle mind, but in some things the village simpleton could have given him cards and trumps. As a young man, especially, what a motley piece of work he was! Yet, with all his unattractive oddities and irritating ways, Pound had a tremendously invigorating and reforming effect on the literary scene. His criticism, if not always as impressively stated as Eliot's, is on the whole more acceptable—except perhaps to scholars. He strikes the rock of his reading and out gushes a torrent of clear water, with a most refreshing taste and an occasional hilarious romp of tadpoles. His critical tone is quite unself-conscious, at times even incautiously blurty; this tone buoys him up and carries him along swimmingly—until, late in his career, he founders in the shallow rapids of his exaggerated baby talk. But until then, whenever he completely changes his mind or admits that he was quite wrong, we never hold these hops and skips against him, nor feel that they seriously detract from his essential rightness. Quite the contrary.

Eliot as a critic is an extreme contrast: cautious, precisian, authoritarian. Was he a scholar? He read a great deal and remembered a lot of it. And he saw ways of using things he had read. He was impressive but he did not exactly fit into a scholar's definition of a scholar. To Professor F. W. Bateson of Oxford, for example, he was "an American poet of enormous talent who happened to live in England . . . the 'learning' in Eliot's earlier poems must be seen as an aspect of his Americanism. As scholarship it is wide-ranging, but often superficial and inaccurate." His stabbing wit sometimes draws blood, though as often it merely punctures the air, and generally alarms the reader into a defensive posture—the very opposite effect of Pound's large-hearted and good-humored buffeting.

Yet Eliot the toplofty critic captured the British literary establishment as a comparatively young man and held it in thrall for the rest of his life. How do we account for that? Let an English man of letters, V. S. Pritchett, answer.

The two great American writers who have settled in England and have taken British nationality in the last half-century have been, primarily, persons who inspire awe. Henry James with his austere and indefatigable conception of the novel as a work of art, T. S. Eliot by the always increasing severity of his revolutionary practice of poetry, gave their English contemporaries a tremendous dressing down. Deliberately circumspect, serious and shocked, almost to the point of being noticeable in the street, these two American men of genius seem aloof from the English imagination which, as a rule, is hostile to intellectual formalizations and is lazy, sociable, sensual and heretical. Even the English feeling for tradition is a feeling for the history of its heresies: in this tradition Eliot and James, on the contrary, have given the sharp call to order.

An intensely serious American who reads more books and reads them more closely (i.e., works harder at them) than the clever but comparatively indolent English dilettante who takes his literary heritage for granted, considering himself and his peers its sole owners and only licensed interpreters, is bound to carry the day. Extraordinary as Eliot's single-handed invasion and conquest may appear, given his ambition, intelligence, and New England persistence, his capture of the British literary scene is comprehensible. Of this period Eliot said later: "In my earlier years I obtained, partly by subtlety, partly by effrontery, and partly by accident, a reputation amongst the credulous for learning and scholarship, of which (having no further use for it) I have since tried to disembarrass myself."

8

In May 1918 Eliot made the first of several attempts to enlist in the U.S. Army or Navy, whichever would take him. Physically he was unfit for either: underweight (137 pounds, fifteen pounds lighter than he had been at Oxford—five feet eleven), with a chronic hernia; but hope was held out to him that he might serve in Intelligence. The red tape unrolled endlessly, but he kept trying to cut his way through it until two days before the Armistice. That summer he and Vivienne spent at Marlow, a pretty village on the Thames, in a cottage belonging to Bertrand Russell. While they were there he wrote *Ode*.

In September, under the auspices of the London County Council, Eliot began a series of eighteen lectures in Sydenham on Elizabethan literature. At a poetry recital in Sibyl Colefax's London drawing room, Arnold Bennett heard Eliot read *The Hippopotamus* and noted in his journal: "Had I been the house, this would have brought the house down."

In January 1919, Eliot's father died in St. Louis. The cable came on January 8, after Tom had left for work, and Vivienne had to keep the miserable news till he came home from the bank. Mr. Eliot had not been close to his son nor, lately, on friendly terms; the news therefore added to Eliot's sense of irredeemable loss. As soon as she could, his mother and the two daughters who still lived with her left St. Louis for good and moved to Cambridge, their natural habitat.

That summer Eliot took his August holiday in France, without Vivienne; alone part of the time, part of the time with Ezra Pound in the Dordogne. There he saw some prehistoric cave paintings ("Art never improves, but . . . the material of art is never quite the same"). And that month he had good news from America. Alfred Knopf had condescended favorably to Eliot's poems and would publish them: "I have read Eliot's little book of poems with immense enjoyment. I do not know whether it is great poetry or not. I do know that it is great fun and I like it." And Eliot made some jottings for a "long poem . . . which I am wishful to finish"—still formless, and without a title. The following year it would have its temporary name: *He Do the Police in Different Voices.*

In October he began another series of lectures, which he gave at Conference Hall, Westminster (at least the addresses of his addresses were getting better) on "Modern Tendencies in Poetry." Lloyds Bank sent him on occasional business trips, about one of which he wrote to Lytton Strachey, who must have tried to get under Eliot's skin with some faint sneer about his hobnobbing with Anglican clergy: "You are very—ingenuous—if you can conceive me conversing with rural deans in the cathedral close. I do not go to cathedral towns but to centres of industry. My thoughts are absorbed in questions more important than ever enter the heads of deans—as why it is cheaper to buy steel from America than from Middlesbrough, and the probable effect—the exchange difficulties with Poland—and the appreciation of the rupee."

The most authoritative critical voice in England issued from the *Times Literary Supplement,* and particularly from its unsigned leading review. In 1919, at the age of thirty-one, Eliot captured this shrine and took over the Delphic voice (or, in his more modest phrase, reached "the top rung of the ladder of literary journalism"). Bruce Richmond, the nonwriting but all-pervasive editor of the *Times Literary Supplement,* had read and liked Eliot's reviews in the *Athenaeum* and wanted to meet him. Richard Aldington undertook to introduce him to the great editor. To Aldington's chagrin Eliot, just back from a holiday in Switzerland, turned up sporting a most unbecoming full beard under his bowler. But Eliot's conversation soon won Richmond, and the beard was not seen again. Eliot learned from Richmond how to take good editing. "I remember how the occasional deletion of a phrase, by the editorial pencil, taught me to temper my prejudices and control my crotchets and whimsies . . . I learnt to write in a temperate and impartial way."*

*Much as he admired Richmond as an editor, Eliot's opinion of him as a man was that he was typical of All Souls, Oxford, in elevating lack of conviction into a strong conviction itself.

On November 13 his first contribution to the *Times Literary Supplement* appeared, a leading article on Ben Jonson. It was impressive. "Of all the dramatists of his time, Jonson is probably the one whom the present age would find the most sympathetic, if it knew him. There is a brutality, a lack of sentiment, a polished surface, a handling of large bold designs in brilliant colours, which ought to attract about three thousand people in London and elsewhere. At least, if we had a contemporary Shakespeare and a contemporary Jonson, it would be the Jonson who would arouse the enthusiasm of the intelligentsia!" But his real work for the year was a long poem about a little old man, *Gerontion*. That, and those jottings for an even lengthier poem.

That winter an access of homesickness swept over him. He had not seen his native country for five years. He thought with particular fondness of his mother: how dearly he would like to see her again! But he could not afford the price of the journey to America, nor the loss of pay from his job that would entail; nor could he afford to pay for Vivienne, even if she would go with him. Perhaps his mother would come to England instead? But Mrs. Eliot felt that she should not leave the United States until her husband's estate was settled.* She promised to come then, as soon as she could. He had that to look forward to.

So he settled down as best he could to the daily round: a drab and constricted life, on the face of it, in a London dingied and diminished by four years of a war that had effectively ended Britain's empire. He got up about five in the morning for a couple of hours' work before breakfast. Twice a day he joined the hurrying, anonymous throng ("A crowd flowed over London Bridge, so many,/I had not thought death had undone so many") that streamed from the drab neighborhoods of outer London to the packed confines of the City, and ebbed back again at day's end. Once at his desk, he was too busy to brood on his own concerns. He was now being paid £500 a year, and his duties had become less routine and much more interesting: settling the prewar accounts of the bank with the Germans, which entailed some fascinating legal questions and a study of "that appalling document the

*Mr. Eliot's will left outright bequests to all his children except Tom, whose share was put in trust and reverted to the estate on his death.

Peace Treaty" (of Versailles). He was held in such esteem by his colleagues at the bank that returning war veterans who protested against the advancement of junior staff over their heads singled out Eliot as an exception.

Home again with Vivienne, in the noise and clutter of Crawford Street—or even worse, with Vivienne ill and absent—he was constantly reminded of the awful predicament of their life. Nevertheless, he knew now where he was going, even if he did not know how he was going to get there. The year saw the publication of two books that made his goal clearer and his progress toward it more certain. In February John Rodker published in London *Ara Vos Prec**—thirteen new poems and a reprinting of *Prufrock*. And in the same month Knopf brought out in New York *Poems by T. S. Eliot,* the same collection, except that in this American edition *Ode* replaced *Hysteria*.

These poems were still so far in advance of the public taste of the day and so liable to be misunderstood as satirical or cynical light verse that Eliot felt it necessary to write to his brother Henry, the only American audience he could talk to and count on, that these poems, no matter how lightly they might seem to tinkle, were in fact "intensely serious." He felt that he had to explain this, to his own brother, because even in England, he said, he was typed as no more than a witty satirist, and in America he expected these poems to be written off as downright disgusting.

It seems incredible now that the first poem in the book, a monologue by Eliot in the guise of a little old man *(Gerontion)* could ever have been mistaken as either satirical or disgusting. John Crowe Ransom, himself one of the craftiest of poets, who at first was slow to recognize Eliot's genius, said of these lines

> Gull against the wind, in the windy straits
> Of Belle Isle, or running on the Horn,
> White feathers in the snow, the Gulf claims,
> And an old man driven by the Trades
> To a sleepy corner

---

*Part of this edition bore the title *Ara Vus Prec.* Years later Eliot explained this error by saying that his ignorance of Provençal was to blame; he was quoting from an Italian edition of Dante whose editor apparently did not know Provençal either.

that they were "wildly beautiful" and "the work of a master of his art."

Pound has let one kitten out of the bag: that Grishkin (in *Whispers of Immortality*) was a real woman, and that he introduced her to Eliot, some time before 1919, in the hope and with the intention that a poem should result from the meeting. This successful experiment, he said, was unique in his experience.

The other book, published in London in November, was *The Sacred Wood*, a selection of Eliot's critical essays which became the bible of his literary followers, and the most influential book of criticism of its generation. As F. O. Matthiessen said, the essays in this book "definitely placed their author in the main line of poet-critics that runs from Ben Jonson and Dryden through Samuel Johnson, Coleridge, and Arnold."

The year also brought him one of the most brilliant and effective of his followers: a young Cambridge don, I. A. Richards, who was halfway between a friend and a disciple. The second time they met was at Eliot's office at the bank. Richards described him as "a figure stooping, very like a dark bird in a feeder, over a big table covered with all sorts and sizes of foreign correspondence. The big table almost entirely filled a little room under the street. Within a foot of our heads when we stood were the thick, green glass squares of the pavement on which hammered all but incessantly the heels of the passers-by. There was just room for two perches beside the table."

And Richards quoted a senior official of the bank: "If you see our young friend, you might tell him that we think he's doing quite well at the Bank. In fact, if he goes on as he has been doing, I don't see why—in time, of course, in time—he mightn't even become a Branch Manager." Richards instead tried to persuade Eliot to accept some sort of academic post at Cambridge, but Eliot, like a wary animal sniffing a trap, declined.

At year's end the pressures on Eliot were mounting to an almost intolerable pitch: the steady pounding of his bank job, the anxious strain of his literary work, the unrestful nights, disturbed by Vivienne's fretful alarms and nervous crises, plagued by his own haunted wakefulness and haunting dreams. Could nothing be done to break this pressure, or at least ease it? One thing he might do was to get them out of this noisy and sordid neighborhood and into a quieter street.

To his other tasks he added house hunting. At last he found a place, a flat in Clarence Gate Gardens, on the north side of Marylebone Road, on the edge of Regents Park. Then Vivienne's health worsened and everything seemed to conspire against them. He was filled with despair and began to doubt that they could ever move or ever find a way out of their thronging troubles.

But the face he showed the world, "infinitely suffering," was also "infinitely gentle." In the hollow round of his skull beneath the skin, unseen, unguessed-at, betrayed only rarely by rumbles and somber gleams, the violent, intemperate, unappeasable volcano.

▬

FOUR

Life Is Very Long

(1 9 2 1 – 1 9 2 5)

1

THAT WAS ONE WAY of putting it—not very satisfactory. It might be said differently, if no more accurately—that the Furies hunted him. He would not have described his situation so melodramatically, himself. He did, however, consider himself "emotionally deranged," and that this derangement had been "a lifelong affliction." Yet there was nothing wrong with his mind, he was sure of that; it was his will that was sick. He could not shake off the constant, pressing burden of anxiety and fear.

Why should he be anxious? What did he fear? To judge by the surface, nothing much seemed amiss. Millions of other London lives looked equally humdrum, equally harassed. He was overworking himself, fourteen and fifteen hours a day, but that was by his own choice, because he was driven by an ambition as fierce as his grandfather's: *to excel.* He wanted to prove to his family in America (particularly to the shade of his disapproving and disappointed father) that he had *not* made a sorry failure of his life, that he could beat those British men of letters at their own game: *that* would show him. Those spare hours—all he could spare and more—after his daily stint at the bank, in which he hammered and whetted his pieces of literary journalism for the *Egoist,* for the *Athenaeum,* for the *Times Literary Supplement,* were devoted to one consuming purpose: to establish himself, the alien, the foreigner, the American, as the dominant voice in English letters.

His love for Vivienne, the deep incurable wound in his life, had begun in anxiety and fear—fear and anxiety over the break with his family, his country, his traditions—and grew into a different profound anxiety about her health, her sanity, and the inevitable lessening of his own love. And there was always the competitive stress, himself against the rest of the writing world; Conrad Aiken called it the "unceasing literary *sauve-qui-peut.*"

The lives of quiet desperation observed by Thoreau would not have been so described or perhaps even felt as such by the New Englanders who led them; to those patient or merely enduring men their lives may well have seemed quite ordinary, the inevitable human condition, only requiring patience or at any rate endurance. But Eliot was aware that his suffering was intolerable, and his desperation drove him to complain, as the ancient Psalmist had complained, before the face of God.

In February 1921 Virginia Woolf noted in her diary that she and Leonard had dined with Eliot at The Cock in Fleet Street: "Pale, marmoreal Eliot was there last week, like a chapped office boy on a high stool, with a cold in his head, until he warms a little, which he did. We walked back along the Strand. 'The critics say I am learned and cold,' he said. 'The truth is I am neither.' As he said this, I think coldness at least must be a sore point with him. . . . But what about Eliot? Will he become Tom? . . . I suppose a good mind endures, and one is drawn to it and sticks to it, owing to having a good mind myself. Not that Tom endures my writing, damn him." By the end of the year they were calling him Tom and Virginia noted with regret that she was no longer frightened of him.

Eliot had not seen any of his family or his native land since just after his marriage, six years before. None of his family had as yet met Vivienne. Now at last his mother, having settled her husband's estate, decided to come, with his favorite sister Marian, and pay Tom and his wife a visit, preceded by a shorter visit from his brother Henry. The young Eliots moved out of their flat at Clarence Gate Gardens so that Mrs. Eliot and Marian could stay there, and went temporarily to 12 Wigmore Street.

That year the German mark began its precipitous rush down the cliffs into the abyss where Hitler waited; as a desperate and ineffective expedient, the French Army occupied the Ruhr. For the rest, small routine catastrophes were noted by the omnivorous, toothless, tasteless press as tidbits or solid sustenance. A Disarmament Conference met in Washington, where Warren Gamaliel Harding had taken up residence in the White House; in Canada, Mackenzie King inaugurated his long gray reign over his wide gray land. The year 1921 saw the beginning of two literary friendships of Eliot's: with Wyndham Lewis and with James Joyce. Neither could be described as warm, although Eliot and Lewis saw a good deal of each other and remained on those terms until Lewis's death—a feat of immense patience and forbearance on Eliot's part, in view of Lewis's abnormal and recurrent suspiciousness.

The two admired each other, up to a point, and each found the other amusing, with an undercurrent of irritation. In the summer of 1921 they went on a walking trip together down the Loire. At Saumur they hired bicycles to ride to Chinon and were going at a great clip when Lewis's handlebars snapped off and he came a cropper. Eliot's spinsterly description of this incident might make a spinster giggle; Lewis's account of Eliot totting up the day's expenses in a notebook rouses a dry grin. On this same trip they spent a few days in Paris, where they met James Joyce for the first time, and Eliot handed him the parcel he had brought from Ezra Pound: a pair of used brown shoes. Joyce and Eliot did not hit it off; each felt chilled by the other's imperfectly concealed arrogance.

Conrad Aiken, his much-enduring old friend, admiring but not uncritical, he sometimes treated with merciless contempt. In *Ushant,* Aiken's characteristically quirky autobiography, he speaks of "that evident streak of sadism in the Tsetse's [Eliot's] otherwise urbane and kindly character, which now and again, as D. [Aiken] well knew, he enjoyed indulging. 'You don't know the meaning of words,' he had once remarked to D., in a sudden such thrust. . . ."

And Aiken describes another occasion, on which he had written a letter of somewhat fulsome praise to Eliot about his latest book. He had written the letter from hospital, the morning after an operation, in great pain and still woozy from ether. Eliot's reply was a printed page torn from *The Midwives' Gazette,* "on which he had underlined in ink certain words and phrases—*'Blood—mucous—shreds of mu-*

cous—purulent offensive discharge.'" Aiken recovered from this Tsetse bite, as he called it, but he never forgot it.

In London that same summer Eliot heard Stravinsky's *Sacre du Printemps,* which made a profound impression on him, and gave him the ambition of achieving in words the effects Stravinsky had accomplished in music. His "London Letter" in *The Dial,* defending and interpreting the *Sacre,* led to a correspondence with Stravinsky and a lifelong friendship.

Eliot's brother Henry came and went; his mother and his sister Marian also, after a longer visit. All of them presumably were anxious about Tom's poor health—and Vivienne's too, for that matter—but it gave none of them cause for immediate alarm. Ezra Pound, who bulked larger in Eliot's life than any of his American family did, quit London this year, and for good. He was sick and tired of banging on editorial doors that were permanently locked against him. He decided that England was hopeless: he would try Paris for a change. Eliot did not admit to any feeling of relief at his departure, but it was almost certainly a good thing for him that this benign bully should remove himself to another parish.

2

By September 1921 Vivienne was so worried about Tom's mental state that she insisted he see a nerve specialist, who told him flatly that he must go away at once, alone, for three months, see nobody and not exert his mind at all. The bank generously gave him leave of absence with pay. Lady Ottoline Morrell recommended Dr. Roger Vittoz of Lausanne; Julian Huxley, when asked, confirmed her good opinion of this specialist.

Eliot did not carry out the doctor's orders to go alone. First he and Vivienne went to Margate, having asked Richard Aldington to look after their cat, "a very good mouser." They spent three weeks at a hotel near Margate

> On Margate Sands.
> I can connect
> Nothing with nothing . . .

then returned home for a week; at last, in mid-November, set out for Lausanne. Vivienne went with him as far as Paris. Eliot was in Switzerland for about six weeks. While he was there he disobeyed another of the doctor's orders: that he was not to exert his mind at all, for there he put together the extraordinary poem *The Waste Land.* "A piece of rhythmical grumbling," he called it later, in the understatement of the century. It was also an amazing effort, unless we are to suppose that *The Waste Land,* in its original version nearly a thousand lines long, was an example of automatic writing; for although Eliot had been collecting bits of it for years, a great deal was written in Switzerland. A considerable accomplishment for a man said to be suffering from an *aboulie* (a French word defined as *absence morbide de volonté*). Eliot did say afterward that "some forms of ill health . . . may . . . produce an efflux of poetry in a way approaching the condition of automatic writing . . . an outburst of words which we hardly recognize as our own (because of the effortlessness). . . ."

Another way of putting it would be that the heat of his mental fever hatched the egg. Conrad Aiken was "entirely convinced" that Eliot's feverish frame of mind was raised to this pitch by anger at a psychoanalyst's opinion (reported by Aiken) that "all that's stopping him [from writing] is his fear of putting anything down that is short of perfection. He thinks he's God." Eliot "was literally speechless with rage . . . but it did the trick, it broke the log-jam. A month or two later he went to Switzerland, and there wrote *The Waste Land.*" However much he wrote or revised in Switzerland, on his way home in December Eliot stopped off in Paris and handed over to Pound the enormous fruit of his "rest cure." Then he and Vivienne, who had also been at a sanatorium, near Paris, went back to London together.

Pound's editing transformed an inchoate collection of poems into the single poem we know. His editing was drastic. He cut out half the lines Eliot had written, making the remainder harder to understand, easier to remember. The main thing he did was to cancel big chunks —the opening fifty-four lines; seventy lines of heroic couplets imitating Pope's *Rape of the Lock;* eighty-three lines telling the story of the wreck of a fishing schooner in the Arctic ice. He also criticized some lines and passages he left in: "Too tum-pum at a stretch"; "photography"; "make up yr. mind." His cries of approval were muted but unmistakable: "O.K." or "Echt." And perhaps the best thing he did was to tell Eliot—and everyone else within earshot—that this poem was a bloody masterpiece. To Eliot he wrote: "Complimenti, you bitch. I am wracked by the seven jealousies. . . ."

Not everyone thought it a masterpiece. Some spotted it as a hoax, and *Time* so reported in its first issue. Christopher Morley called it "high-spirited spoofing"; John Crowe Ransom (who afterward changed his tune) thought it "insubordinate, unequal," and impermanent; to Amy Lowell it was "a piece of tripe . . . Tom is an intellectual and an intellectual cannot write a poem. . . ." Edmund Wilson and Gilbert Seldes, who could tell a hawk from a handsaw, hailed it as a triumph. To William Carlos Williams it was an atom bomb, and he hated it for that reason.* Van Wyck Brooks thought it "like a great hollow gong, echoing from beginning to end; there is no mistaking an Eliot line; there is hardly an Eliot line that is Eliot." Yvor Winters did not think well of it: ". . . it is a broken blank verse interspersed with bad free verse and rimed doggerel. . . . The method is that of a man who is unable to deal with the subject, and resorts to the rough approximation of a quotation. . . ." Evelyn Waugh's father, in his review of the poem, spoke darkly of "drunken helots" —the Spartans, according to him, used to encourage orgies among their slaves in order to disgust decent people; and this was the only conceivable purpose of such poetry. Though at first *The Waste Land* brought him little honor and loud jeers in his own Midwestern country, it did win over his mother. He had written to her that he had put much of his life into the poem; she therefore tried to read it with sympathy, she reflected on it and—feeling a little giddy with daring —accepted it.

When Conrad Aiken reviewed the poem for the *New Republic* he told Eliot he had called his review "An Anatomy of Melancholy," whereupon Eliot turned on him "with that icy fury of which he alone was capable, and said fiercely, 'There is nothing melancholy about

---

*The mutual dislike that grew up between Eliot and Williams was rooted in something very like class distinction. There was all the difference in the world between Ezra Pound's condescending but warm-hearted jeers at Williams as an incoherent immigrant (he was a second-generation American, half Portuguese) and Eliot's cold disdain, dismissing him as "of local interest perhaps." Eliot and all his works drove Williams to helpless rage.

it!' " Aiken quietly explained that the reference was to Burton's famous treatise, which also contained an extraordinary amount of quotations.

In England, A. P. Herbert said he preferred Oscar Hammerstein; A. E. Housman's sympathy was not engaged; Arnold Bennett couldn't see the point; Sir Edmund Gosse was not amused. To others the poem was completely incomprehensible, or hateful, or both. It is hardly too much to say that Eliot himself, at first, did not regard *The Waste Land* as a great poem, but was gradually persuaded that it might be, perhaps was. The year after it was published he wrote to Ford Madox Ford that in his opinion there were thirty good lines in the poem (out of 433), and specified them: "the water-dripping song in the last part." Did he really not know? Vivienne knew. In the margin of the typescript, alongside the forty lines beginning

Filled all the desert with inviolable voice

and ending

"What shall I do now? What shall I do?"
"I shall rush out as I am, and walk the street
With my hair down, so. What shall we do tomorrow?
"What shall we ever do?"

she penciled W O N D E R F U L and then again *wonderful wonderful*—quite disregarding Pound's denigrating and picky grumbles about the same passage.

The literary establishment, which always feels itself mocked or threatened by anything new, set its face against the mocking threat of this new kind of poem. It was not so much a poem, in the accepted sense, as a drama with no stage directions, no plot, and no listed cast of characters. But those with eyes to see and ears to hear, especially the young, who were not shocked, because they neither knew nor cared what rules Eliot was breaking, recognized *The Waste Land* and welcomed it. One of them, afterward headmaster of Eton, remembered after fifty years the impact the poem made on his generation: "Here was someone who could give expression to our own deep, but hardly understood, doubts and uncertainties, and do this in language of unforgettable beauty, so that lines from the poem have haunted me constantly ever since."

Why did Eliot himself feel so unsure of what he had written that he meekly submitted to the cancellation of half the poem, and accepted most of Pound's scolding strictures on the rest of it? No one likes being edited, and Eliot, of all people, was not accustomed to making such obeisances. In this case he carried his submissiveness so far that when Pound had reduced the *Death by Water* section (Part IV) to the ten lines beginning

Phlebas, the Phoenician, a fortnight dead,

Eliot suggested that they throw out this marvelous baby with the rest of the bath. Was this simply pique? And in writing to John Quinn, the New York Maecenas to whom he gave the only copy of the original poem, Eliot said, "In the manuscript of *The Waste Land* which I am sending you, you will see the evidence of his [Pound's] work, and I think that this manuscript is worth preserving in its present form solely for the reason that it is the only evidence of the difference which his criticism has made to this poem. I am glad that you, at least, will have the opportunity of judging this for yourself. Naturally, I hope that the portions which I have suppressed will never appear in print, and in sending them to you I am sending you the only copies of these parts." And in an earlier letter to Quinn he voiced his fervent hope that, now the mess had been wiped up, no more should be said about it: "You will find a great many sets of verse which have never been printed and which I am sure you will agree never ought to be printed, and, in putting them in your hands, I beg you fervently to keep them to yourself and see that they never are printed."

Quinn was an honorable man, and did keep them to himself; perhaps, had he lived long enough, he would have carried out in lawyerly fashion Eliot's fervent plea to "see that they never are printed." But Quinn died at an unexpectedly early age, and the manuscript became the property of his niece, who apparently was unaware of its existence; it was "lost" in the welter of Quinn's papers. In 1958 she discovered the manuscript and sold it to a private collection, housed in the New York Public Library, for $18,000.

Eliot was still alive then, and lived for seven more years. Why was he not notified of the discovery or consulted about the manuscript's disposition? No satisfactory answer has yet been made. Ten years later, three years after Eliot's death, his widow was informed of the manuscript's whereabouts and was given a microfilm copy, on the understanding that she would keep quiet about it until the library issued a public statement later that year, on the day of publication of John Quinn's biography, *The Man from New York*. In 1971 Mrs. Eliot brought out the facsimile edition of the original *Waste Land*, including all those passages which her husband had fervently begged Quinn to suppress.

How did Valerie Eliot get around this particular veto of her husband's? Very simply. She said that he had changed his mind, and had told her so. In an interview in *The Observer*, February 20, 1972, she was reported as saying: "We never thought it [the missing manuscript] would turn up, but Tom told me that if it did I was to publish it. 'It won't do me any good,' he added, 'but I would like people to realize the extent of my debt to Ezra.' " Pound himself said, after the lost typescript reappeared: "The more we know of Eliot, the better." Until this capsizing statement of Mrs. Eliot's, it had been generally supposed that Eliot had *not* changed his mind, and that he had several times expressed the hope that the lost manuscript was lost forever.

We must of course accept Mrs. Eliot's statement. Who should know better than she what her husband said to her or did not say? And yet this awkward question must be raised as well: Did she quite realize what initial effect the printing of these "never-to-be-printed" passages might have on Eliot's reputation as a careful and cunning poet? For students of T. S. Eliot or of poetry in general, Valerie Eliot's edition of *The Waste Land* is valuable and useful in showing work in progress and the disarray that progress entails. It was obviously a labor of love and wifely piety (slightly marred by a fistful of misquotations and misprints in her Editorial Notes). Nevertheless, although a monument to good intentions, the book would seem to show that without Pound's shaping hand *The Waste Land* would have been a jumble of first-rate, second-rate, and even third-rate verse in which some hard beauties were embedded that Eliot himself was apparently incapable of distinguishing from the surrounding rubble. Pound did not organize the chaos of the poem, which remains chaotic: by his delving and chucking out the chaos was channeled and the stream quickened.

And yet, are the canceled verses really as bad as all that? To the anonymous, rather nasty mind of the reviewer in the *Times Literary Supplement,* some of the suppressed lines blow the gaff on Eliot's guilty secret: that he hated and feared women—in short, that he was a homosexual. This supposition is not only nasty but ridiculous. If Eliot at times felt a horror of women, he was not the first mother's son to be so afflicted; if he was sometimes given to the contemplation of the cold comfort of his own sexuality, he was not the first there either. There are more damaging passages. The twenty-two lines of *Dirge,* surely one of the most horrible descriptions ever written of a drowned body, are further uglified by naming the disintegrating corpse Bleistein, "a dead jew." But aside from giving new life to rumors of Eliot's homosexuality (easy to refute) and antisemitism (not so easy), most of these discarded poems and passages, looked at a second time, do no serious harm to Eliot's reputation *as a poet,* nor does their quality altogether explain his nervous anxiety that they should never be published. If he had wanted to ensure their nonappearance, why did he not destroy these passages himself, or ink them out on the pages he sent to Quinn? Why should a writer enjoin his literary executor to destroy work that he himself might have destroyed, if he meant what he said? There is something not strictly honest about such a behest.

Only a few of Eliot's canceled lines are so bad, even out of context, that they excite derision. These, from the eighty-three lines deleted from Part IV *(Death by Water)* are perhaps the worst. A terrible storm has driven the fishing schooner far north, and the horrified sailors see they are about to crash into a wall of ice. At the last moment one of them says, or thinks:

> My God man there's bears on it.
> Not a chance. Home and mother.
> Where's a cocktail shaker Ben, here's plenty of cracked ice.

It is just as well for Eliot's reputation that these uproariously awful lines have not passed into the language. But look at the next two, which attempt the impossible by trying to express the *sound* of silence, the drowned silence which swallows the ship and the sailors after the storm's "illimitable scream," and with an echo of the Homeric phrase *poluphloisboio thalasso:*

> And if Another knows, I know I know not,
> Who only know that there is no more noise now.

Eliot achieved a more successful onomatopoetic effect in the final line of the poem (as Pound left it): the downpouring rain of

Shantih shantih shantih.

In his published verse Eliot has shown himself a sardonic master of the knife edge, whose foot never slips into the sentimental or the unconsciously ridiculous, but in another deleted passage, five lines of religious paradox, beginning with the opening line of the Anglican burial service

I am the Resurrection and the Life

end with the ludicrous and bathetic Buddhistry

I am the fire, and the butter also.*

And, whether it was Pound or the sobriety of second thought that persuaded him, Eliot did well to abandon his original, hilarious title for the poem: *He Do the Police in Different Voices.*†

The original opening, fifty-four lines of casually sauntering prosy verse about a night on the town (presumably Boston), is better out. Its omission, like most of Pound's editing, helps to speed and intensify the poem. But there are other passages whose deletion is not an unarguable improvement. Admirable lines such as these:

Kingfisher weather, with a light fair breeze . . .
A porpoise snored upon the phosphorescent swell,
A triton rang the final warning bell
Astern, and the sea rolled, asleep . . .

And those seventy lines of heroic couplets in the manner of Pope-in-modern-dress? As Eliot later reported, Pound had said, "Pope has done this so well that you cannot do it better; and if you mean this as a burlesque, you had better suppress it, for you cannot parody Pope unless you can write better verse than Pope—and you can't." Eliot agreed, although he felt a twinge of reluctance: he had consid-

---

*Speculation about *The Waste Land* still goes on. Eliot's admission that it was "just a piece of rhythmical grumbling" is taken with a larger pinch of salt than the recipe called for. The latest discovery (by Craig Raine in the *Times Literary Supplement*, May 4, 1973) is that *The Waste Land* "is a Buddhist poem about reincarnation."

†For non-Dickensians it should be explained that this is a quotation from *Our Mutual Friend*. Betty Higden, a poor widow, likes to have the newspaper read to her by her adopted son, Sloppy. "You mightn't think it, but Sloppy is a beautiful reader of a newspaper. He do the Police in different voices."

ered them "an excellent set of couplets." It is quite true that they are not as good as Pope, but they are better than most such imitations, on a par with Pope's own imitation of Chaucer, and they read more entertainingly than most of Swift's verse, for example.

It was Eliot's frugal habit to save unused lines and bits of poems for later use; it is noteworthy that he revived very few of the hundreds of lines expunged by Pound. He kept and developed the second half of *Song for the Opherion*, perhaps partly for the pleasure of the jangle-juddering rhyme

> The wind sprang up and broke the bells
> Is it a dream or something else . . .

Why did he bury forever two finished or nearly finished poems, *Elegy* and *Exequy?* He would no doubt have said that they did not measure up to his exacting standard (screwed to the sticking point by Pound); perhaps he was even more afraid that they gave too much away.

Besides her applause, Vivienne contributed at least two lines to *The Waste Land:*

> If you don't like it you can get on with it, I said.

and

> What you get married for if you don't want children?

Much has been written about the scheme, the symmetrical plan of *The Waste Land,* an illusion which Eliot, by the solemn mockery of his appended Notes, has done much to foster. But the scheme, such as it is, is mostly afterthought. The jagged bits of glass in a kaleidoscope seem to form patterns and to complement each other, but only because the mirror makes it seem so: without the optical illusion their meetings and matings would appear quite haphazard.

3

Prufrock had put Eliot on the literary map of England. *The Waste Land* made him an international figure. His great year was 1922, which not only saw the publication of *The Waste Land* on both sides of the Atlantic, but marked the start of his own literary journal, the

Criterion. At the beginning of the year he had added to his literary chores that of London correspondent of the *Nouvelle Revue Fran-çaise.* He was already sending "London Letters" to Schofield Thayer's *Dial* in America; by year's end the pressure of his own work had forced him to give up both these jobs.

At the Sydney Schiffs, in Cambridge Square, one of the literary houses he frequented in London, Eliot met Lady Rothermere, who liked literary lion cubs and perhaps hoped to train this one. If so, she must soon have discovered that Eliot was no cub and would not respond to training. But when she learned that he wanted to edit his own literary quarterly, she offered to pay the bills, up to a certain figure, and he accepted with alacrity. The first issue of the *Criterion* (Vivienne suggested its name) appeared on October 15, 1922. Its leading feature was *The Waste Land,* without the Notes. The *Dial* also printed the poem in its November number, and awarded it the annual *Dial* prize of $2,000.

In the *Criterion* Eliot felt that his whole career was at stake. He did not expect the quarterly to make money or to be a popular success, but he hoped that it would set a high standard and that it might be acclaimed for doing so. If it fell flat, he feared he would "have to retire to obscurity or Paris like Ezra." The magazine never gave the slightest promise of making money—the circulation at its peak was nine hundred, and was usually less than half that—but its quality was severely respectable and its tone lofty, tinged at times with that frosty contempt that makes intellectuals shiver with delight or shake with rage. It was definitely highbrow but on the whole well written, and occasionally entertaining. And though its readers were few, they included a dominant minority of the literary establishment. To be the editor of the *Criterion* was like being a doctor hanging out his shingle in Harley Street: it was not only a good address but it bespoke authority.

In his progress from critic to arbiter Eliot laid the foundations and built a large part of his critical edifice in the form of book reviews. The books he was careful to choose or to be assigned were nearly all integral or capable of being integrated with the principal courses of literary masonry. As an arbiter he did not cease to be a critic, and he was not infallibly even-handed: he tended to magnify the virtues of those whom he found praiseworthy, and to minimize the virtues of those he disliked. In short, though cleverer and better read than most, like everyone else he exaggerated a little. In his more didactic essays a faint note of scolding—rather like an orthodox Communist explaining the Five-Year Plan—gives the impression that he is addressing an infant class, and not a very bright one, either.

But his critical prescriptions, in the *Criterion* and elsewhere, were generally unexceptionable, balanced, boring, often on the dull, safe-and-sane side, but sometimes flashing with insight or illumined by uncommon sense. Henry James was "the most intelligent man of his generation . . . he had a mind so fine that no idea could violate it. . . . Mr. Chesterton's brain swarms with ideas; I see no evidence that it thinks." Eliot's comment on Othello's final speech: "What Othello seems to me to be doing in making this speech is *cheering himself up.* . . . Poetry is a superior amusement: I do not mean an amusement for superior people. . . . If we talked extempore exactly as we write, no one would listen, and if we wrote exactly as we talk, no one would read. . . . Tradition . . . cannot be inherited, and if you want it you must obtain it by great labour."

Speaking of the tendency of Shakespeare critics to substitute a Hamlet made in their own image for Shakespeare's: "We should be thankful that Walter Pater did not fix his attention upon this play. . . . Immature poets imitate; mature poets steal; bad poets deface what they take, and good poets make it into something better, or at least something different. . . . England . . . has produced a prodigious number of men of genius and comparatively few works of art. . . . Milton's celestial and infernal regions are large but insufficiently furnished apartments filled by heavy conversation. . . . Kipling might have been one of the most notable of hymn writers. . . . The worst fault that poetry can commit is to be dull. . . . The chief use of the 'meaning' of a poem, in the ordinary sense, may be . . . to satisfy one habit of the reader, to keep his mind diverted and quiet, while the poem does its work upon him; much as the imaginary burglar is always provided with a bit of nice meat for the house-dog. . . . Verse must be at least as well written as prose."

Edmund Wilson, most learned, judicious, and generous of American men of letters, was soon to write these words of high praise: ". . . Eliot's opinions, so cool and even casual in appearance, yet sped with the force of so intense a seriousness and weighted with so wide a learning, have stuck oftener and sunk deeper in the minds of the postwar generation of both England and the United States than those of any other critic."

Eliot wrote apologetically to Richard Aldington about his own prose style, which he said was based partly on his two years' study of F. H. Bradley's writing, and partly on a fondness for rhetoric inherited from his forbears, who had been immersed in the law, the church, or politics. He knew, he said, that this made his own prose style rather creaky and pompous, but by this time there was nothing he could do about it.

On a dull day, Eliot could out-dreary and out-pedant the dreariest and most pedantic academic, e.g.: "That there was a family of Tourneurs is certain; the precise place in it of Cyril is, as Mr. Nicoll freely admits, a matter of speculation." He sometimes carried his posture (it was only occasionally an imposture) of solemn scholarship to such lengths that it is impossible to say whether he himself drew the line between parody and pedantry. His friend John Hayward preserved an exchange of eleven letters between Eliot and a German professor which were entirely concerned with the problem of whether Satan, described by Milton in *Paradise Lost* as "prone," was lying on his belly or on his back. Did Eliot think this was funny, or did he just think it was fun?

He knew how to shock the reader by a show of contemptuous familiarity with names generally held in some awe—"the humble Welsh family of Tudor," or "Donne . . . the Reverend Billy Sunday of his time, the flesh-creeper, the sorcerer of emotional orgy." Or "Thomas Hobbes was one of those extraordinary little upstarts. . . ." He speaks with an admiration it is hard not to find significant of Bradley's "habit of discomfiting an opponent with a sudden profession of ignorance, of inability to understand, of incapacity for abstruse thought. . . ." And he sometimes makes judgments which only omniscience should attempt: "Huysmans, by the way, might have been much more in sympathy with the real spirit of the thirteenth century if he had thought less about it, and bothered less about architectural lore and quotations from philosophers whom he may have read but certainly did not understand. . . ."

In the preface to *For Lancelot Andrewes* Eliot announced that he had "in preparation a trilogy: *The School of Donne; The Outline of*

Royalism; and *The Principles of Modern Heresy."* As Edmund Wilson dryly pointed out: "these books were never written,* but they became very influential."

Many readers by now have noted the obvious discrepancies between Eliot's precepts (criticism) and his practice (poetry). As Leonard Unger says, "His criticism urged a program of the classical, the traditional, and the impersonal, while he was producing a poetry which is poignantly romantic, strikingly modernist, and intensely personal."

It must be remembered that Eliot's work on the *Criterion*, like all his literary work at this period, had to be done after banking hours. And even before the *Criterion* was launched, his days were so much more than brimful that his health, never sturdy, once more began to falter. In Paris, Pound was much disturbed to hear that Eliot was going to pieces again, less than three months after his "cure" in Switzerland. Pound thereupon decided to rescue him from the bank. This was to be done by guaranteeing Eliot an income of £300 a year, to be raised by thirty anonymous donors giving £10 each. Bel Esprit, Pound's code name for this well-meant scheme, came to nothing, partly from lack of donors but largely because Eliot balked at this kind of help.

Vivienne too had taken a turn for the worse. For the last six months of the year she was on a Spartan diet and a strict course of treatment that resulted in insomnia. At Christmas she came to the table for dinner for the first time in months. In the spring her doctor advised country air, so they found a small cottage near Chichester where Vivienne spent six months, and Tom went down for weekends. The medical expenses were huge: a specialist from London twice a week, the local doctor sometimes twice a day. She became very ill with something the doctors called septic influenza, wasted away to skin and bone, and on seven or eight occasions Eliot despaired of her life. One of the regimens prescribed for this illness was the Plombières treatment (so called from the French spa where it originated), later known as high colonic irrigation, a nostrum then just coming into medical fashion. Eliot's annual holiday was spent at

*Perhaps the last one was: *After Strange Gods* has the subtitle *A Primer of Modern Heresy.*

her sickbed, and left him exhausted and numb: 1923 was a bad year.

Middleton Murry, who much admired Eliot, had taken over the moribund *Nation* and intended great feats with it. He now offered Eliot the literary editorship, but could not promise that the job would last longer than six months. Eliot declined the offer, feeling that his new duties would take up so much of his time and energy that none would be left for his own work. He wrote about this proposal to Quinn, adding, "I am worn out. I cannot go on." Quinn immediately sent him $400, promising that this would be the first of four annual payments, to which Otto Kahn would add $200 (if Eliot left his bank job). Quinn hoped that he might get this temporary subsidy up to at least $1,000 a year. Since Eliot did not leave the bank, Kahn's contribution was not forthcoming.

The year 1924 was perceptibly better, although halfway through it was darkened by the death of John Quinn, at the early age of fifty-four. Though he and Eliot had never managed to meet, they had written to each other so fully and frequently that they had developed a mutual liking and admiration. Quinn's death was also a blow to the many writers and painters in England, Ireland, and France whom he had encouraged and helped to support. Vivienne, who seems never to have been completely well, this year and the next must have had periods of fairly good health, for in these two years she contributed no less than eleven pieces of fiction, prose, and verse to the *Criterion*. These contributions were signed by various pseudonyms (Fanny Marlow, Feiron Morris, Felix Morrison, F.M.) but Vivienne's authorship is authenticated by Professor Donald Gallup, whose authority was T. S. Eliot himself.

Eliot took a great interest in Vivienne's writing and went over it carefully, occasionally coming to her rescue when she was stuck, but interfering as little as possible with the actual writing. He once said of her that she was the only woman he knew who had a mind like a man. She was paid, presumably, at the same niggardly rate* as other *Criterion* contributors, including Eliot, who, in all the seventeen years he conducted the magazine as editor, took not a penny of pay.

By the evidence of these *Criterion* pieces, Vivienne was a writer

*For one sketch, *Thé Dansant,* for example, Vivienne was paid £1.10.0.

of felicity and charm. Why she wrote nothing after 1925, or at any rate was not published in the *Criterion* after that year, is a tantalizing question that cannot be answered until the secrets of all Eliots are disclosed. An even more tantalizing question is, How much of a hand did she have in writing those heroic couplets that were dropped from *The Waste Land,* and of which a shorter version appeared later in the *Criterion* as part of a sketch known to have been written by her? One line is identical:

> Her hands caress the egg's well-rounded dome,

and four other lines have only slight variations. Which is the original, and who wrote it—Eliot or his wife?

Bertrand Russell spoke of Vivienne's "impulses of cruelty" toward Eliot. Something of the sort appears in one of her stories in the *Criterion*:

> Sibylla, looking round the room, saw the American financier leaning with exaggerated grace against the eighteenth century marble fireplace. She went up to him confidently. "Hullo," she said, but he only smiled. . . . "He *is* rather unsatisfactory," Sibylla thought, and, glancing up at him, she was struck afresh by his strange appearance. The heavy, slumbering white face, thickly powdered; the long hooded eyes, unseeing, leaden-heavy; the huge protuberant nose, and the somehow inadequate sullen mouth, the lips a little reddened. His head was exceptionally large, and not well shaped; the hair thin, and plastered tightly down. "Yet somehow," she thought, as she watched him, "although in a way he is such a hideous man, he has the air of being good-looking, distinguished-looking anyhow, and I like him—if only he would—what? What is wrong, what missing?"*

This kind of public teasing is exciting, both to the teaser and the teased; it is also risky. The excitement inheres in showing off, before an audience consisting largely of strangers but including some friends and even intimates, a trapeze act which has of course been well rehearsed and is therefore not nearly so dangerous as it looks—but is dangerous, all the same.

As Eliot very soon discovered, an editor's job is by no means confined to midwiving manuscripts; it also includes the nursing of stubbed egos and the soothing of tantrums. Ezra Pound was by now so muddy-booted with crotchets that very few editors would let him

---

*Cf. *The Waste Land,* 1.113: "What are you thinking of? What thinking?"

in the door. In spite of their old friendship and his gratitude for past help, even Eliot found it less and less possible to publish Pound's peculiar diatribes. In 1923 he wrote to Quinn: "Apart from the fact that he is very sensitive and proud and that I have to keep an attitude of discipleship to him (as indeed I ought) every time I print anything of his it nearly sinks the paper."*

Wyndham Lewis was one of his most difficult patients, and Eliot continually had to cope with Lewis's paranoiac suspicions that Eliot was party to a conspiracy against him. It is not surprising that at times Eliot's patient denials and explanations thinned into asperity. He and Lewis were not so much friends in the ordinary sense as complementary confidants, mutual conveniences. Only a few months later, Eliot was leaning against Lewis as if he were a wailing wall: "I am ill, harassed, impoverished, and am going to have 5 teeth out. I have managed to avoid seeing anyone for a very long time. I have several enemies."

Another contentious character, Eliot now found, was his patroness. Lady Rothermere invited Eliot to come and see her in Switzerland, one of those invitations from the rich and powerful which is rightly understood to be a summons. At their interview she voiced, at considerable length, her dissatisfaction with the *Criterion*. It was not, to her mind, chic enough; in fact, it was not chic at all. She informed Eliot that, after a certain date, she would pay no more of the magazine's bills.

Almost before he had begun to absorb the effects of this grievous blow, rescue was at hand. It was the Old Boys' network (the deliverer and prop of so many faltering British enterprises and enterprisers) that did it. At a weekend at All Souls, Charles Whibley put a word in Geoffrey Faber's ear. Whibley was a cantankerous literary journalist of the old school; Faber a scholarly businessman just starting his own publishing firm. The results of this word-in-ear transformed Eliot's life. First, Faber undertook to underwrite the *Criterion*, starting in January 1926; second, he offered to take Eliot on his board of editors, at "a much better" salary than the £600 a year he was now

*In 1924 Pound and Eliot moved farther apart in actual fact: Pound left Paris for Italy. In July he was in Bressanone with Olga Rudge, who there gave birth to his daughter Mary; in Paris, two months later, his wife, Dorothy, gave birth to his son Omar. These were his only two children.

being paid at the bank. Eliot accepted both offers thankfully. In November he left Lloyds Bank and entered the publishing firm, where he happily remained for the rest of his life. Frank Morley, his compatriot and colleague, on why Eliot was offered the job: "He was a gentleman; he was literate; he was patient; he got on well with difficult people; he had charm; and, he had been in the City. He had good qualifications for a man of business, and it was as a man of business, I suggest, that he was taken on." (Eliot himself said that Geoffrey Faber wanted a "talent scout.")

Now that his banking days were over, he could admit that they had not been so bad, that they had even been, in some ways, beneficial. And compared to schoolteaching, banking was a rest cure. If he had not had to earn his living and could have given all his time to poetry, that might, he thought, have had "a deadening influence" on him. As it was, the rationing of his time had made him concentrate, and had prevented him from writing too much. And the work he had done at the bank was, in itself, some of it, quite interesting. In his last year in the City, for example, he had written a monthly article (unsigned, of course) for the Lloyds Bank *Economic Review,* on foreign currency movements.

As for his own writing, he had begun and abandoned an experiment that at first had looked promising: a play about Sweeney. A slim volume of his criticism, *Four Elizabethan Dramatists,* was published in 1924, and the following year his gloomiest poem, *The Hollow Men.* At the end of the year 1925 Faber & Gwyer brought out a book of his collected verse: twenty-six poems in all, four of them in French.

But he thought he would never write another poem. His poetry-writing days, he told himself, were done.

—

FIVE

You Don't See Them, But I See Them

(1 9 2 6 – 1 9 3 2)

1

THERE IS A SENSE of guilt so profound that, even though it visit a man only in sleep, it will remain horribly present for some moments after he wakes; and if it return to haunt his dreams as a recurrent nightmare, he will never be able to shake off the possibility that this fearful messenger is telling him the truth: in spite of all the daylight evidence that exonerates him, he is indeed guilty of murder—a murder committed so long ago that he has succeeded in putting it almost out of his mind, and no one suspects him. He knows that he is guilty, and that his guilt will soon, inevitably, be known. Is his sense of condemnation the bitter fruit of some mad or bloody crime committed by one of his forbears? Or is it a glimpse of the hidden, unbearable reality ("the burden . . . is intolerable") that shadows our waking life? We have various medical tags for this not uncommon complaint, and some theological labels too, of which the most popular is "Calvinist." It is apparent that T. S. Eliot was a lifelong sufferer.

His friend Herbert Read said of him: "I always felt that I was in the presence of a remorseful man, of one who had some secret sorrow or guilt." He was born with a sense of sin, or, if that is too much to swallow, let us say he learned about hell and damnation when he was an infant, at his mother's knee. Why did he never develop a stomach ulcer? His Calvinist ancestors all informed him that God is an angry God, and some of the language in the Anglican liturgy did not contradict them: "We acknowledge and bewail our manifold sins and wickedness, Which we from time to time most grievously have committed, by thought, word and deed, Against thy Divine Majesty, Provoking most justly thy wrath and indignation against us."

At Harvard, in Paris and Oxford, and in his early years in England, he seems not to have outwardly offended against the straitjacket rules of his religious upbringing, although he was obviously attracted by Hindu or Buddhist belief. Might he not have felt welcome in the Church of Rome? An odd little scene in Rome itself might seem to lend some likelihood to such a possibility. In the fall of 1926 Eliot and Vivienne accompanied his brother Henry and his wife to Italy. On their second day in Rome they went to see St. Peter's, which impressed them, and they all acknowledged this in their different fashions. Vivienne said, "It's very fine, isn't it?" Henry Eliot said nothing. His wife was much struck with Michelangelo's Pietà. Tom Eliot rather embarrassed them by kneeling, "right at the front entrance."

Why, then, when at the age of thirty-eight he was received into the Anglican Church, did he feel like a foster child who had at last come home? There must have been a complex of reasons, acknowledged or unacknowledged. Samuel Smiles might have advanced one which Eliot would doubtless have rejected out of hand: that this was another step in a process of self-betterment; that, just as Boston had been a better address than St. Louis, and London a better address than Boston, so the Church of England was a cut above the Unitarian Church. Yet Eliot might have admitted that he felt a certain aesthetic attraction to the Church of England, superficial as that may have been compared to his innermost feelings. The practices and possessions of the established church in England diverted and allured him. They had something of the authoritarian and grandfatherly aura of the New England church of his childhood, but also something much more appealing: an ancient tradition, a shadowy but also a more impressive authority ("to kneel/Where prayer has been valid"), based on a mystical belief that in "the laying on of hands," generation after generation, there is a continuity of practice and performance from the time of Christ himself, and bridging, however narrowly and rudely, the schism with Rome. This belief in the pedigree of the Anglican Church enabled Eliot to become an Anglo-Catholic. Although it might have seemed that there was nothing in theology or church history to prevent him from going all the way to Rome, the Church of England was on his road and suited him well.

Although his acceptance of Anglican authority shocked many of his followers, who now began to talk of him sadly or bitterly as if he had indeed been their lost leader, who had left them just for a riband to stick in his coat, there was nothing sudden or surprising about his conversion. In fact "conversion" is too loud a word for Eliot's reception into the church. He was merely re-entering the house where he had been born and brought up. Those who had seen him emerge and thought he was leaving for good were mistaken: he had only been for a stroll around the block.

It is true that during that ramble he indulged in some cane twirling, ogling, and other forms of showing off, but nothing for which he could be arrested or even reprimanded, except by those solemn and somnolent elders who think that clever young men should be suppressed. The famous *Hippopotamus*, a favorite weapon of those who delighted in taking the mickey out of the church, on closer inspection was seen to be disrespectful but not irreverent. *A Cooking Egg* might seem to laugh at notions of personal immortality and the hope of heaven; but in heaven's name why not? If not much can be said in defense of *Mr. Eliot's Sunday Morning Service*, it is not because it sails blasphemously close to the wind but because it is so unabashedly pretentious. The poem has justly been characterized as "obscure, precious and bombastic." *Sapient sutlers, piaculative pence, polyphiloprogenitive, superfetation of τὸ ἕν*—if this isn't showing off with a smirk and a vengeance, what on earth is it? For only one stanza should it be spared:

> But through the water pale and thin
> Still shine the unoffending feet
> And there above the painter set
> The Father and the Paraclete.

And even here there are at least two unnecessary words, inserted to pump up the smooth tire of the meter.

Eliot would not have said that he was "bettering himself" by joining the Anglican Church; in fact he might have said, and almost did, that he was deliberately enlisting on the losing side. Democracy, the predominance of the common man, was the winning side, at least in England. Nine years before, Eliot had written: "The forces of deterioration are a large crawling mass, and the forces of development half a dozen men." And of his own day: "there never was a time so completely parochial, so shut off from the past." He believed that the attempt to achieve a non-Christian civilization would collapse into another Dark Age, and that the church's task would be to survive this era and then redeem the world.

Did he believe all the articles of the Christian faith, and did he renounce the devil and all his works? Or did he regard the church as being somewhat in the nature of a political party, its members sharing a common loyalty and purpose without necessarily subscribing to all the party's beliefs—if indeed a *party* can be said to hold beliefs? These are questions to which Eliot presumably found a working answer. His review of Bertrand Russell's *What I Believe,* written in this same year, seems to hint that his religious faith, while it conformed to the Christian creed, was not altogether confined by it: "I am amazed at Mr. Russell's capacity for believing—within limits . . . I cannot subscribe with that conviction to *any* belief. . . ."

It was more than an amused attraction to an old-fashioned institution that Eliot felt, and it was more than a snobbish or antiquarian interest that drew him to the Christian faith secreted somewhere on the church's premises. He was a Dives of the intellect in torment, whose letters from Hell could indicate his position but not alleviate it. The bad reputation of Christianity could not have escaped Eliot's attention. But we must remember that he was born and brought up in a corner of "the church's" tent—that nonexistent "church" whose purely theoretical "unity" is made up of countless mutually hostile sects all claiming to be the quintessence of "Christian"—and that he therefore took sectarian religion for granted and did not find it shocking.

Though the peaceable Unitarian Church had been completely committed to the northern side in the bloody Civil War, a war which he personally considered a disastrous mistake, he saw nothing amiss in that commitment and presumably did not regard it as characteristically Christian. He might not have agreed with most non-Christians that systematic, bloodthirsty cruelty was, if not brought into the world, carried to its highest pitch by the Christian church, whose most powerful and largest sect, the Roman, has fought for two thousand years, tooth, nail, and aspersorium, to keep or regain control of an integral church which, except for a few years at the very beginning, has never existed! And the various schismatic sects have fought back, to preserve their independence and to enlist more followers. To many Christian sects besides the Roman Catholics, all other Christians are damnable heretics.

The belief that one can know God and therefore know His will is perhaps the only real heresy of which mankind can be guilty. This frightful illusion leads inevitably to the correction of others whom we imprison, torture, or kill for the good of their souls. Thus the Roman Catholic Hilaire Belloc, on a Puritan:

> He served his God so faithfully and well
> That now he sees him face to face, in hell.

Would Belloc have admitted the possibility that he himself might be serving the devil?

The history of Christianity is a long record of relentless bloody-mindedness: massacres and murders, persecutions, witch hunts, destruction of Catholic churches by Protestants (and vice versa), torture, killing, enslavement, repression. How on earth could this endless parade of atrocities have emanated from the teaching of Jesus? Christians, having forgotten Christ (if they ever knew him) now quarrel bitterly among themselves over the niceties of the form in which he should be remembered.

Belief in God is an extreme last resort: finally there is nothing else to believe in. Belief in God, shaky, uncertain, and indefinite as it must be, is nevertheless also a great relief from the ridiculous "waste sad time" that stretches before us and after, and our only consolation for history, that unrelieved record of man's inhumanity to man. Was it some such considerations as these that decided Eliot to enroll himself as an Anglo-Catholic? In England he was surrounded by such evidences of Christianity as the Martyrs' Memorial in Oxford, the ruined abbeys, monuments to Christian hate, the country churches scarred by the hammers of Cromwell and his saints. May it not have been these paradoxical, apparently irreconcilable facts—not only in spite of them but because of them, because the time-serving, addlepated, brutal yet somehow wise and angelic Church of England could in a sense reconcile such contradictions, merely by gathering them all together—that enabled Eliot to feel at home in the Anglican Church?

Furthermore, worship—to worship a god—is a natural human impulse, a natural need as old as man's life on earth. Those spontaneous outbursts of praise and thanksgiving, almost like bird song, that well up in all human beings at times and which most of us suppress or divert into other channels or allow ourselves to express only by thanking "the world" for its beauty—as if "the world" knew or cared, or could take credit for its own creation!—this natural need was strong in Eliot. And the Anglican liturgy supplied the want he felt and could not always, of himself, provide.

If it would be too much to expect that he took this step with enthusiasm or joy (his was not a nature easily visited by such feelings, nor did the church encourage their display), we may be reasonably sure that it brought him relief and serenity, or at any rate the means of acquiring them. What was it about the Anglo-Catholic faith that so appealed to him? Here we can only guess, but our guesses can follow the hints he left us. For one thing, he must have been drawn by the *incomprehensibility* of the Christian faith (Anglican version). The church's language, the faint and lessening echo of the words of Christ, is itself a foreign and almost forgotten tongue in which for nearly two thousand years priests have elaborated a commentary on the mysteries of the Christian faith. Attempts to disembalm the fundamental rudiments of Christ's teaching from the bejeweled and encrusted liturgy by modernizing and "clarifying" the language are well meaning but generally fatal: such attempts falsify, distort, or cheapen the meaning and eat away the magic.

And that there is something magical, and healingly so, in the repetition of time-polished phrases that have acquired an incantatory ring, many generations of Anglican churchgoers will testify. Who can fail to be moved by the Lord's Prayer, the only prayer we have that was supposedly uttered by Christ himself, the simplest and most impressive prayer in the whole liturgy; yet who can honestly say he understands it? And who would undertake to translate the Creed, or bring its language up to date? "Begotten of his Father before all worlds"? "God of God, Light of Light, very God of very God"? "I believe in the Holy Ghost, the Lord, and Giver of Life, Who proceedeth from the Father and the Son"?

Some incomprehensible phrases or sayings must be left embedded in the poetry that is their proper setting. These are not to be confused with the "hard sayings" that we should rack our hearts and minds to understand. For those who cannot believe in the equality of man but who recognize the existence of different ranks, and feel themselves one of a superior class (as Eliot undoubtedly did), the parable of the publican and the Pharisee is a case in point. When the Pharisee gives thanks that he is not as other men are, and gives his reasons, he speaks for all who feel in any way superior to their fellow men; the publican's prayer ("God be merciful to me a sinner") knocks the props out from under all human differences, leaving us all equal in the sight of God, who sees more than we do.

Nevertheless (and out of God's sight) we cannot help feeling superior to some people, especially when we obviously *are* superior! Eliot was in many ways a modest man, who thought little of himself, or tried to. But how could he deny that he was cleverer than most men? He had a better mind, and used it better, than most of the people he met. Humility, he said, is endless. But it must also have a beginning. Why was Eliot so concerned about humility? Was it because he deeply desired what he had not? To him humility was a virtue, the most highly prized of all. But, like Christianity itself, humility is not popular nowadays. To D. H. Lawrence, who without pride could never have lifted himself up by his bootstraps, humility was no virtue whatever, but a dirty little piece of class-conscious nastiness.

Hints of arrogance, or of something not akin to humility, are not far to seek in Eliot's poetry:

> (Why should the agéd eagle stretch its wings?) . . .
>
> Then fools' approval stings . . .

Eliot's image of the tiger is not, like Blake's, something fearful and admirable and apart from us, but a man-eater, a paradoxical extension of the "infinitely gentle, infinitely suffering thing": "Christ the tiger . . . the tiger springs in the new year. Us he devours." And the tiger's cousins, the graceful, decorative white leopards in *Ash-Wednesday*, though they appear in postprandial satiety, are man-eaters (or poet-eaters) too, and have already devoured his legs, heart, liver, and brains.

In *Lines for an Old Man* the tiger appears again: irritable, pent-up, full of hate and lusting for blood, delighted in the prospective slaughter of his inferiors, the dolts, the ignorant young, the fools and madmen who are his natural enemies.

> Reflected from my golden eye
> The dullard knows that he is mad.
> Tell me if I am not glad!

These are violent images, and argue violent feeling. And they reverberate a clangorous discord with the "infinitely gentle, infinitely suffering thing," the sweet, sad music of the "perpetual angelus." In Eliot's view, a poet is a man who at times has to suffer more than he can bear. Writing a poem under these horrible circumstances is the only way he can save himself. Poems are made in hell. Who then would aspire to be a poet?

But all men are liars, said the Psalmist; Laura Riding (who may be his direct descendant) reminds us that poets too are men.* To hear poets talk about themselves ("purifiers of the dialect of the tribe," "a poet must himself be a true poem," etc., etc.) you might think they inhabit a height from which they can look down on the saints. But in hearing poets talk about each other you realize how down-to-earth they really are and how closely related. Indeed, many of them share the same middle name: backbiter. And if the writing of a poem, or the poem itself, is the be-all and the end-all of the poet's tortured existence, why does he bother to get it published, or even keep it?† Not nearly enough, surely, has been made of the fact that the man who is universally regarded as the best poet who has ever written in English wrote his best poetry for the purpose of entertainment—and made no attempt to preserve it, beyond what he must have considered its natural span of life.

Rimbaud, Kafka, Shakespeare, all seemed to share a rather odd

---

*". . . truth begins where poetry ends. . . . I have initiated enough poets into the idea of linguistic discipline for truth's sake, in the past, to know how verbally insensitive to considerations of truth poets can be, though behaving as persons born privy to it."—Preface to *Selected Poems* (Faber & Faber, London, 1970).

†W. H. Auden once sketched out his utopia. The Swiss were excluded from it, for some Audenesque reason—and newspapers as well: news was to be spread about by the barbers in their barber shops. Poets would not be allowed to publish their poems; but they could write them out as broadsheets, which would then be sniffed and, if approved, passed from hand to hand by the buzzing, pollinating barbers.

feeling about their writing. Rimbaud stopped writing before he was thirty and went into trade—thus showing that he equated poetry with juvenilia. Kafka left instructions with his literary executor that all his writings were to be burned (although apparently he could not bear to burn them himself). Shakespeare simply made no attempt to preserve anything he had written except his sonnets and two extremely artificial set pieces. Why? Because he wrote his plays for money? Because in that kind of writing he had no pride of authorship? Because so much of his work was collaboration or rewriting someone else's version? Because he felt that a writer should not take himself too seriously?

A poet, like the spider, spins his poem out of his own vitals. But a spider doesn't mass-produce its web. Why should a poet *publish* his poetry? Why should he want to? Shouldn't the relief of having concocted the poem suffice him? Obviously it does not. He wants others, as many others as possible, to see and share his expressed feeling and presumably applaud what he has done. Eliot wanted a wider and wider audience. When he speaks of Dante or Shakespeare—or Yeats —he can use the phrase "great poetry" or "great poet" without embarrassment; but when he talks about poetry itself—what its nature is, what its role is—he becomes hesitant, defensive, ambiguous, almost shamefaced. The most he will say about poetry is that it entertains us, it gives us pleasure!

And yet he took his own poetry with the utmost seriousness. Herbert Read said of him, "As the years passed he became just a little pontifical, and would refer to his own writings in a tone of voice that was a shade too solemn. He would use expressions like 'Valéry, Yeats, and I'—with perfect justice, but one was rather checked by the calm acceptance of a status that one felt should be left to others to confer." What has Eliot's poetry, this private creation, this private possession, to do with us? How can it mean for us what it meant for him? Why did he publish it? And if it aims at being universal poetry, why did he try to keep its meanings so private? More awkward questions to be added to our list.

Milton's Law (that he who would be a poet must be himself a true poem) is no law but a counsel of perfection, obviously far removed from the way things are. It's all very well for Milton to say that a poet must himself be a true poem: he never is. Milton, for one, cowardly and cantankerous, was not an agreeable character, and his life was more like a bad novel than a good poem. Then is the opposite of Milton's Law true? In that case, the loveliest and the best poetry could be written by monsters. We can perhaps go so far as to say this: that we can count ourselves fortunate not to be married to a poet, or have one as a parent, or live with one at close quarters. One poet of my acquaintance would, I strongly suspect, define a poet as "a man who has something so wrong with him that he must be exempted—at times, at any rate—from behaving with ordinary care or even decency." Shakespeare did not have to worry about the size of his audience. That was given to him; the number of people who could crowd into the Globe Theatre. And it may be doubted that he thought of himself as a poet but, as in Eliot's sensible definition, as a writer who sometimes wrote poems, among other things.

Does a modern poet think about his audience—what sort of people they are, and how many? Nowadays, when publishing is almost a branch of publicity, a poet can hardly avoid, somewhere along the line, thinking in these terms. He may not take his "readership" into account while he is writing a poem; but when the book containing that poem is printed, jacketed, advertised and on sale, he cannot fail to take an interest in the audience that takes an interest in him. He is curious about the people who read him, and wishes there were more of them.

This results in an ambivalent attitude on the poet's part. He writes for himself, and for the rare souls who are intelligent and sensitive enough to appreciate him, and he knows and is glad that he and they are few, the few who "really matter." At the same time he dreams of a vast (well, vaster) audience that will hang on his every word and smite their thighs in a thunderclap of applause; and he is reduced to bitterness and scorn at the spectacle of less intelligent, less gifted poets whose readers far outnumber his own.

But if poets are not totally concerned with truth, who else is more concerned? They seem to take it for granted—and the rest of us seem to agree with them—that when they speak as poets they are always under oath. Do they never perjure themselves?

When Yeats says

> Nor dread nor hope attend
> A dying animal;

> A man awaits his end
> Dreading and hoping all;

what sort of truth, or how much of the truth, is he telling? How does he know how a dying animal feels (or how a dying man feels, for that matter)? If he is thinking of an animal dying alone, of "natural causes," as grizzly bears and elephants are said to do, then his statement might be defended, at least as imaginatively possible. If, however, his statement must include the last moments of a monkey cornered by a leopard, there are photographs to prove him wrong: the monkey may have no hope, but he is obviously attended by dread and despair.

There are poets, in every age, who either do not consider themselves bound by this oath of truth-telling or are not aware of it or are not conscious of having failed to measure up to it. Yet it may be said in general that the more conscious a poet is of his role the more he feels bound by this oath. Eliot felt himself so much more bound to truth than to poetry that he ended up by saying in a poem, "The poetry does not matter."

Eliot's poetry, almost from the very first, had been religious—a question requiring an answer ("Do I dare/Disturb the universe?") or an answer requiring a question ("The tiger springs in the new year"). After *The Hollow Men* in 1925, for two years Eliot wrote no poetry, and thought he would never write any more. What a grim finale that would have been: not with a bang but a whimper. But the fountain had not after all dried up. Writing the Ariel poems to order (for the highbrow Christmas card trade) siphoned up *Ash-Wednesday* and *Marina,* the very purest Pierian. "Not all of us can share Eliot's faith," says B. Rajan, the Indian critic, "but all of us can accept the poetry because nearly every line of it was written while looking into the eyes of the demon."

Eliot also had a great deal to say about religion, alas, when he was writing prose. (Prose is rational, religion is not.) In his critical writing his attitude and feeling can hardly be called Christian, except of a scolding, ultramontane, Holy Office sort. This un-Christian attitude is especially noticeable when he writes about Christianity. "In the present ubiquity of ignorance, one cannot but suspect that many who call themselves Christians do not understand what the word means, and that some who would vigorously repudiate Christianity are more

Christian than many who maintain it. . . ."

The critic is finally unsatisfactory, and must be, because he is not God. He writes at times as if he were. And he writes generally as one who, if not actually possessing the godlike attributes of omniscience and omnipotence, is certainly on their side and in their neighborhood. But it is only "as if": everyone, including the critic himself, knows that neither his knowledge nor his power is absolute, and that when the clock strikes twelve he must divest himself of the costume that hides his nakedness.

Eliot's purest and most acceptable religious statements are all to be found in his poetry. "Teach us to care and not to care/Teach us to sit still." A saying of holy simplicity, embodying the same sort of tiny but tremendous moral leap—but Eliot's stillness goes much further—to be felt in the difference between the two sermons in Camus's *Plague;* in the first the preacher said "you," in the second "us." For most of us (not being saints) religion comes through only in bits and pieces, in certain phrases in the liturgy: "Hear what comfortable words our saviour Christ saith"; or "newness of life." As we become familiar with Eliot's poetry we find, to our grateful surprise, that many of his lines are devotional; they too are "comfortable words." Some of them may seem to be cold comfort, but that is comfort of a kind, and the only kind Eliot had to give.

"Modern man has heard enough about guilt and sin," says C. G. Jung. "You've had punishment enough," says Norman Cameron. Not so, says Eliot; we have nearly lost our sense of sin, and had better find it again.

Eliot's sense of guilt seems not only to have been built into him but to have been centered on two peculiar obsessions which he stated as general truths: that every man wants to murder a girl; that sex is sin is death.

> Any man has to, needs to, wants to
> Once in a lifetime, do a girl in.

Though murder may be latent in most of us, is that true of *all* of us? And the orgasm, that sneeze of fire that culminates the sexual act, is merely, according to Eliot, a foretaste of death—the real article, and not just "the little death" of French erotology:

> Those who suffer the ecstasy of the animals, meaning
> Death

Why not say

> Those who suffer the ecstasy of life, meaning
> Death

and be done with it? This is a man who sees life itself in terms of "the white flat face of death."

Was Eliot what oriental mystics call "an old soul"—near the end of his wheeling course? He did give off, occasionally, some of the odors of sanctity; but if you had asked him whether he was a saint he would have replied "Hell, no!" (or the Eliotesque equivalent "By no means!"). This Melchizedek of poets, in his apparent mockery of the church, sometimes seemed to verge on blasphemy: "For thine is the boredom and the horror and the glory." In his defense he could have cited the Nicene Creed: "Maker . . . of all things visible and invisible." If we accept the universe we surrender all responsibility for it to God, whose responsibility includes a knowledge and understanding of evil far beyond ours. God is therefore the creator of boredom and horror as well as of glory. A hard saying, to be accepted if possible, not necessarily understood.

2

Eliot came home to Mother Church on a June day in 1927, in the parish church at Finstock, in Herefordshire, not far from Oxford. Vivienne was not with him. First he was baptized (as a Unitarian, whose church does not recognize such sacraments, he had never been baptized). The officiating priest was the Reverend W. T. Stead, also an American, whom Eliot had met in London at Ezra Pound's, and who had recently been appointed chaplain of Worcester College, Oxford. The two sponsors, Eliot's godparents, were both Fellows of Worcester. Immediately after his baptism Eliot and Father Stead drove in to Oxford, whose bishop confirmed him in his private chapel.

At his baptism the priest had asked him, "Dost thou renounce the devil and all his works, the vain pomp and glory of the world, with all covetous desires of the same, and the carnal desires of the flesh, so that thou wilt not follow, nor be led by them?" and he had answered, "I renounce them all."

Five months later, on November 2, he made a further renunciation. He gave up his American citizenship and became a British subject. Eliot never spoke his full mind about his native land, but in 1928 he wrote a preface to Edgar Ansel Mowrer's *This American World*, and presumably these sentiments of Mowrer's were not very different from his own:

> . . . [the] mass of latter-day immigrants was recruited largely from the European proletariat. In their own countries their individual immaturity was not apparent because people of their class in Europe received their civilization with their orders from above. . . . Left to themselves and to win our favor, the new arrivals became more "genuinely American"—that is, immature—than the natives.
>
> In the absence of recognized tradition, the tone in the U.S. is set by the really undeveloped masses. Our half-educated, self-opinionated citizens can do what they like, read what they like, think as badly as they like, enforce what mental and moral tyranny they like. . . .
>
> The winning of the West transformed the type of governing class. . . . Puritanism was useful and survived, while culture was superfluous and perished. . . . When, after the Civil War, the South ceased to count in anything but statistics and elections, the aristocratic tradition of culture was dead.

From the start Eliot was a faithful churchgoer. He disliked sermons but went to early Mass at least once a week. There he acknowledged and bewailed his manifold sins and wickedness whose remembrance was grievous, whose burden intolerable. By most secular standards and to all appearances he led a blameless life. Why, then, did he feel so guilty? His desire to bury his private life with him in the grave argues more than an instinctive shyness. Did he feel remorse not only for what he had done and for what he had not done but for what he was going to do? The point at which tenderness turns into treachery is imperceptible. It would have been quite impossible for Eliot to say which was the exact moment when he knew that he was going to leave Vivienne, "for her own good," or to put his finger on that earlier moment when at last he persuaded himself that his desertion of her was necessary for her health, if not for her salvation.

Because the evidence of his poetry points to the strong probability that Eliot suffered or had suffered from *horror feminae,* we must not be led into the specious assumption that he was homosexual. It is peppery, glaring little men like Evelyn Waugh who are sexually suspect—as his diaries bear witness. Eliot's suppressed desire was not for his fellow man but for his wife, who, when she saw that look in his eye, screamed with laughter, declined the gambit, showed fatigue, went to bed with a headache rather than with him. Perhaps only those who, like Eliot, were brought up in the strict, asexual, pious American tradition, which teaches small boys that their deepest yearnings are shameful, could either understand or sympathize with his case. Englishmen of comparable social background might find his plight incomprehensible, the nearest British parallel to his sexual education being among the devout working-class Welsh or Scots.

Without the support of the church, without the extra strength which he felt was given him by his attendance at Mass, by his prayers and by his attempts, daily renewed, to lead a Christian life, Eliot thought that he could never have survived these years. Pain is also a form of work, and even more tiring. Pain works upon the passive sufferer to the point where exhaustion or unconsciousness intervenes. Until exhaustion numbed his pain and sapped his passion nearly to nothing, Eliot suffered "the torment of love unsatisfied," very occasionally "the greater torment of love satisfied." When he married Vivienne he had been passionately in love with her, which frightened them both. Furthermore he was ashamed of his feelings, as he had been trained to be. Bertrand Russell said that Eliot was ashamed of his marriage; if so, it may not have been for the social reasons that Russell assumed but because he was disconcerted and abashed by the violence and "animality" of his passion.

Since adolescence he had been haunted by sexual demons, terrified lest they become apparent ("You don't see them, but I see them"), desperately determined not to let them get the dominion over him. Laforgue's languid, dandiacal, parsonic pose was just the protective disguise he was looking for, a disguise he further elaborated in the "objective correlative" and the lines purloined from other poets, lightning rods to draw down fire from heaven and to deflect it from himself. Nevertheless, like a thread of scarlet through the drab monochrome of his life, hidden ("O hidden") but never quite concealed, ran the trilling wire in the blood.

The evidence? Scanty but striking. From *Gerontion:*

In depraved May . . .

Excite the membrane, when the sense has cooled,
With pungent sauces, multiply variety
In a wilderness of mirrors.

If *The Waste Land* is the anaphrodisiac poem it has been called, surely it is consciously so? There was a certain French writer who so feared and hated his own sexual nature that on the rare occasions when he succumbed to it he could be heard muttering, as he left the brothel, *"Ah, j'ai perdu un livre! J'ai perdu un livre!"* Eliot was not one to guard his long-preserved virginity for the sake of writing—no man who believed, as he did, that scripture outranks poetry could do that—but he feared his sexual nature and, like Augustine of Hippo, wanted to be rid of it.

> O the moon shone bright on Mrs. Porter
> And on her daughter
> They wash their feet in soda water

This is a bowdlerized version: in the original Australian ballad, the word is not *feet*.

At one point in *The Waste Land* he put himself in Augustine's shoes:

> To Carthage then I came
>
> Burning burning burning burning
> O Lord Thou pluckest me out
> O Lord Thou pluckest
>
> burning

From *Ash-Wednesday* this startlingly graphic description of that female pudenda that roused in him such shame and such desire:

> a slotted window bellied like the fig's fruit

From his last poem, *Little Gidding* (though an old man now, to his way of thinking, his primary complaint is the dwindling of sexual pleasure):

> Let me disclose the gifts reserved for age
> To set a crown upon your lifetime's effort.
> First, the cold friction of expiring sense
> Without enchantment, offering no promise
> But bitter tastelessness of shadow fruit . . .

and at the end of the poem:

> The intolerable shirt of flame
> Which human power cannot remove.
> We only live, only suspire
> Consumed by either fire or fire.

The fire of lust or the fire of purgatory: he knew which one he prayed to undergo, as he remembered also the irremovable, unbearable shirt of flame he had once worn.

There are other lines and phrases that might be cited, and there must be many more whose sexual references are so successfully hidden that they will never be known. The acts of exorcism he performed in his poetry were not enough in themselves to rid his swept and garnished house of the evil spirits that threatened to dispossess him: for that, he felt that he had to have the assistance of superhuman power. No distant, deist, Unitarian God could have sustained him. The God he needed, on whom he could lean his whole weight, was God who had become man, an infinitely gentle, infinitely suffering incarnate thing, recognizably human, unknowably divine.

Vivienne, Church of England from birth, was a typical Anglican: bored, unbelieving, a nonstarter who went to church only on "special occasions," for a wedding, a christening, or a funeral, as she might have gone to Ascot or to Trooping the Colour. She gave Tom's churchgoing no overt encouragement or support, but she was an almost perfect proving ground for the exercise of the Christian virtues. Three years before, she had been close to death, and she never again really got her head above the waves of ill health. She was not a "good patient": she complained, she demanded, she required constant attention and continual sympathy; she was subject to fits of violent temper; she made scenes. Drugs were not yet the doctors' panacea that they became a generation later, but drugs were certainly prescribed for some of Vivienne's various illnesses, and she took them. Presumably they had some effect on her, sometimes a good effect. To that extent but, it seems probable, to that extent only, she might be said to have been "addicted" to them.

When everything has been said in her favor that can be said, the glum fact remains that she was, to put it as mildly as possible, hard to live with.* A less long-suffering, less resigned, more hopeful man than Eliot might well have found her impossible, and a good deal sooner than he did. Her response to his sexual advances was more and more frequently to retreat into a raging migraine. Did she really want a husband at all? Gradually but certainly it became clear to him that she would have preferred him as a brother, a son, anything but the lover he had longed to be. She was fond of him, but not "in that way." Waiting on her, sitting up with her, sometimes far into the night, already tired from his day's work at the office but having looked forward to this precious spare time for his own writing; trying to calm her nerves, trying to reassure her ("What is that noise now? What is the wind doing?"), listening to her wild accusations and suspicions and patiently, patiently reminding her that she herself knows they are wild—these unremitting vigils ended by turning him from a husband into a lay nurse, a night watchman.

The only times he had to himself were when she was asleep or away, in a recuperative country cottage or a hospital. It became the accepted thing to invite Tom Eliot for a weekend without his ailing wife. Poor Vivienne. The spirit went out of her, as it had gone out of their marriage, long before he left her. No more stories, sketches, verses from her to be scanned and polished by Tom and then printed in the *Criterion*.

There are always compensations, perhaps even in hell. By 1925 Eliot was known, by his English contemporaries, as a coming man (they had not yet noticed that he had passed them and was, in racing parlance, "going away"). They were pleased at being friends with this solemn creature, and in their rather catlike way showed it by mocking him. At the dining table at Lady Ottoline Morrell's Garsington Manor, the handsome young painter Duncan Grant was asked his opinion of someone's painting. He screwed up his face and batted his eyes like a mountain in labor (in his case the necessary preliminaries to speech) and produced the mouselike reply, "Very interesting."

---

*A psychiatrist, after reading Vivienne's diaries, had this to say of her: "The young girl is neurotic, feels insecure, particularly about her femininity. She suffers from psychosomatic illnesses. . . . In the end there is a picture of a full-blown paranoia with delusions. Absurd and pathetic as her delusions may appear, they are her reality. Her suffering is real . . . most likely a gifted person, at the same time vivacious and morose and 'complex'—a combination which can be very attractive if difficult to live with."

Eliot leaned over the table and inquired, "And what, precisely, do you mean by 'very'?" This set the table on a roar and the phrase became enshrined in the Bloomsbury jokebook.

Sometimes the mockery was not intended kindly. Richard Aldington, who had been Eliot's friend and predecessor as assistant editor of the *Egoist*, turned on him in a parody biography, *Stepping Heavenward*. Eliot appeared in this as the blessed Jeremy Cibber, whose life some people explained "as a case of chronic constipation." Cibber's first words, when he was nearly three, were: "Mother, why *precisely* does the refrigerator drip?" Cibber "made few intimate friends and spoke very rarely, but listened carefully." He developed "the famous oblique method which Cibber made so formidable, i.e., always to create by destruction, to seek truth for oneself by exposing the errors of others." When Cibber married, his wife was the chief sufferer. "Could she help it if his presence—owing to the will of God no doubt—drove her into wild neurasthenia? After all, it must be rather a shock to think you are marrying a nice young American and then to discover that you have bedded with an angel unawares. . . . For him God was not a passion, but a theorem; and he could never quite prove the theorem."

Eliot must have been aware that behind the friendly faces there were often such flickerings of spite. He knew his literary colleagues well and mistrusted them accordingly, though his carefully cultivated public urbanity betrayed no sign of this mistrust. Only rarely did he lay bare the tooth of wit: "Bishops are a part of English culture, and horses and dogs a part of English religion." His public friendships were numerous and grew with the years; his private friendships remained few. The tally of his real friends and the number of those who claimed to be his intimates would not have matched, by a long chalk. His brother Henry, his sister Marian, Mary Hutchinson, Emily Hale, Mary Trevelyan, the McKnight Kauffers—were there many more than that?

Conrad Aiken, acknowledged as his privy peer, stood in a special, uneasy relationship with him; Ezra Pound, who had "discovered" and harangued him to his great benefit, and had then mooched off on his own mazy concerns, did not come back again until they were both old men. The New York lawyer John Quinn and Harriet Weaver, editor of the *Egoist*, were two people for whom he rightly felt admiration and trust. But his official friends, e.g., Charles Whibley, Geoffrey Faber, John Hayward, Father Eric Cheetham, all shared an unattractive, chilling quality; none was what the British call "a nice man." Eliot wrote of his friend Charles Whibley: "One always feels that he is ready to say bluntly what everyone else is afraid to say. Thus a feeling of apprehensiveness, conducive to attention, is aroused in the reader." Eliot evidently tried hard to be friends with Wyndham Lewis, whose talents he found as attractive as his morbid suspiciousness was repellent, but after Lewis's death Eliot finally admitted that he had never really liked him. It was women, and not many of *them*, with whom Eliot felt at home.

Work was the only remedy for the miseries of his domestic life. He made it his habit to take on more duties than he could readily handle. He became a churchwarden at St. Stephen's; he wrote for a church paper and edited it (i.e., wrote the whole issue himself during the regular editor's absence on holiday); every fortnight he attended a meeting of the Chandos group (laymen and clergy who met at the Chandos Restaurant in St. Martin's Lane to discuss church affairs). No one in the firm of Faber & Gwyer (in 1929 it became Faber & Faber)* worked any harder, certainly, than Eliot. He became locally famous as the most accomplished blurb writer in the office ("I don't know how to grow asparagus, or how to improve your lawn tennis, or the best diet for a six-month-old baby, but I have to write blurbs about them"), all foreign correspondence and foreigners who could not speak English tended to find their way to him, as well as the most abstruse manuscripts and the writers most difficult to handle. Of the books listed in ten of Faber & Faber's catalogues, eighty-four blurbs were written by Eliot. (Sample, announcing *The White Goddess*, by Robert Graves: "A prodigious, monstrous, stupefying, indescribable book.")

There were two other Americans on Faber's board: Frank Morley and Morley Kennerley. On the Fourth of July, a date that meant nothing to the English, this trio usually managed some sort of explosive celebration in the office—once by setting off firecrackers in a coal scuttle they maneuvered under the table until it rested between

---

*There was only one Faber, but it was decided that doubling the name "sounded nicer" and imparted confidence.

Geoffrey Faber's feet. These schoolboy pranks were taken in good part; another of Eliot's japes did not go down so well. He faked a letter from the town clerk, announcing to the directors that an equestrian statue by A. J. Munnings and including figures of all the directors was to be erected in Russell Square—to be made of concrete, since marble was too expensive.

Such rare effervescences were a safety valve in a life of unrelieved hard work, the greater part of it hack work and drudgery. For, besides his full-time job as a publisher, Eliot put together four numbers of the *Criterion* each year* and wrote a commentary for each number; he also wrote book reviews, articles, and lectures. The prestigious lectures he was invited to give at the beginning and end of this six-year period (1926–1932) show pretty clearly the position of authority he had now attained. In January 1926 he gave the first of eight Clark Lectures at Cambridge; in the winter of 1932 he went to the other Cambridge to deliver the Charles Eliot Norton Lectures at Harvard.

He had already paid his respects to the easygoing ways of his contemporary men of letters in England. "One may even say that the present situation here has now become a national scandal impossible to conceal from foreign nations; that literature is chiefly in the hands of persons who may be interested in almost anything else; that literature presents the appearance of a garden unmulched, untrimmed, unweeded, and choked by vegetation sprung only from the chance germination of the seed of last year's plants. . . . The British writer, who shrinks from working overtime or at weekends, will not find these ideas congenial."

Eliot knew there was something too stiff and proud in the way he wrote prose: it was the penalty he paid for having learned to beat the British man of letters at his own game. He could not unlearn the habit of writing pontifically. But he did not shrink from working overtime, and he cultivated his garden unceasingly. *The Sacred Wood* had made his name as a pre-eminent critic: during this period *For Lancelot Andrewes, Essays on Seneca, Dante,* and finally *Selected Essays* secured that pre-eminence. His report of what he saw from his hard-attained height was not hopeful; announcing his position as

---

*For one of its seventeen years, 1927–1928, the *Criterion* became a monthly.

"classicist in literature, royalist in politics, and anglo-catholic in religion,"* he proceeded to reprehend and oppose the spirit of the age. Commenting on Baudelaire's inability to regard the sexual act lightly, as "just a good roll in the hay," Eliot commented: "The sexual act as evil is more dignified, less boring, than as the natural 'life-giving,' cheery automatism of the modern world. For Baudelaire, sexual operation is at least something not analogous to Kruschen Salts."† And he performed one of his most teasing and graceful *veronicas*, which is still a stumbling block to many brave, outraged bulls: "Poetry is not a turning loose of emotion, but an escape from emotion; it is not the expression of personality, but an escape from personality."

The year 1930 saw two of Eliot's narrowest escapes: *Ash-Wednesday*, perhaps the most beautiful, certainly the most heartrending and heartbroken of Eliot's poems, dedicated to Vivienne and his farewell to her; and *Marina*, unique among all of Eliot's verse in having a humanly hopeful ending.

When Conrad Aiken reviewed *For Lancelot Andrewes*, he asserted, in effect, that Eliot had tried to dodge something undodgeable: "Again and again he [Eliot] took elaborate pains to evade or minimize the problem of personality: even going so far as to maintain that the work of art is an *escape* from personality: a very revelatory view . . ."

In August 1932 Eliot and his wife went in their tiny Morris, an uncertain performer which Eliot drove uncertainly, from London to the Frank Morleys' farm for the christening of his goddaughter Susanna. Vivienne noted remorsefully in her diary that Tom had a hard time getting her up and dressed and ready to leave, but that he had been very patient and gentle with her, only reminding her that they were keeping two old people (Frank Morley's parents) waiting, and that the old lady had come out of the London Clinic that very day. They also spent a weekend together at the Woolfs' cottage at

---

*Phrases lifted from the *Nouvelle Revue Française*, which had applied them to Charles Maurras fifteen years earlier. Commenting on Eliot's choice of the word "royalist," Bernard Bergonzi points out that "no native Englishman, writing as a subject of the impeccably bourgeois George V, could ever have described himself in this way."

†Which were advertised with a picture of a man bounding out of bed in the morning, as "giving you that Kruschen feeling!"

Charlotte Stearns Eliot.

Henry Ware Eliot.

TSE, age seven,
and Annie Dunne.

TSE, age about eight,
at Gloucester, Mass.

The Eliot house—Gloucester.

TSE, age ten, from a portrait by his sister Charlotte.

TSE and Howard Morris as Harvard freshmen in their room at 22 Russell Hall.

TSE (front row, third from left) and the other members of the 1910 *Advocate* board. Conrad Aiken is fourth from left, second row.

Vivienne Eliot at Garsington Manor.

Emily Hale.

Emily Hale.

TSE, John Hayward, Christopher Sykes.

TSE, age sixty-seven.

TSE in Nassau, January 1959.

Rodmell. A photograph of Vivienne on that occasion, standing next to Virginia Woolf and Tom Eliot, shows her, a drab little figure, much shorter than either, staring down at the ground, her face shadowed by a broad-brimmed straw hat, her hands clasped in front of her, her toes turned in, her shoulders hunched. All three of them are too thin; but Vivienne looks miserable; she looks ill. In September there was a merry dinner at the Three Arts Club, with Ralph Hodgson, Mark Gertler, the painter, and other friends.

Before he left for America Eliot read the proofs of *Sweeney Agonistes*, which Faber & Faber would publish in December, while he was out of the country. These two "fragments of an Aristophanic melodrama" are introduced by two epigraphs, one from Euripides, the other from St. John of the Cross—a characteristic Eliot left-and-right. Perhaps one of the reasons this experiment was broken off was Eliot's inability to make Sweeney talk in character, when it came to brass tacks. "I gotta use words when I talk to you," says Sweeney. Fair enough. But "Birth, and copulation, and death"? Sweeney wouldn't talk that way: he would never say "copulation." Eliot knew what word Sweeney would have used but could not bring himself to use it. What he was after was "poetry standing naked in its bare bones" —and this was not it: "copulation" still has its pants on.

In mid-October Vivienne and her brother, Maurice, went with Tom to Southampton to see him off for America. As the *Ansonia* drew away from the dock and they waved good-bye, Vivienne's tears were no more than could be expected from a wife who would not see her husband again for six long months.

Tom knew, though he tried to hide the knowledge from himself, that he was never coming back to her.

SIX

—

Teach Us to Care and Not to Care

(1 9 3 3 - 1 9 4 7)

1

ELIOT finally convinced himself, as he *had* to convince himself, that he had done Vivienne irreparable harm in marrying her, and that he was intensifying and prolonging the harm by allowing the marriage to drag on. He was bad for Vivienne; she was ruinous for him. If he was to save them both, or either of them, he must separate from her. But, like most sensitive people, he hated scenes. And he knew that, if he broached even the edge of the subject to Vivienne it would mean an intolerable, excruciating, endless series of scenes. He must break it to her some other way. There was no right method: he would have to pick the least bad he could find. He told himself that it would be a mercy killing; himself replied: No, murder.

What a precarious situation: for a human being to feel, for a moment, clean! Too many things can topple us into horror and self-disgust, too many things will not bear thinking of: the half-drowned fly in the water closet that we try (and fail) to flush out of sight; the daily occasions when some fellow sufferer begs us for a mouthful of bread and we give him a stone. . . . The list of our murderous cruelties is endless, and abominable. In a sense, we are only a bad smell contained in human skin.

What did it mean to Eliot, what did he feel, hearing this collect at early Mass on a winter morning? "That we may cast away the works of darkness, and put upon us the armour of light, now in the time of this mortal life. . . ." What if, in casting away this darkness, we also cast off the human being who loves and depends on us? Whatever we may think of the general human condition, some particular human situations are impossible—impossible to resolve without doing someone else great hurt and mischief.

How should it be done? Divorce was out of the question, even had there been grounds, and there were none, under the prevailing law. Although he and Vivienne had been married only by a registrar in a civil ceremony, he considered himself bound to her, according to the strictest Christian laws of marriage, for life. By these laws they could never be divorced, nor could he marry again while she was alive. But long before he sailed for America in September 1932 he had made his plans to leave her. He would break the news to her by letter; though they would both continue to live in London, he would see to it that they never met. He would continue to support her, and through her family and other surrogates would keep a protective eye on her.

This fifteen-year chapter of Eliot's life began in agony—the kind of agony that must accompany the planned, deliberate murder of a wife or child—and ended in a flare-up of terrible remorse, when the long-drawn-out act ended at last, as it had to, as it was meant to do, in Vivienne's death. After her death there would be no more poetry, only plays which he said were in verse. (To all eyes but his, the verse was mostly written in invisible ink.) By the time she died, the love that had once joined them had died too. "Died" is perhaps a misleading word: it might be truer to say that his love for her was transmuted into poetry (what a comfort *Ash-Wednesday* must have been to him —but not to her!). And for her he became a beloved absent son, to whose absence she was never reconciled.

That frantic, driven woman, racked by fears and anxieties and suspicions, exacerbated if not caused by chronic ill health, still turned, awkwardly and painfully, like a stunted heliotrope, toward the best and truest person who had ever happened to her, who had been, however unhappily, her lover, husband, and friend.

2

Eliot's return to Harvard, which he had not seen for seventeen years, was (you may say) satisfactory. He was now a Londoner, the length of whose domicile in England exactly balanced the years of his youth in St. Louis. But Boston (in effect, Cambridge and Harvard) was still the native city of his spirit. It represented for him, as St. Louis never could, that American past in which his family had played a significant part. It was the city where he still had more family and friends than anywhere else. His mother had died there in 1930, but sisters and cousins and aunts, not to mention friends, still abounded.

A new friendship that dated from this visit was with Theodore Spencer, a young Harvard professor of English who was one of Eliot's most appreciative critics and warmest admirers. Like Eliot, he was physically languid but mentally on fire; he died untimely in 1949. Harvard itself was almost a family demesne: Eliot House, where he stayed, was named after a distant cousin who had been president of the university. To have been chosen as Norton Lecturer was in itself honorific, and the lectures, published later under the characteristically leaden title, *The Use of Poetry and the Use of Criticism*, were arrestingly orthodox, now and then primly hilarious, and mounting firmly to collar the rich and modest assertion, "From time to time, every hundred years or so, it is desirable that some critic shall appear to review the past of our literature, and set the poets and the poems in a new order." It was apparent to his audience that they were gazing on that critic.

In his study at Eliot House he held open tea parties. To one of them the Boston *Herald* sent a snide reporter, with small sympathy for this visiting expatriate:

His accent is an obvious pose. But it is not half-baked, like so many English accents: it goes the whole hog, and he nearly gets away with it. . . .

A discussion about what makes a poem good ended inconclusively. Good poetry has "something." Eliot's formula for making poetry is to catch that "something" and mix it with water. Water consists of images and words which your reader easily catches hold of. You use it according to what you think your reader can bear. Masefield is watery. Eliot's poetry is about 100 proof.

Personally, Eliot seems to be all water. His manner is all a superimposed form and pose, which his special type of readers swallow with joy. But sometimes when he is silent he seems to enjoy watching them swallow.

From the time of Dickens, the visiting British lecturer in the United States has been traditional. In 1932 lecturing was the only way Eliot could pay for his trip. Besides the prestigious Norton Lectures at Harvard, he lectured at Yale, the University of Virginia and Johns Hopkins, and gave addresses at Vassar, Milton Academy and to a gathering of Unitarian ministers in Boston. The three lectures at the University of Virginia were published (1934) under the title *After Strange Gods*. This book was never reprinted. It got him into more trouble than anything he ever wrote. Subtitled *A Primer of Modern Heresy*, it was a statement of Eliot's unpopular (and, as he considered, Christian) beliefs on various subjects: the American Civil War, blasphemy, D. H. Lawrence, Thomas Hardy, W. B. Yeats. In a later foreword he wrote: "In a society like ours, worm-eaten with Liberalism, the only thing possible for a person with strong convictions is to state a point of view and leave it at that." He never actually recanted any of the obnoxious statements he made in these lectures, but he did give the impression that he was rather sorry he had made them.

His strictures on the Civil War ("certainly the greatest disaster in the whole of American history; it is just as certainly a disaster from which the country has never recovered, and perhaps never will . . .") would go down better in Virginia than in the North. But when he asserted that in "the society that we desire . . . reasons of race and religion combine to make any large number of free-thinking Jews undesirable," he started a hue and cry of "antisemitism!" which has not yet been stilled. Like most Americans of his background, he was not consciously or openly antisemitic. He merely reflected the pejorative feeling of his class and region about Jews; that they are partly comic, partly sinister—an attitude imported from England, where it was voiced by Shakespeare and Dickens, to name only two.*

Eliot was certainly never a Fascist, but that libel may have been fomented by statements like this (from *After Strange Gods*): "The number of people in possession of any criteria for discriminating between good and evil is very small." And his dislike of Thomas

---

*All his life long this raven kept coming home to roost. When taxed with the charge, Eliot would say, "I'm a Christian—and therefore not an anti-Semite." But Emanuel Litvinoff, a Jew from London's East End who progressed from Communism to the rank of wartime major in the British Army, and who felt he needed Eliot as a man needs bread, could not forgive him for republishing after the war his early poems apparently tinged with antisemitism. Litvinoff, himself a poet, wrote a poem attacking Eliot and read it at a poetry evening at the Institute of Contemporary Art in London. To his consternation he was told just before he began that Eliot was in the audience. A week later Eliot lay gravely ill, and Litvinoff heard the news with a heavy heart.

Hardy led him into the untenable position that in one of Hardy's stories, *Barbara of the House of Grebe*, "We are introduced into a world of pure Evil. The tale would seem to have been written solely to provide a satisfaction for some morbid emotion."

This unfortunate slip of the judgment drew a piercing rejoinder from Katherine Anne Porter: "Of all evil emotions generated in the snake-pit of human nature, theological hatred is perhaps the most savage. . . . My own judgment is that Hardy's characters are in every way superior to those of Mr. Eliot, and for precisely the reason the two writers are agreed upon. Hardy's people suffer the tragedy of being, Mr. Eliot's of not-being . . . they are the sinister chorus of the poet's own tragedy, they represent the sum of the poet's vision of human beings without God and without faith, a world of horror surrounding this soul thirsting for faith in God."

That pawky poet Robert Frost once said, "[Eliot] doesn't want people to understand him. I want people to understand me, but I want them to understand me *wrong*." In Possumy mood Eliot was certainly not above playing tricks on his audience. In the winter of 1932 he told a hall full of Vassar girls, before reading *Ash-Wednesday*, "The three leopards in the next poem are, of course, the world, the flesh and the devil."

He was in Baltimore for nearly a week that winter, to lecture at Johns Hopkins (the Metaphysical Poets) and to give a reading before the Poetry Society. He stayed in Baltimore with his old Harvard friend George Boas, who had become Professor of Philosophy at the Hopkins. (Eliot had a bad cold and asked Mrs. Boas to refuse as many invitations for him as she could.) Boas was delighted to see his admired friend and mentor again. But soon afterward, when he read the lectures Eliot gave at the University of Virginia, he was deeply wounded by Eliot's statement about "free-thinking Jews." Boas's comment was, "I felt that in that case I could relieve him of one of them and did."

Eliot also spent two days with Mrs. Bayard Turnbull, whose parents-in-law had endowed the lectureship that had brought Eliot to Johns Hopkins. Scott Fitzgerald, a Midwesterner eight years his junior, was then living as a tenant on the Turnbull place, in the barnlike Victorian house where Mr. Turnbull's parents had once lived. Fitzgerald had a deep admiration for Eliot, whom he considered the greatest of living poets, and had sent him an inscribed copy of *The Great Gatsby* in 1925. Eliot's reply had praised the book as "the first step that American fiction has taken since Henry James." There had been several exchanges of letters, in which the half-educated and careless Fitzgerald had persistently misspelled Eliot's name and at least once had failed to date his letter, for which Eliot could not resist calling him to account.

The two first met at a dinner in Baltimore. In the course of the evening Fitzgerald was called on to read some of Eliot's verse, which he did with unabashed animation. On the afternoon of Eliot's arrival at the Turnbull house Fitzgerald came to see him, and the two went off for a long walk. Mrs. Turnbull remembers seeing them start off across the lawn, toward the abandoned roadbed of a narrow-gauge railway track that ran for miles between woods and meadows. She wished she might have heard their conversation, which she was sure was "immensely articulate." Might they have touched, though obliquely, on their common problem of gifted but difficult wives? Quite possibly. When Eliot returned from his walk, Mrs. Turnbull showed him her copy of *The Divine Comedy,* and told him with some pride that she had read it. *"Begun* to read it," he corrected her.

When Fitzgerald next wrote to his friend Edmund Wilson he told him that he had spent an afternoon and evening with Eliot. "I read him some of his poems and he seemed to think they were pretty good. I liked him fine."

In Princeton Eliot found again his old friend Paul Elmer More, who had settled there. More, a shy, scholarly, religiously doctrinaire man of letters, was an intimate but not a close friend of Eliot's for many years, and stood in a special relation to him. More too was born in St. Louis, twenty-four years before Eliot, and took his degree at Washington University before proceeding to Harvard, where he became assistant professor in Sanskrit. After several years as an associate professor at Bryn Mawr he gave up his academic career for literary journalism. He was a contemporary and for a time an ally of Irving Babbitt, but eventually parted company with him, as Eliot did, on the question of religion.

More's shyness was so acute that it sometimes fell upon him even in his own house. When his two young daughters had a guest for tea or lunch, More would do his awkward best to make conversation, but the minute the meal was over he would rise thankfully from his chair, exclaiming, "Well, I must get back to my books!" and so escape.

He had narrow tastes—narrower than Eliot's—but deep theological feelings. Eliot considered their spiritual biographies so similar as to be grotesquely so. They did not meet often or correspond frequently, but both men talked and wrote to each other from the heart about the state of their souls. Eliot once expressed to More his incomprehension of those people who do not feel the emptiness at the core of life; and confessed that it was his own awareness of this central nothingness that had driven him to accept the partial panacea of Christianity. Further: that Hell exists, and for those who do not believe in life after death, Hell establishes itself here on earth; that people go to Hell of their own choice, and cannot leave it because they cannot change themselves sufficiently to make the attempt.

More had small sympathy for Eliot's poetry. He detested *The Waste Land* and said so, and once criticized Eliot's punctuation in *Ash-Wednesday*. This so nettled Eliot that he asked More why he bothered to discuss theology and philosophy with an ignoramus like himself but attacked him on the one subject in which he was perhaps the world's foremost authority: the punctuation of poetry.

It might seem astonishing that Eliot should have confided to More his plans to separate from Vivienne, and long before he had broken the news to Vivienne herself, until one recalls other occasions when he entrusted intimate information to comparative strangers.

Very occasionally a watery gleam of something like humor (clerical humor) was reflected in the Eliot-More correspondence: as when Eliot commented on the nature of bishops, saying that they are no help to ordinary mortals because they are too busy, cannot afford to have opinions and have no time to read; or tacked on a postscript asking More to recommend a good book on Original Sin.

On June 24, 1933, Eliot sailed on the *Tuscania* from Boston to Greenock. From there, instead of returning home, he went to stay at Frank Morley's farm in Surrey. In a letter to Morley he attempted a seasick grin: a grotesque and horribly off-key imitation of jauntiness: "O Boy say that Good. I'll be seein' yuh." Eliot's lawyers had drawn up a Deed of Separation, and the papers had been served on Vivienne, together with a letter from Eliot explaining—or trying to explain—what he was doing. He stayed for several months with the Morleys, and then went to London, where he became a paying guest at Father Eric Cheetham's presbytery in Grenville Place. Father Cheetham was the Vicar of St. Stephen's, Gloucester Road, which then became Eliot's church and remained so for the rest of his life.

Like many Anglo-Catholic priests, Father Cheetham seemed not altogether masculine. A pastime to which he was seriously addicted was dressmaking. Yet he was a forceful and eloquent preacher, and a confessor who attracted penitents. He appointed Eliot Vicar's Warden in 1934, a position he continued to hold for twenty-five years, until Father Cheetham's death. When Eliot found out that he should have been formally elected and that his appointment was highly irregular, he characteristically appealed to the archdeacon for an act of indemnity for everything he had done as warden. (The archdeacon told him to forget it.)

When Father Cheetham died, Eliot contributed a memorial note about him to the parish paper: "Eric Cheetham was very lovable and was also, at times, extremely irritating: and one loved him the more for the irritation he caused. There was more than one occasion on which my fellow Warden and I, having gone by appointment to discuss some problem with him, were obliged finally to leave in a state of exhaustion and frustration, because Father Cheetham had done all the talking and had not given us the opportunity to say what we had come to say or to ask the questions to which we needed answers." For seven years Eliot continued to be Father Cheetham's lodger, until the blitz in 1940 upset London's domestic arrangements. At that point Father Cheetham went underground, to the basement of the Albert Hall, and Eliot retired to his friends, the Mirrlees, in the country at Shamley Green and to his office in Bloomsbury.

Vivienne did not submit meekly to this enforced separation. On being served with the papers, she immediately started a campaign which went on for years (though gradually it became intermittent) to get Tom home. She wrote wild letters, she telephoned his office, she sent notes to him there by her faithful old ex-policeman, Janes, who continued to do odd jobs for her (and who was also in Eliot's confidence and pay); she even advertised for him, or tried to—or said she did. On September 17, 1934, the anniversary of the day, two years before, when Eliot had left for America, she sent this advertisement to the Personal column of the *Times:* "Will T. S. Eliot please return to his home 68 Clarence Gate Gardens which he abandoned Sept. 17th 1932. Keys with W.L.J." [Janes]. Whether or not she actually sent this notice to the *Times,* it was not printed. She wrote notes to Eliot saying that the front door was open for him every night from ten-thirty until eleven, and signed her name and Polly's. She went several times to performances of *The Rock,* hoping to catch a glimpse of him.

She joined Sir Oswald Mosley's British Union of Fascists—or at any rate signed up as a member. The idea of conspiracy, even so far-fetched a conspiracy as international Jewry, appealed to her. But discipline and party regularity did not. She bought a uniform and showed up for some demonstrations (usually too late to join in) and went to meetings when she felt like it and felt up to it.

Everyone conspired (against her, she thought) to protect Eliot: the telephone operator at Faber & Faber, Eliot's secretary there, Geoffrey Faber himself, not notably a patient or kindly man, all fobbed her off with the utmost patience and kindness. Even the faithful Janes was at bottom more Eliot's man than hers, and sent written reports to him on her whereabouts and doings: "I have not seen or herd from Mrs. Eliot since she came last Sunday week and took away the Tin Base." Eliot's life was fuller and fuller of literary and business affairs; all she had left was her increasing ill health and her static misery.

3

In these fifteen years, 1933 to 1947, the years of Eliot's middle age, the years of his greatest accomplishment, he pursued three interwoven careers: those of layman, publisher, and poet. He played more parts than these. To that stout disbeliever Edmund Wilson, one of Eliot's favorite roles (Wilson listed six)* was *the Anglican clergy-*

---

*The others: *the formidable professor, Dr. Johnson, the genteel Bostonian, the Christian, the oracle.* W. H. Auden said there was a lot of conscientious churchwarden in Eliot, but also a twelve-year-old boy, "who likes to surprise over-solemn wigs by offering them explosive cigars or cushions which fart when sat upon. It is this practical *man,* "one of Eliot's most successful, if not most exhilarating, impersonations. You can hear how the voice is handled in the droning and monotonous recording he has made of the *Four Quartets.* Eliot makes clergymen's jokes, he laughs a clergyman's laugh; you could swear he wore a turned-around collar."

Some of these disguises, at least some of the time, Eliot put on with a wink, or the hint of one; perhaps the only guise it would really have disconcerted him to admit was the *connoisseur of cheese.* Hugh Kenner* gives a hilarious account of a lunch with Eliot at the Garrick Club. After close examination Eliot refused to recommend the Stilton; he passed the Red Cheshire, but with no enthusiasm; at last he discovered a toadstool-yellow cheese of which no one could tell him the name. "He then achieved with aplomb the impossible feat of peeling off a long slice. He ate this, attentively. He then transferred the Anonymous Cheese to the plate before him, and with no further memorable words proceeded without assistance to consume the entire Anonymous Cheese."

4

Eliot's passionate purpose in becoming a declared Christian was to turn his back on Hell and his face toward Heaven. Was St. Stephen's, Gloucester Road, a solid steppingstone on his way? Eliot thought it was. Without hoping to follow either his reasons or his steps, let us look at the steppingstone.

The walls of St. Stephen's hold the quite explicable splendor of Edwardian green and gold: an overlay to the solid Victorian (1866) underpinnings. The normal gloom of dim religious light suits its style. When the lights are on, various uglinesses emerge. The reredos reaches up a stone disc to cover the center of the smallish rose window, which glows deep blue. The exaggerated height of the can-

---

joker who suddenly interrupts the churchwarden to remark that Milton or Goethe is no good." Neither Wilson nor Auden cited another disguise which Eliot wore often in his early days: *the old man.* Eliot himself sometimes liked to stand on his head and score his own published criticism with such mocking marginalia as "double talk"— "well well!"—"typically TSE word"—"very TSE in one period."

*Hugh Kenner, *The Pound Era* (London: Faber & Faber, 1972).

dles on the altar give a Bernard Buffet effect; the statue of St. Stephen Martyr, standing just below the chancel and facing the nave, is slightly Modigliani. The saint wears a long robe with a belt in which he carries some of the stones of his martyrdom. Red hanging lamps denote the reserved sacrament. There is a faint smell of stale incense. The pews are so squeezed together that worshippers kneeling on a hassock must press their buttocks against the seat.

If you telephone to inquire about an eight o'clock Mass on Sunday you are told that Masses are at seven, eight, and eleven; and then warned sharply that "this is not a *Catholic* church, you know." The congregation is fairly large for an eight o'clock Anglican Mass: ten women, two men. The liturgy follows a line rather spikier than the Book of Common Prayer directs; the congregation differs about the proper times to stand, sit, or kneel. The priest (blest office of the epicene) recites his lines in a severe nasal voice, no quarter asked nor given. When he passes along the communion rail with the chalice he tips it lightly to each mouth; no communicant reaches up a hand to touch and guide it. Ben Jonson, who after his relapse to Rome was so delighted at once again receiving the sacrament "in both kinds" that he seized the chalice and drained it to the last drop, would not have been well received, one feels, at St. Stephen's.

At this church Eliot worshipped for more than forty years; here he was a churchwarden, here he came regularly with his second wife during his last eight happy years; here family piety has placed a memorial tablet inscribed with the worst three lines he ever wrote:

> We must be still and still moving
> Into another intensity
> For a further union, a deeper communion*

What is it about churches like St. Stephen's that is attractive to some, repellent to others? What is there, of the same sort of alternating current, that turns people on and off about the Church of England, or any other Christian sect? Why do Christians hate each other so? *Is* there such a thing as religion? We know that there is such a thing as St. Stephen's. It is not the only place to go but perhaps the

*On the tablet, the last line is inscribed without a comma.

best we can find. We know that Christ lived, and Buddha; we hope against hope that God lives.

As layman, Eliot fulfilled the duties of churchwarden at St. Stephen's, was a faithful attendant at early Mass, wrote articles defending or admonishing the Anglican Church, addressed Anglo-Catholic congresses and similar meetings. It was his church work that got him into playwriting. After his abortive attempt to finish *Sweeney Agonistes,* he was persuaded to write a pageant for a church-building fund in London. *The Rock* was so successful, in its limited field, that his friend George Bell, formerly Dean of Canterbury and then Bishop of Chichester, invited him to write a play for the Canterbury Festival of 1935. The result, *Murder in the Cathedral,** became the best known of all his plays.

An experimental theater in London, The Group, put on several performances of *Sweeney Agonistes.* Vivienne went to see it and sat in the front row. When *Murder in the Cathedral* moved from Canterbury to London's Mercury Theatre, she booked a seat in the stalls, where she found herself sitting next to Aldous Huxley and his wife, Maria. No sign, though, of Tom. But when she saw a notice that he was to speak at a book exhibition put on by the *Sunday Times* on November 18, she put his three latest books in a satchel, tucked Polly under her arm, and set off for the lecture room.

She arrived there just ahead of him, and in the crowded doorway turned and faced him, saying "Oh, *Tom.*" He took her hand, said, "How do you do?" and walked quickly past her. During his lecture she stood up, holding Polly high so that he might see her; and she kept nodding at him encouragingly. When he had finished, and while the audience was still applauding, she pushed her way up to the speakers' table, clutching her satchel and letting Polly off the lead. The little dog made for Tom and jumped up at him in delight, but he paid no attention. Vivienne produced the books from her satchel, and said, "Will you come back with me?"

He said, "I cannot talk to you now." He signed his name in the books, and left. That was the last time they ever met.

---

*Eliot's uncertain first title was *Fear in the Way.* His proposed title for *Four Quartets* was *South Kensington Quartets.* He was better at finding names for the characters in his dramatic verse and in his plays.

5

Eliot felt a need for support and, if possible, sympathy, for his desertion of Vivienne. He even looked for support in unlikely quarters—perhaps it was mainly in such quarters that he could best hope for vindication. Although he and James Joyce were never on intimate terms, he wrote to Joyce that he had separated from his wife, and drew a cool Irish reply: "Thanks for writing to me. One needs a huge lot of patience in these cases."

In the summer of 1934 a Unitarian parson from Boston, Dr. John Carroll Perkins, decided to bring his wife and his niece for a six-month holiday to Chipping Campden, Gloucestershire. Mrs. Perkins was a keen gardener and a collector of gardens. She liked to take color photographs of every Cotswold flowerbed that took her fancy. The Perkinses were old friends of Eliot's family; as for their niece, who was a younger contemporary of Eliot's, she and Tom had been fast friends for twenty-five years—ever since his undergraduate days at Harvard. Dr. Perkins rented Stamford House, and the adjoining Stanley Cottage for his niece, and this arrangement was repeated every summer until the war. In 1934 Eliot paid the first of many visits to Stanley Cottage. His hostess's name was Emily Hale.

In these last years of peace, other home ties tightened or tugged at him. In June of 1935 the Harvard Class of 1910 met in Cambridge for its twenty-fifth reunion. Eliot did not attend, but he rendered an account of himself for the class report, in the light terms the occasion demanded. "I am obliged to spend a great deal of time answering letters from Ezra Pound, but my firm pays for the stamps. . . . I never bet, because I never win. I have travelled a little in foreign parts, such as California, Scotland and Wales; but I become more and more sedentary, although I have only put on seven pounds in twenty-five years [he now weighed 165 pounds]. . . . I am afraid of high places and cows. I like detective stories but especially the adventures of Arsène Lupin. I tend to fall asleep in club armchairs, but I believe my brain works as well as ever, whatever that is, after I have had my tea. . . ."

Contemporary observers have described the exterior Eliot of this period. The descriptions do not always match perfectly, but they fit. Wyndham Lewis pictured him as a man nearly at the end of his tether. "With Mr. Eliot . . . appearing at one's front door, or arriving at a dinner rendezvous . . . his face would be haggard, he would seem at his last gasp. (Did he know?) To ask *him* to lie down for a short while at once was what I always felt I ought to do. However, when he had taken his place at a table, given his face a dry wash with his hands, and having had a little refreshment, Mr. Eliot would rapidly shed all resemblance to the harassed and exhausted refugee, in flight from some scourge of God."

William Empson showed him the respect due to an admired elder, but watched him all the same with a skeptical and twinkling eye. "He has a penetrating influence, perhaps not unlike an east wind. . . . 'Do you really think it necessary, Mr. Eliot,' I broke out, 'as you said in the preface to the Pound anthology, for a poet to write verse at least every week'? He was preparing to cross into Russell Square, eying the traffic both ways, and we were dodging it as his slow reply proceeded. 'I had in mind Pound when I wrote that passage,' began the deep sad voice, and there was a considerable pause. 'Taking the question in general, I should say, in the case of many poets, that the most important thing for them to do . . . is to write as little as possible.' The gravity of that last phrase was so pure as to give it an almost lyrical quality. A reader may be tempted to suppose that this was a snub or at least a joke, but I still do not believe it was. . . . There was a party (I forget everybody else in the room) where Eliot broke into some chatter about a letter being misunderstood. 'Ah, letters,' he said, rather as if they were some rare kind of bird. 'I had to look into the question of letters at one time. I found that the mistake . . . that most people make . . . about letters, is that after writing their letters, carefully, they go out, and look for a pillar box. I found that it is very much better, after giving one's attention to composing the letter, to . . . pop it into the fire.' "

6

In *The Complete Poems and Plays of T. S. Eliot,** two of Eliot's precedent remarks have been removed: the dedication of *Ash-*

*A new edition was published in 1969, four years after his death, and seems certain to become notorious among Eliot scholars for the number and carelessness of its misprints.

Wednesday to Vivienne ("To My Wife"), and the acknowledgment originally printed before *Four Quartets:* "I wish to acknowledge a particular debt to Mr. John Hayward for general criticism and specific suggestions during the composition of these poems." This salute confirmed a friendship, already of seventeen years' standing, that was to last altogether more than thirty years, and was finally terminated by Eliot's second marriage.

When Eliot visited Cambridge in 1926 to give the Clark Lectures, six of the more promising undergraduates were chosen to have breakfast with him. One of them was John Hayward, of King's College, already under sentence of gradual death from muscular dystrophy (in laymen's language, creeping paralysis) but not yet confined to a wheelchair. Though noted for his sharp tongue, he was gregarious: he had a good bass voice, and sang in musical societies; and in one undergraduate play he took the part of a whole procession of prisoners under torture behind the scenes, "producing some of the most blood-curdling Grand Guignol noises ever heard in Cambridge." John Hayward was a surgeon's son, one of three children, born and brought up in Wimbledon, a suburban address of which he was not proud. His school was Gresham's, in Norfolk, which, though of an ancient foundation, was not in his view sufficiently distinguished. Not until he got to King's College, Cambridge, did he feel socially secure. He liked fashionable and titled people, and joked about his snobbery—as if he could erase it by joking. At this early morning meeting everyone was so gripped by shyness that no one spoke for a full minute. Finally Hayward said, "Mr. Eliot, have you read the last volume of Proust?" Eliot replied, "No, I'm afraid I have not." Again, silence. This was the beginning of a notable friendship.

After taking his degree at Cambridge Hayward went to London, where he established himself as a professional man of letters, re-editing such English classics as Rochester, Swift, and Donne, and eventually becoming the autocratic editor of *The Book Collector.* His flat in Bina Gardens was the seat of a jolly good fellowship, rocking with intellectual bawdry and highbrow jokery-pokery. A beautiful young Russian actress, frightened by the prospect of her first evening there, especially by the presence of T. S. Eliot, found everyone very

friendly and the entertainment—a showing of early Chaplin films—
hilarious.*

Hayward loved parties and dining out, and managed to get about
a good deal, even with his wheelchair. He evolved an effective tech-
nique for riding in a taxi. "Tip me back, head first, don't be alarmed,
driver," he would say as his chair was pushed into the cab. A record
of the highjinks at Hayward's flat, under the name of *Noctes Binania-
nae*, was privately printed for the delectation of the regular members, who appeared in it under nicknames: Geoffrey Faber was Coot;
Frank Morley, Whale; Eliot, Possum or Elephant; Hayward, Spider
or Tarantula.

Though not an eminently clubbable man, Eliot believed deeply
in men's clubs and joined a good many; apparently they represented
for him an almost irresistible mingling of civic duty and private
pleasure. He was already a member of the Oxford & Cambridge; now
he joined the newly formed Burke Club, a serious Tory dining club
made up of Members of Parliament and journalists;† and The Club,
an eighteenth-century foundation consisting mainly of peers, with a
few such right-thinking commoners as Desmond MacCarthy and
John Betjeman. Later he became a member of the Garrick, and the
Athenaeum. To Eliot, a club was not simply a convenience to be
used. When Herbert Read told Eliot he was thinking of resigning
from his club, the Reform, Eliot said with concern, "But don't you
think you *ought* to go on supporting it?"

As Eliot said of himself, joining committees was in his blood; he
was always being asked to serve on one, and hardly ever refused. Not
all of them were intended to get things done. Some had less practical
purposes: to clear the air, to clear the mind, to explore a situation.
Some of the clubs he joined were simply committees in thin disguise.
One such was The Moot, an occasional gathering of first-rate intel-
lects who met to consider the Larger Questions, treated each other
with great respect, and rarely agreed. His membership in this
learned body is chiefly of interest for one small but significant fact:

*She later brought in a minority report on Eliot: "He was hard. Kindly? I don't
think so. And he could be *very* angry."

†One of his fellow members, W. Collin Brooks, was a friend of Valerie Fletcher's
family and, when she later applied for the job of Eliot's secretary, Brooks recommended her.

the signature he put to a paper he wrote for The Moot was "Metoi-kos"—a Greek word meaning "resident alien."

It was the war that brought Bina Gardens and its nights to an end. Lord Rothschild, shocked at Hayward's helpless isolation in London, took him off to his own house in Cambridge, where he was well cared for till the war was over. Eliot left his lodgings in St. Stephen's clergy house and alternated between Shamley Green, near Guildford, where he spent long weekends with his friend Mrs. Mirrlees and her daughter Hope,* and the Faber offices, where for four days a week he worked, slept and fire-watched.

The first year of the war saw the end of the Criterion. It also saw the beginning of Eliot's career as a playwright. It would hardly be correct to say of the Criterion that it failed financially, for it had never even attempted to succeed in that way. Not popularity but influence ("to be understood by a few intelligent people is all the influence a man requires") was what the Criterion was after; Eliot had hoped that the quarterly would foment and enliven intellectual commerce throughout Europe. That it signally failed to do; and as the war clouds gathered on the horizon, clearly visible to the naked eyesight of plain men though imperceptible to experts, the national boundaries of Europe became ramparts, excluding or discouraging all such peaceful palaver. Would the Criterion have been a more inspiriting force if Eliot had been a more inspiring editor? There are those who think so. Nevertheless, for seventeen years the Criterion had raised a respectable standard to which at least a few just men repaired. If its performance had not been a triumph, it had not been a disaster either.

Six months before England declared war on Hitler's Germany and two months after the Criterion's last issue (in January), The Family Reunion opened at the Westminster Theatre in London, and ran for only five weeks.† Nevill Coghill, the Oxford don whose musical version of The Canterbury Tales has had one of the longest runs in West End history, greatly admired the play, but listed its basic

---

*The married daughter, Margot Coker, had a large country house near Bicester where Eliot liked to stay. There her brother, General W. H. B. Mirrlees, introduced him to the local hunting set—among them Ernest Simpson, ex-husband of the Duchess of Windsor.

†After the war it was revived and played at the Mercury Theatre for three months in the winter of 1946–47; a later revival, in 1956, did not do so well.

flaws. "The supreme flaw is the daring introduction of the Eumenides as 'the objective correlative' of Harry's guilt and expiation. . . . The second great flaw lies in Harry's character; it is hardly too much to say that he is odious. [But] whether we love Harry or loathe him, the intuition that created his character is faultless; it is the very portrait of a certain kind of soul in the throes of religious conversion." If it is going too far to say that Harry is largely autobiographical, it is not too much to say that he is Eliot's mouthpiece. Another principal character, Agatha, as we shall see later, was probably based on an American lady who loomed large in Eliot's life.

Though attempts to understand oneself often slide into attempts at self-justification, it does seem to have been Eliot's instinct to put a finished (or even an unfinished) work aside and try a different sort of experiment. This tendency would partly explain his growing preoccupation with the theater—as also his amazing assertion (amazing, that is, for a poet) that "the poetry does not matter." Each of the four plays he wrote after *Murder in the Cathedral* was based on a Greek tragedy and written in a kind of verse-form that was a double first cousin to lucid prose. In each successive play the verse became less apparent. The "verse," as defined by Eliot, consisted of a line made up of three, sometimes four, stresses, with a caesura separating one stress from the other two.

Most of the time the result was indistinguishable from prose. Here is a speech by Dr. Warburton in *The Family Reunion*, not broken into lines of "verse" but printed as the prose it is: "I needn't go into technicalities at the present moment. The whole machine is weak and running down. Her heart's very feeble. With care, and avoiding all excitement she may live several years. A sudden shock might send her off at any moment." In the last play, *The Elder Statesman*, the verse was not only inaudible but virtually nonexistent: the poetry no longer mattered.

The man who worked closely with Eliot on all his plays, and produced them all, the man from whom he learned his stagecraft, was an old Etonian named E. Martin Browne, a devout Anglican and professor of religious drama. Though an admirer of Eliot and in almost complete sympathy with him, as a man of the theater Browne kept a cool head about his plays. He considered *The Family Reunion* "a masterpiece, but not a successful play." Eliot himself later turned on his own play and savaged it more fiercely than any of its other critics. "I should either have stuck closer to Aeschylus or else taken a great deal more liberty with his myth. . . . [The Furies] never succeed in being either Greek goddesses or modern spooks.* . . . [M]y sympathies now have come to be all with the mother, who seems to me, except for the chauffeur, the only complete human being in the play; and my hero now strikes me as an insufferable prig." Eliot exaggerates: the play remains an extraordinary piece, if not quite a masterpiece, far superior to his later, "better made" plays. He never again came as close as this to writing a great play.

In June 1940 Eliot went to Dublin to give the first annual Yeats memorial lecture at the Abbey Theatre. In the morning, "An old charwoman came, lighting a fire in my room and pulling the same kind of tub from under my bed, which made me feel as though I were a boy again, and back in Missouri."

Work, church, work, office, committees, lectures. From now on these would be the principal nouns in his life; and the verbs would be as heavy as the nouns: broadcast, lecture, speak, edit, listen, write (anything but poetry). Like everyone in Britain, like almost everyone in the world, his daily life bore the extra burden of wartime, when more than usual had to be done with less.

Besides his extracurricular fire-watching, Eliot put himself at the disposal of G.I.'s in London who wanted to see him, or were told they should want to. Sergeant James A. Fechheimer was one of five who visited him one evening in his office, taking along a copy of the American edition of *Four Quartets*—the first copy of the poem Eliot had seen in print, since the English edition was not yet out.† Another G.I., John Stanley, who hadn't the slightest idea who Eliot was, heard him talk about poetry at a Red Cross club and thought him patient and amiable, and noted that he smoked a lot and was generous about passing around his cigarettes. As for Eliot's remarks about poetry,

*One of the fundamental awkwardnesses of the play was that the Furies were twice required to appear on the stage, in the embrasure of a window, though they never spoke. They also—a piece of high camp!—had to wear evening dress. In some productions they did not appear: their presence being signaled by a sudden change of light. That didn't work either.

†The *Four Quartets* were published one at a time: *Burnt Norton* in 1935 (as the last poem in *Collected Poems: 1909–1935*); then, after a lapse of five years, *East Coker* in May 1940; *The Dry Salvages* in 1941; and *Little Gidding* in December 1942. (Each of these three was first published in *The New English Weekly*.) The first edition of the whole poem was brought out in the U.S. in May 1943, eighteen months before the first U.K. edition.

which Stanley hated, he didn't understand a word.

There are chapters, or at least paragraphs, in Eliot's life that cannot be set forth with any certainty, not because the facts have been concealed but because they are not yet available. Such a paragraph is the five weeks in May and June 1942 that Eliot spent in Stockholm with his friend Bishop Bell. It is known that a delegation of anti-Hitler Germans, including Hans Schönfeld and Dietrich Bonhoeffer, went to Stockholm and had a series of meetings with Bishop Bell—about plans to overthrow Hitler and end the war—and that Bell later reported to Anthony Eden and that nothing came of it. Whether or not Eliot was privy to these abortive talks we do not know. At any rate, he was not present when the Bishop reported to the Foreign Secretary.

7

Most of Eliot's holidays were business trips, or combined with business trips. When he went to Paris to lecture in May 1945 he held a reunion with his old friends Sylvia Beach and Adrienne Monnier, whom he had first met with Joyce, twenty-five years before, and brought them much-needed tea and soap. When he went to the United States, and particularly New York, his talk became livelier. New England primness might even rouse the rascal in him, as when, after a lecture, a very proper lady congratulated him on his youthful appearance and wondered how he kept it: "Gin and drugs, madam, gin and drugs!" In New York, when a young publisher of the spoiled priest type asked him if he agreed that most editors are failed writers, he replied: "Perhaps, but so are most writers."

Eliot's opinion of Carl Sandburg, as a poet, was never printed but did not need to be. Sandburg, on the other hand, greatly admired Eliot. They met, once, in a publisher's office in New York. Sandburg, pointing at Eliot, cried: "Just look at him! Look at that man's face—the suffering, the pain! You can't hold *him* responsible for the poets and critics who ride on his coattails!" Eliot grinned and said nothing.

When he was in England, unless he was with one of his few intimates he kept watchfully in his shell, though occasionally a sharp peck would bring out the tip of an antenna to see what sort of bird was there. A canny and worldly lady, meeting him for the first time and wanting him to remember her, asked him, "How intelligent do you think Richard de la Mare* is?" He flashed back at her, "By whose standards—yours or mine?" Both of them saved the day by roaring with laughter.

Murder in the Cathedral had been Eliot's first theatrical success. He learned a good deal in the course of adapting what he had written to the demands of the stage, absorbing in the process many suggestions and a good deal of criticism. He was an amenable student. He was also a frugal Yankee who detested waste, so that when he was persuaded to change or to drop a favorite phrase or line or passage from the text of his play, he pigeonholed it for future use. From these leftovers from *Murder in the Cathedral* came the beginnings of a new long poem, *Burnt Norton*.

It was on one of his visits to Emily Hale at Chipping Campden that she took him out to see a restored eighteenth-century manor house, Burnt Norton, so called because its original owner had set fire to the house in 1737 and was burned up with it. The house became the seat of the earls of Hawtrey, but was standing empty when Eliot saw it.† Set on a wooded hillside with a sweeping view of the Cotswolds, the house is surrounded by steep lawns and a formal garden, with the dry pool (two, in fact) described in the poem.

When *Burnt Norton* was first published, in 1935, to an already bewildered world it seemed, in Dame Helen Gardner's words, "almost impenetrably obscure." After Eliot conceived the idea of adding three other poems and linking the four together, some inklings of what he was up to began to appear; *Burnt Norton* was partly explicable by the parts that came after it. Eliot had written obscure poems before, but *Burnt Norton* was also notably different from anything he had done. The tone was elevated and calm rather than intense, the language comparatively simple, quiet, didactic. No wild beauties here. Whatever it was that Eliot was trying to say, it was apparently almost a philosophical statement, the summing up of his life's experience.

Three years later he told his fellow-poet George Barker that po-

*Son of the poet Walter de la Mare and a fellow director of Faber & Faber.
†It is now an expensive private school for fifty "maladjusted" boys.

etry, whether it is only a brief visitation or a lifelong employment, is sure to be a vexation to the poet. He is bound to feel, again and again, that his ability to write poetry has vanished, and that he must either repeat himself or stop altogether. These dry periods, said Eliot, are unpleasant but salutary; he himself had experienced several of them, and while they lasted could have sworn he would never be able to write again—or else he sweated over a piece of work only to find it was no good. These times, in fact, seemed to have covered most of his life. He might have published much more than he had, if he had not constantly told himself that nothing is worth doing a second time.

Two years before the war Eliot had made a pious pilgrimage to East Coker, the Somerset village where the Eliot family had lived before emigrating to the Massachusetts Bay Colony in the seventeenth century; he took half-a-dozen photographs of the place. Now he formed the idea of expanding *Burnt Norton* into a series of poems, and started writing the second, *East Coker.** Since it is almost a truism that poets, like mathematicians, do their best work before the age of thirty, it may seem extraordinary that *Burnt Norton* was finished when Eliot was forty-seven, and the last and best of the *Quartets, Little Gidding,* eight years later.

8

In 1940 *East Coker* was ready to publish. For many British readers, it was exactly the kind of thing they wanted to hear. Thirty years afterward Professor Freeman Dyson, who had been in the R.A.F. Bomber Command, remembered how welcome the poem had been: "We did not need Churchill's oratory to tell us that we could take it. We liked much better the quiet rhythms of T. S. Eliot, whose *East Coker* appeared in May 1940, and sold out five printings by February 1941:

> There is only the fight to recover what has been lost
> And found and lost again and again; and now, under conditions

*". . . *Burnt Norton* might have remained by itself if it hadn't been for the war. . . . You remember how the conditions of our lives changed, how much we were thrown in on ourselves in the early days? *East Coker* was the result—and it was only in writing *East Coker* that I began to see the *Quartets* as a set of four."

That seem unpropitious. But perhaps neither gain nor loss.
For us, there is only the trying. The rest is not our business.

Writing poetry in the Eliot mode was as complicated a maneuver
as Perseus' killing of the Gorgon, and required as many implements:
hat of darkness, winged sandals, razor-sharp sword and mirror-shield.
He must never look the Gorgon in the face, but sight her periscopi-
cally in his shield and then strike home. If he made a clean hit the
result was there for all to see: the bloody head, the snaky tresses still
hissing and writhing in death, the face of such beauty and such horror
that it turned a beholder to stone. "Any man wants to do a girl in"?
Why didn't Sweeney say, more accurately, that to escape the Furies
a poet must hunt down and kill their cousin, the Gorgon?

Eliot was now in his early fifties, an age when most poets are
either dead or decaying, or garrulously parodying their earlier selves.
A dangerous time for a poet. But Eliot had insured himself against
this occupational hazard by eschewing the *profession* of poetry
(professionally, he was a publisher, editor, and critic, who sometimes
wrote poems); and by making it an inflexible rule never to do the
same thing twice. In the winter of 1941, a grim winter for war-locked
Britain, he was in the very midst of the struggle with his last major
poem, *Four Quartets*. In February he finished *The Dry Salvages*,*
the third of the series, and by July he had begun the fourth and last.
Little Gidding, his favorite (as the youngest child often is), was published in December 1942. Except for a few faint gleams and flashes
in his later plays, that was the final appearance of T. S. Eliot the
poet.

Little Gidding, its stern beauties as yet unsuspected by the world,
was still in the press on a day in November 1942 when Eliot took tea
with Lady Colefax at her house on Lord North Street, near Westminster Abbey. An American journalist, an admirer of Eliot's, made a
third. They sat in Lady Colefax's bandbox of a sitting room, a fat little
fire on the hearth and the blacked-out London fog outside. The
conversation tinkled among the teacups; their remarks verged on the
prim. There are stubborn and brittle Americans who can stay in

---

*One of the foremost authorities on Eliot and Pound, Professor Hugh Kenner, said
of this poem, "It is my argument . . . that . . . the whole of *The Dry Salvages* is a
parody." Another authority, Herbert Howarth, thinks it "the greatest of his poems and
among the great poems of his time." We shall just have to wait till they settle it.

England for twenty years without acquiring an English accent or losing their own; Eliot was not of that unalterable breed.

The journalist watched him, but with bated eyes; he seemed to be holding himself together, almost as if he were a piece of riveted china; if he lowered his carefully held cup without rearranging his carefully held feet (but of course he did!) he might break in two. How deracinated he seemed, thought the journalist: how non-English (and how non-American) his polite accents were, how carefully he was dressed and with what propriety his hair was combed. Does he seem to Lady Colefax as uprooted, as *outlandish* as he seems to me? And how does he appear to himself? Most Americans, the journalist thought, would consider him quite Anglicized; but few Englishmen would mistake him for one of themselves.

Into the midst of this engrossing tea party, and smashing it 'to bits like a clumsy, waggy-tailed big dog, bounded the beaming and complacent, the ruddy and rotund figure of Harold Nicolson. A most unwelcome interruption. Not, however, to Lady Colefax, who hailed the intruder with enthusiasm. Nicolson, fresh from the House of Commons, was full of himself as always, and bursting with hot-off-the-griddle political gossip. The next half hour was a whooping, giggling monologue, prickly with first names and bursting with inside-stuff lingo, interspersed with screams of delight and encouragement from Lady Colefax. None of this incomprehensible club talk could be of any interest whatever to an outsider—which of course was a large part of its charm for the insiders. By the poet's complete absence of expression and his utter silence, the journalist gathered that Mr. Eliot shared his acute boredom. With the fragile tea party in fragments on the sitting-room carpet, as soon as they decently could Mr. Eliot and the journalist took their separate leaves.

9

For such a precisian as Eliot there could be little margin of safety:

> The common word exact without vulgarity,
> The formal word precise but not pedantic,
> The complete consort dancing together.

And like many clever men, Eliot was at times obtuse. Like the Edwardian butler in *Punch,* he never chips or cracks—when he breaks he smashes utterly. Only Eliotolatry can explain the admiration for such a line as this, from *The Waste Land:*

Inexplicable splendour of Ionian white and gold*

This obtuseness is manifest in the ponderosity of such unpoetic "poetry" as this (which is here transcribed as prose—and prose of doubtful syntax—to show it as it really is): "It seems, as one becomes older, that the past has another pattern, and ceases to be a mere sequence —or even development: the latter a partial fallacy, encouraged by superficial notions of evolution, which becomes, in the popular mind, a means of disowning the past. The moments of happiness—not the sense of well-being, fruition, fulfillment, security or affection, or even a very good dinner, but the sudden illumination—we had the experience but missed the meaning, and approach to the meaning restores the experience in a different form, beyond any meaning we can assign to happiness."

Examples of Eliot's failure of musical ear abound in his later poems. They are first to be seen (italicized for emphasis) in one of the choruses from *The Rock:*

The great *snake* lies ever half *awake,* at the bottom of the
   pit of the *world, curled*
In folds of himself until he awakens in hunger and moving
     his head to right and to left prepares for his *hour* to *devour.*
But the Mystery of Iniquity is a pit too deep for mortal
     eyes to *plumb. Come*
Ye out from among those who *prize* the serpent's golden *eyes,*
The worshippers, self-given sacrifice of the *snake. Take* . . .

The common practice among modern poets is to use rhyme so lightly, so unemphatically, that it is scarcely noticeable. It is as if Eliot had tried to hide or camouflage these flat-footed rhymes, at least to the eye, by tucking them inside the lines. The eye may miss some,

---

*For "inexplicable" Eliot first wrote "inviolable," then "joyful"; and "Corinthian" for "Ionian." (The columns in the nave of St. Magnus Martyr are in fact Ionic, with trimmings.) To prove that the first seven syllables of this line are not only cacophonous but unpronounceable, try saying them out loud without frothing at the mouth. And what on earth does the phrase mean? Why should splendor be either explicable or inexplicable?

but the ear is not deceived. Eliot's obsession with these rub-a-dub internal rhymes reached its nadir in *Ash-Wednesday*, where their clamor nearly ruins Part V of that beautiful poem, like a lovely room marred by jarring echoes:

Where shall the word be *found*, where will the word
Resound? Not here, there is not enough *silence*
Not on the sea or on the *islands*, not
On the *mainland*, in the desert or the *rain land*,
For those who walk in darkness
Both in the day time and in the *night time*
The *right time* and the right place are not here
No *place* of *grace* for those who avoid the *face*
No time to *rejoice* for those who walk among *noise* and deny the *voice*

Will the veiled sister pray for
Those who walk in darkness, who *chose* thee and *oppose* thee,
Those who are *torn* on the *horn* between season and season, time and
        time. . . .
Who will not go *away* and cannot *pray:*
Pray for those who *chose* and *oppose* . . .

These insistent rhymes, that din in our ear like a jarring cymbal too frequently struck, put us in mind of the popular songs that haunted Eliot's youth.* The same trick, used again and again by Eliot to enhance the intensity of the passage cited above, not only fails to do so but, by drawing attention to itself, dissipates the reader's attention. And if to our ears, contemporary with Eliot's, such lines tremble on the verge of the ludicrous, will not a later generation find them laughable? Except for a brief passage in *The Dry Salvages*, the poems after *Ash-Wednesday* are free of this fungoid flaw.

10

A new kind of poetry, like a new kind of music, is not likely to be immediately understood, or even to be granted a patient hearing.

*For example, *Do You Ever Think of Me?*
        . . . and when your eyes
        Disguise
        The same old loving lies
        They tell so tenderly . . .

Four Quartets were not immediately understood, but so great was Eliot's reputation by the time they appeared that they were given a reception in which reverence contended with awe. Before the critical faculty at last reopened its bemused eyes and took a good look at what was in front of it, some readers had blurted out appreciative ejaculations that were later seen to have missed the mark. For example, a French critic: *"Je suppose que le quatrième quatuor, Little Gidding, porte le nom d'un petit garçon cher à T. S. Eliot. A ce petit garçon, l'auteur veut léguer trois pensées: que la vie est dure, qu'elle est composée d'échecs et qu'elle est sans cesse un recommencement . . ."*

Let it be a lesson to all of us. The scholars continue to peck away at Eliot's poems like sparrows picking at horse shit that still smokes with life and still gives off its fresh ammoniac fumes. There are many less attractive examples of ingenious erudition pursuing its own tail. Does it matter whether or not we know that the sausages mentioned in line twelve of *Triumphal March* come from Aristophanes' play, *The Knights?* It does not matter. The kind of allusive, learned, buried-treasure poetry Eliot wrote beckoned encouragingly to the scholarly approach; and though occasionally he publicly deprecated the critical Sanhedrin, he himself was a Pharisee. His attempts (if they were genuine attempts) to explain his own poetic practice leave most of us in a state of enlightened mystification. Take the famous —the notorious—"objective correlative." This hideous phrase, it will have to be admitted, was coined by Eliot himself. What on earth does it mean? Well, as nearly as you can put it into plain, unscrunched English, it means a verbal image that works on the reader the same way it worked on the writer.

When the "objective correlative" does work, it's like hitting the jackpot on a fruit machine: three white leopards in a row, lady. This can only happen when the reader sees and takes in all the references Eliot has used. If the reader gets some references but not all of them, it's like seeing two white leopards but not three: a partial picture and no jackpot. If the reader fails to recognize any references at all, he still has the pleasure of the slight exercise of pulling the lever and hearing and seeing the smooth whirring blur of a cunningly contrived mechanism.

Four Quartets were presented, and accepted, as a major poem.

Were they great poetry? Were they in fact poetry at all? Or did they consist of short poems linked by passages of prose, as Arthur Symons had long ago suggested that all long poems must be? Poetry has not yet been defined to everyone's satisfaction, but examples of it are generally recognized. If the *Quartets* were printed as prose, the lodes of poetry would be luminous, the shale in which they lie would not. Look!

What might have been is an abstraction remaining a perpetual possibility only in a world of speculation. What might have been and what has been point to one end, which is always present. . . .
. . . Internal darkness, deprivation and destitution of all property, desiccation of the world of sense, evacuation of the world of fancy, inoperancy of the world of spirit; this is the one way, and the other is the same, not in movement but abstention from movement; while the world moves in appetency, on its metalled ways of time past and time future . . .
That was a way of putting it—not very satisfactory: a periphrastic study in a worn-out poetical fashion, leaving one still with the intolerable wrestle with words and meanings. The poetry does not matter. It was not (to start again) what one had expected . . .
So here I am, in the middle way, having had twenty years—twenty years largely wasted, the years of *l'entre deux guerres*—trying to learn to use words, and every attempt is a wholly new start, and a different kind of failure because one has only learnt to get the better of words for the thing one no longer has to say, or the way in which one is no longer disposed to say it. And so each venture is a new beginning, a raid on the inarticulate with shabby equipment always deteriorating in the general mess of imprecision of feeling, undisciplined squads of emotion. And what there is to conquer by strength and submission, has already been discovered once or twice, or several times, by men whom one cannot hope to emulate—but there is no competition—there is only the fight to recover what has been lost and found and lost again and again; and now, under conditions that seem unpropitious. . . .
We must be still and still moving into another intensity for a further union, a deeper communion. . . .
What we call the beginning is often the end and to make an end is to make a beginning. The end is where we start from. And every phrase and sentence that is right (where every word is at home, taking its place to support the others, the word neither diffident nor ostentatious, an easy commerce of the old and the new, the common word exact without vulgarity, the formal word precise but not pedantic, the complete consort dancing together) every phrase and every sentence is an end and a beginning, every poem an epitaph.

11

On January 22, 1947, in Northumberland House (a mental hospital), Green Lanes, London, N.16, Vivienne Eliot died.* The causes of death given on her death certificate were syncope and cardiovascular degeneration. Her age was reported as fifty-seven; she was in fact fifty-nine, the same age as her estranged husband.† Her death was not noted in the *Times*. Her only brother informed John Hayward, who in turn told Eliot; he and Maurice went together to her burial. Three days later a memorial signed by T. S. Eliot was printed in the *Times*—not to Vivienne but to Professor Karl Mannheim, one of Eliot's distinguished fellow members of The Moot.

> A restless shivering painted shadow
> In life, she is less than a shadow in death.

Yes, but that did not begin to say it all. When she died it was terrible; but it was a relief. That too was terrible. Friends who were close enough, like John Hayward and Christopher Sykes, saw that Eliot's grief was abnormally great, and showed unmistakable traces of remorse. It even seemed to Eliot that he was being punished for a failure of memory—or was it for remembering too well? Through his tears he said to Hayward, "I've not a single second of happiness to look back on, and that makes it worse."

> Teach us to care and not to care
> Teach us to sit still

That prayer was still needed.

The year ended for Eliot with a whimper. As he complained in a letter to Desmond MacCarthy, his chronic hernia was acting up again, and he would have to have all his teeth out.

---

*Her brother, Maurice, who visited her there shortly before her death, stated emphatically that she was then no more mad than he was.

†At some point in her marriage she had changed the spelling of her name from Vivienne to Vivien; but her death certificate returned to the original spelling.

SEVEN

"Meeting Is for Strangers"

(1908–1957)

EZRA POUND's helping hand, throughout Eliot's early career and particularly in the shaping of *The Waste Land*, has always been known; the only thing unknown about that help, its extent, has now been cleared up by the publication of *The Waste Land*'s original version, with the marks of Pound's editing. But there are other facts of Eliot's life that are not widely known: one of them was his nearly lifelong association with Emily Hale. It was more than a friendship, definitely not a flirtation, something a little less than a love affair but very like a long engagement. A forty-eight-year-long smile and shake of the hand? Not to Emily's mind, and not on Emily's part. She was his oldest friend, and perhaps his closest.

Emily Hale was born in Chestnut Hill, a suburb of Boston, on October 27, 1891, just three years later than T. S. Eliot, but in the proper place. A younger brother died in infancy, so that in effect she was an only child. Her father, Edward Hale, was an architect who became a Unitarian minister like her uncle, John Carroll Perkins. Another uncle, Philip Hale, was the music critic of the Boston *Evening Transcript*. Emily's claims to Bostonian properness (the right church, the right art, the right paper) were thus impeccably registered—as Eliot's, except by ancestry and by adoption, were not. But both of them had the same Unitarian, bluestocking background. Her father was assistant minister (but no kin) to the famous Edward Everett Hale, author of *The Man Without a Country*, at the South Congregational Church in Boston.

Both her parents died when she was a young girl, and she went to live with her uncle and aunt, Dr. and Mrs. Perkins. She and Eliot met perhaps as early as 1908. She was a "finished" young lady of seventeen, recently graduated from Miss Porter's celebrated academy at Farmington; he was a twenty-year-old undergraduate at Harvard. Their meeting place is uncertain. Was it a dance at Brattle Hall, or a tea, or a luncheon? If it was a dance, what was she wearing? Something long and light-colored, her dark hair down her back. He was a tall, skinny boy in a dark suit, with a shy, engaging grin and brilliant gray-green eyes.

Did he take her to Harvard-Yale football games? To dances in Boston? Or did they prefer a walk along the Charles and then tea at some chaperone's house? We know they went on skating parties together. And did he show her his poems? Did he confide to her what his own mother did not yet know and that he hardly dared say to himself: that it was poetry he was after, not philosophy? No one now living knows the answer to these questions. One day, however, they may be answered.

How deeply was Emily's heart engaged in this friendship? And what about Tom's? When he set off for Europe in 1914, not to return for eighteen years (except for that brief, unhappy visit to his family in the summer of 1915) he was twenty-five, she twenty-two: old enough to be in love though hardly at the age for two cautious New Englanders to commit themselves. We may hazard a guess—that she was "fond of him," that he *liked* her very much but preferred for the present to go it alone. She could understand that and accept it. For both of them the future was long and lofty.

Then came the unexpected, buffeting word of his almost furtive marriage to some English girl with the fancily spelled (socially suspect) name of Vivienne. Once she had recovered from the shock of this painful news and had come to terms with its implications, it must have chastised and then chastened her opinion of him—"altered" would perhaps be too drastic a word. He was less wise than she had thought him, more unstable, liable to the awful daring of a moment's surrender. He was not after all the paladin she had made of him. But he was still the most talented person she knew and fundamentally a dear boy; she was sure great things lay ahead for him. This was a rude interruption of their intimacy, but no more than an interruption; the friendship, momentarily severed, knitted itself together and survived, stronger than ever.

Nevertheless, he would have to endure the consequences of his youthful folly; he must work out his salvation with diligence. Meantime she had her own life to live. She would not, herself, use so evangelistic a word as "salvation," but perhaps "living her own life" came to much the same thing. She liked proper speech and she liked people to speak properly. Speech became first her study and then her career. Speech led her to drama: she found that she not only had a good speaking voice but that she was a natural actress. As one of her former pupils said, "There never was such a lady for a gesture and a pose." Some of her friends thought she would certainly have gone on the stage had her uncle not forbidden her.

After Tom Eliot's marriage several years went by before they met again: for one thing, U-boats in the Atlantic did not encourage wartime travel, but letters went back and forth; they kept in touch. She heard of his labors at the bank and of his literary schemes and accomplishments; he heard about her scholastic life and the gossip of the academic Rialto. If he did not always send her copies of his books as soon as they were published in England, she could always read them in their American editions. And in 1922, when the first number of his *Criterion* appeared, she would have been a charter subscriber, or on the free list. They met in many places, over many years: in California, when she was on the faculty of Scripps College; at Chipping Campden, in those six summers when she was there with her uncle and aunt; at Northampton, Massachusetts, when she taught at Smith; at Andover, when she was at Abbot Academy. The brightest days of her life were those that marked his visits to her.

Was it from him or from others that she learned of the failure of his marriage? When he came back to Harvard in 1932 to give the Charles Eliot Norton Lectures she must have seen him; she was teaching then at Smith College, where she was to stay for many years. Did he tell her that he was not going back to his wife? He had not yet broken the news to Vivienne herself, so we may hope that he said nothing to Emily either.

Her life and career were a complement to his: as student and teacher of speech and drama she was a sounding board for his poetry, perhaps a testing ear for the phrases that had to ring memorably and true; and a scanning eye for the dramatic lines that had the seasoned air of lines that have been looked at long (some said for six months). This is not even to hint that Emily was consulted about any of his poems-in-progress; but it may reasonably be conjectured that on more than one occasion he may have shown her an unpublished poem that was finished or even in a semifinal state. In the case of at least one of his plays, *The Cocktail Party*, the typescript passed back and forth between them several times.

The only two poems Eliot is known to have written to her are both light verse: *The Country Walk* ("Among the beasts that God allows/ In England's green and pleasant land,/ I most of all dislike the Cows . . .") and *Morgan Tries Again* ("Now you jist try your paw —let it come from the 'art—/ At a birthday oration to honour Miss 'Ile"). Neither has been published. But it was she who introduced him to Burnt Norton, the opening scene of the first of the *Four Quartets*, and the person who is hidden in the "you" and half the "we" of the introductory lines may well be Emily.

> Footfalls echo in the memory
> Down the passage which we did not take
> Towards the door we never opened
> Into the rose-garden. My words echo
> Thus, in your mind.

We get a glimpse of her in *La Figlia che Piange:*

> Stand on the highest pavement of the stair—
> Lean on a garden urn—
> Weave, weave the sunlight in your hair—
> Clasp your flowers to you with a pained surprise—
> Fling them to the ground and turn
> With a fugitive resentment in your eyes:
> But weave, weave the sunlight in your hair.

And in Eliot's most ambitious and least successful play, *The Family Reunion,* she has a whole character to herself: Agatha. She is the strongest character in the play and the only one who from the first is aware of what is really happening.

This is the plot, such as it is: Harry, Lord Monchensey, has just returned to his ancestral home after a three-year absence; he has been traveling restlessly with an unloved wife, who has recently been lost at sea (did she jump overboard or did he push her? He says he pushed her). The family of which he is the head—his mother, uncles, aunts, and a younger cousin, Mary—are gathered to welcome him, hoping that he is home to stay. From his favorite aunt, Agatha, Harry learns that she and his father had been in love, that his father had wanted to kill his mother but had been dissuaded by Agatha, not from sisterly love but because his mother was pregnant. Agatha went away, to a life of scholarly spinsterhood as head of a woman's college, Harry was born, his father died. When he learns this closeted secret, which liberates his own, Harry sees the Furies that have been pursuing him in a new light, not as avengers to be fled from but as angels to be followed. Before he leaves, to follow in their train, he says to Agatha, "Shall we ever meet again?" She answers:

> "Shall we ever meet again?
> And who will meet again? Meeting is for strangers.
> Meeting is for those who do not know each other."

When Eliot was given an honorary degree by the University of St. Andrews, Emily went to witness his triumph. For the occasion she had bought a brightly colored flowered dress. She walked from the station, carrying her party shoes in a bag, and when she got to the house where the reception was to be held after the ceremony, she changed into her good shoes in the shrubbery. Everyone else was in drearily correct clothes. When she was introduced to her hostess, Lady Drummond, she made a complimentary remark about her garden, whereat Lady Drummond looked her up and down and boomed, "Miss Hale has brought her garden with her!" As an expert on snubs, Emily liked to tell this story on herself.

More even than Eliot's, her humor was of the head rather than the midriff: it smiled and hummed like a cat or a teakettle; no roars or unseemly sobs of mirth. Her wit did not lend itself to quotation: it was a part of her total style. Eliot's own style, his costume, accent, and manner, was not altogether free from a hint of artificiality; Emily's style was as much a part of her as her backbone. You could not quite say that she was mannered; you could not fail to observe that her manners were impeccable. In some ways a rather odd and difficult person, she was one of those people who, almost embarrassingly, always "do the right thing." With small means, she was generous to a fault. She had many friends, but no close ones.

Before a large party in Northampton Emily sent a huge bouquet of white flowers to her hostess, who was much impressed but who stuck to her own taste. She dismantled the bouquet and added the white flowers to various other vases and pots. When Emily arrived and was profusely thanked by her hostess she looked around, and said in her charmingly clear voice, "Very nice, my dear, but one should never use anything but all white flowers—nothing else is worthy of nature."

Her favorite pupils knew of her friendship with Eliot. She often read his poems aloud in class, and with a favored few she would share carefully chosen excerpts from his letters to her. The excerpts were never very interesting, and she read them as impersonally as if they had been written by some dutiful college boy to an old aunt. But ah, the passages not read! They were what interested the girls. One of her students once asked her whether Eliot was an easy writer. She thought the question over, with many turns and preenings of her proud head, then in her peerless diction she said, "Well, my dear, I believe that Tom enjoys the actual process of writing but finds it quite difficult to think of anything to write *about.*" When the same girl, half in earnest, gave her fair warning that she intended some day to write the life of Emily Hale, she smiled and said, "My dear, you will need to sharpen many pencils."

Eliot sent her a typescript of *East Coker* before the poem was published, and she read it aloud to her special girls. It was an experience they remembered. They gathered in her austere rooms in the sad Massachusetts dusk. Emily was smoking one of her consciously worldly cigarettes. She offered them sherry like a communion rite (a worldly communion with the world beyond Northampton). She arranged herself in a dim slide of light, took up the typescript of *East Coker*, and began to read it as if it were a love letter from God. When she had finished and they had recovered their breath, one of them said, " 'The dawn wind slides and wrinkles'?" "No, no. Wrinkles and slides. Tom is always so good about the sea."

"And that other extraordinary line at the beginning: 'The earth which is flesh, fur and faces'?" (That was how she had pronounced *faeces—faces.* She made no comment. Perhaps Miss Porter's had taught her to pronounce Latin that way; she was not mealymouthed, and she was never known to make another such slip.)

Emily had her detractors, even her enemies; but "her girls" adored her. Her table at Laura Scales House at Smith, where she ate all her meals, was not popular with most of the girls in the house, partly because Miss Hale had the reputation of being an affected snob, partly because no one at the table could leave until she had finished, and she was an excruciatingly deliberate eater. She used both knife and fork, in the English fashion, and cut everything up very fine. It was an ordeal for the impatient to sit and wait while she corraled and subdued a small round-up of peas. Nor would she condone in others behavior she would not indulge in herself: she was quick to show her disdain for any lapse of taste or manners. She made even a weekday college lunch into a decorous ceremony, with courtly conversation. Shortly after a Christmas vacation one of the girls at her table, a fat Chicago debutante, complacently complained, "I just can't seem to get the smell of *champagne* out of all my clothes!"

Miss Hale sniffed. "How very disagreeable!"

What she found disagreeable was quite clear. Emily's voice was dry, clear, immaculate, lit by the splendid diction that was her stock-in-trade; a voice with a good deal more quality than any in the British royal family. Her accent was pure old Boston,* not bogus British. She aged slowly and well, keeping her long slender figure, long fine face, long sensitive mouth, long nose, long neck, long legs. Her dark brown hair was always constrained in a decorous bun. Her eyes were blue, cool as the North Atlantic. The fashion at Smith in the thirties was to dress dowdily, but Emily followed her own fashion. She wore her clothes, which were invariably plain, often severe tweed suits, with such style that they looked stylish, and she held her head as though it carried a garland of flowers or a tiara. Her smile was frequent, small, and significant; it could be chilling.

At first glance you might have taken her for a prim Boston spinster, but if you looked again you began to see her: her physical grace, her talent for gesture and pose. She had an instinct for dramatic effect, a natural felicity of repose and motion: her leaning against it

---

*One of the three places, according to George Gordon, Professor of English at Oxford in the 1920s, where "standard English"—as opposed to the impure vowels and swallowings of London or Oxford—could be heard. The other two: Richmond (Virginia) and Edinburgh.

would indeed have embellished any garden urn. And she knew her own quality. Did she see herself as a princess in disguise? She enjoyed disconcerting those who were too gross to recognize her for what she was. When Koussevitzky, the famous conductor of the famous Boston Symphony Orchestra, came to Northampton, the bigwigs of the college faculty were all agog and vying with each other to lionize him. But because of his friendship with Emily's Uncle Philip, it was Emily the great man sought out. "He came with his car and chauffeur and tucked me in under a fur lap robe and *off* we whizzed—to the *great astonishment* of *certain people*—"

On a full-dress occasion she could be counted on to rise to it. One Valentine's Day there was a fancy-dress party at Laura Scales House, and everyone was invited to come "as a book." Emily came as Edith Wharton's *A Backward Glance.* Her gown, a bequest from her mother or her aunt, was Edwardian, pale green silk; her hair was dressed, her neck bejeweled, her elegant shoulders sloped, her elegant bosom was suggested. She carried an old silver hand mirror and held it at artful arm's length, peering imperiously into it. Her dramatic entrance brought down the house.

She was by nature mysterious and secretive: a lady of significant silences, a lady of barely hinted-at situations. When she announced to one of her intimates the arrival of a new letter from Eliot, she never mentioned his name. "My dear, you will be interested to know that I have heard today from *our friend*—." Not a companionable person, except with the few people she really liked. She preferred the company of men; when she shared a house with another woman it was always with someone much older. More than her faculty mates she liked her dog, a great Norwegian elkhound with a name no one could spell—pronounced Brrrr, like a shiver. She was devoted to this handsome and dignified animal. Together, she in her big-cat coat, they used to stride through the dry leaves and meager snow of a Northampton winter day.

She liked to shock the girls who thought her prim and prudish, and once at dinner told the famous story of Margot Asquith's encounter with Jean Harlow, the sexpot movie actress. Jean Harlow kept calling Margot Asquith by her first name, or kept trying to: she pronounced it Mar*got.* Finally Margot set her right. "No, no, Jean. The *t* is silent, as in *Harlow.*" It sometimes happened, however, that her broadsides flew too high and passed harmlessly through the rigging, leaving the target quite unscathed. Once in a restaurant Emily collided with a group of girls from a school in the Berkshires called Fox Hollow. Emily found their manners in general and their respect for herself defective, and undertook to bring them down a peg.

"Just *what* is the name of your school, my dears? Fox Hollow? I've heard of a Fox*croft*. But Fox *Hollow*? And when was your Fox *Hollow* founded, my dears? 1931? Extraordinary. You see I teach at a school called Abbot Academy. The oldest girls' school in the United States." This withering blast had no effect whatever.

At the wedding reception of one of her girls she was one of the last to come along the receiving line. As she got to the bride she said, "My dear Nancy, I do wish you all happiness and I must tell you that you have a large smudge of lipstick on your teeth." Her wedding present was an English edition of *East Coker*, inscribed "From Emily Hale, a friend of T. S. Eliot." Years later she retrieved this book, saying, "I shall be seeing Tom soon," and mailed it back with an added inscription: "From T. S. Eliot, a friend of Emily Hale."

When she lived in Northampton she was elected president of the women's club, and remained so for several years. Her attitude toward the club was possessive, and her manner toward the rank and file (who were definitely not out of her top drawer) patronizing. As a result, she was not re-elected. Shortly thereafter she left Northampton and moved to Andover.

Her code of right conduct included many bits of worldly wisdom. A friend once asked her to lunch at the Ritz in Boston. The friend was not a seasoned patron of the Ritz, but she was punctual, like Emily, and when she had prowled the lobby for half an hour, between the Arlington and the Newbury Street doors, she began to be worried. Then behind her she heard Emily's unmistakable tones. "My dear, I *feared* that you might be lost. I have been waiting for you for *forty* minutes. *Up*stairs, my dear, is where one meets at the Ritz."

And when she was visiting one of her former girls Emily said, "I regret to observe, my dear, that you are head and shoulders above some of the company you keep."

The ex-pupil laughed and said, "Well, aren't we all?"

"Perhaps, perhaps." A small smile. "Except, of course, on infrequent occasions. Infrequent and almost invariably transatlantic."

Emily smoked, but never more than five cigarettes a day. She sometimes had a drink before dinner: only one. A cigarette and a drink were part of the small formalities of which her outer life was composed: an outward and visible sign of her inward and spiritual strength. She held herself in, and she had a great deal to hold in—deep feeling, strong convictions. When she felt obliged to speak out she spoke out, even at the risk of giving offense. One of her dearest friends, a much younger woman and a former pupil of hers, had made a marriage of which Emily deeply disapproved. On a visit to her Emily made this startling speech: "Beware the weapons of the weak. The strong have no defense against them. Little as I care to seem to meddle, I must as an old and valued friend give you my impression of your difficulty. My dear, you *must* free yourself from a crippling alliance while there is yet time to save yourself. I know whereof I speak. A very dear friend of mine was involved, early in life, with a weak and selfish and seriously unstable partner. For many years I observed the disastrous effects of this marriage—the blighting, debilitating, irreversibly destructive effects of it *on my friend*. Do not delude yourself that *you* are sane and strong and stable enough to withstand the violent onslaughts of weakness—" and more, much more, to the same effect.

Emily's high standards of conduct applied rigidly to herself and to her real friends—most especially to "her friend." She had condoned his youthful lapse, which she considered unworthy of him but still forgivable. She had endured with him his prolonged expiation. She understood and at least partly sympathized with his conviction that as long as Vivienne lived he was not free, and that only by this unremitting atonement could he hope to transform the Furies that hunted him into the bright angels whom he might hunt. When Vivienne died at last, Emily was fifty-six, Tom nearly sixty. Too late to marry now? She might have thought so, and might have reconciled herself to that prospect. For eight more years their platonic affair went on (there were other Egerias in England of whom she was unaware, as they were ignorant of her). But then, like a thunderbolt from a clear sky, the unexpected, unacceptable, stunning news that at the age of sixty-eight he had *married his secretary*.

Eliot's marriage to Vivienne had been a hateful shock, because it was an admission of a weakness that had no place in her picture of him. That marriage had been almost a crime, yes: but a crime of passion. But at sixty-eight to marry his secretary, in a wedding that seemed to her almost as hurried and clandestine as the first, that was too much: to marry beneath him *twice!** Such stooping diminished him to a point where he was no longer clearly visible to her—no longer visible, that is, as the fastidious and almost faultless man she had deeply wanted and almost completely believed him to be. If he was capable of making the same mistake twice, repeating the folly of youth in the foolishness of old age, he could not be the person she had known, admired, and loved. In the words of his own mouth he stood convicted.

> Do not let me hear
> Of the wisdom of old men, but rather of their folly . . .

Had she never known him? Was it only a smiling image to which she had given her devotion? That possibility she would not discuss even with herself. She must save something to shore against her ruins. Was it not enough and more than enough that she must admit herself mistaken in having been certain that she knew him? Was it not obvious now that she had not really known him at all? The man of whom she had been so sure now stood revealed as a rather unpleasant stranger. It was enough; it was in fact too much. But it was not grief that she felt, or heartbreak; no, she told herself, it was anger, revulsion, scorn. Anger that she could have been so hoodwinked, revulsion that she had very nearly swallowed something quite disgustingly inedible, scorn at an object not fit to be on her plate.

One of her Chipping Campden friends, also a Unitarian, read Emily's case more simply. She thought "poor Emily was incurably and most uncomfortably in love for so many frustrated years, always believing that if she were patient long enough, her moment of glory would assuredly arrive. But it didn't, and when Mr. Eliot married his second wife, the poor woman nearly went out of her mind and became a great embarrassment to her friends in Camden, including my sister and me, with whom she stayed. She had been

---

*This New England point of view would seem to be corroborated by the Virginian. In these same words Lady Astor deprecated the marriage of a young compatriot, first to a French count, then to the son of an English earl.

such a delightful and cultivated friend, it was grievous to see her so changed. . . . The last time I heard from her would be mid-1950's when she hoped to persuade me to go for a Continental holiday with her, but I realised how very changed she was and managed to wriggle out of it. But about that time while I was away, she did come and stay with my sister here in Camden, and a very great trial she was in every way, no longer the dear and cultivated companion of prewar days. . . ."

Thus ended Emily's precarious happiness. After such knowledge, what forgiveness? Her idealized, doted-on Tom! Was this a mature man, or a senile one? By now both of them had experienced the horrible betrayal of youth into middle age, a defeat whose shame and bitterness could be borne only by grace of "the partial anesthesia of suffering without feeling"—as Eliot put it. With wrinkling skin, sagging muscles, and failing senses come calloused feeling, thinness of thought, blurred perception. Emily and he went through the same experience, not together but at the same time, and she understood what was happening to her. Could it be that he partly missed the meaning? Was she, being a woman, more in tune with her time of life? How else can we explain his turning away from her to someone younger ("O my daughter"), a betrayal unforgivable because it was an attempt to deny their common lot; while her steadfastness toward him ceased only when there was no longer anyone there to turn to —anyone she could recognize? In many ways she was like him, perhaps too like him: intelligent, elegant, arrogant, immensely discriminating. So her life, which had been nourished and sustained by her belief in him, fell into dust and ashes. Dust and ashes.

Still, it was her life, and she had to live it. And live it she did, in her familiar, dauntless style. She continued to teach until her unwilling retirement at sixty-five; then her aunt died and left her some money: she went on cruises, endowed a building in a black college in North Carolina, played Mrs. Higgins in *My Fair Lady* "with ease and aplomb," to deafening plaudits. "Every speech, every move, every gesture all had one thing in common: they were all the right ones." Arthritis began to bother her. She told a friend: "I am better of my arthritis—I lead a busy life in church and community activities —but *not* a gay life. . . ."

Not long after Eliot died, his widow paid a visit to the United

States and went to see Emily at Andover. If we ever have an account of that meeting, it will not be Emily's. The encounter may have served its purpose—at least the two women came away with an impression of the other's appearance, and to some extent with a hint of her reality—but the meeting was never repeated.

In 1969, five years after her ex-friend T. S. Eliot's death, Emily went into hospital in Concord. A Christmas letter to her was sent back stamped DECEASED. RETURN TO SENDER.

Eliot, as they are apt to say of many good men, was no saint, but as men go he was a good man. Can a good man be looked down on? There is always somebody better than we are; and sometimes it is their misfortune to see it. Should Tom Eliot and Emily Hale have married? Were they ever actually engaged? To some of her friends Emily certainly gave the impression that they were. Was it a lucky escape for her, or for him, or for both of them, that their lives turned out as they did? No one can possibly know the answer—not yet, at any rate.

Emily once wrote what she called a "treatise" about her friendship with T. S. Eliot, with some idea of publishing it. Then she decided that it was too intimate. Friends who should know say they know she destroyed it. Nevertheless, many of the facts and feelings this "treatise" recorded may still be extant in the letters she deposited in the University Library at Princeton: all the letters Eliot wrote to her. By the terms of her bequest and by her promise to him, they and the story they tell may not be seen by anybody until January 1, 2020.

There are a good many letters there from Eliot to Emily—more than a thousand.

—

EIGHT

Old Men Ought to Be Explorers

(1948–1957)

1

THE YEAR 1948 was a high point in Eliot's life: he was awarded not only the Nobel Prize but the Order of Merit, the most prestigious and exclusive honor in the British showcase (limited to twenty-four life members); he started his new career as playwright; he preached his first and only sermon; and he began a nine-year tenancy at 19 Carlyle Mansions, Cheyne Walk, with his friend John Hayward—in a third-floor flat immediately below the one Henry James once occupied.

Of these happenings, the sermon came first. It was preached on March 7 in the chapel of Magdalene College, Cambridge, where Eliot was soon to be made an honorary Fellow. It was not a great sermon, but Cambridge has heard worse. Its typescript, preserved in the college library, shows an interesting Eliotism: time and again he crosses out a short Anglo-Saxon word (e.g., *words*) and substitutes a longer Latinism *(persuasion)*. The sermon was largely about his early antireligious influences (George Eliot and Herbert Spencer) and the regurgitation induced in him by Montaigne and Bertrand Russell— "certainly the reverse of anything the author intended. . . .

". . . But I do not go out to an early communion on a cold morning in order to convert my housekeeper, or to set a good example to the night porter of my block of flats before he goes off duty. . . . So I think that influence by example can be only the by-product of a Christian life. . . . For most of us the occasion of the great betrayal on the clear issue will never come: what I fear for myself is the constant, daily, petty pusillanimity. . . . Penitence and humility . . . are the foundations of the Christian life."

The Institute for Advanced Study in Princeton, the American synonym for Oxford's All Souls, offered him a visiting fellowship, which entailed no duties and gave him the time and the peace to do his own work. Eliot accepted the offer, and in September 1948 set sail for New York, cabin class, on the *America* of the United States Lines, his unfinished play, *One-Eyed Riley* (later to be called *The Cocktail Party*) in his baggage. In Princeton he took rooms in Alexander Street, convenient to Trinity Church, where he went to early Mass nearly every morning. He intended to stay at the Institute through the winter. Not long after he arrived, however, came the news that he had been awarded the Nobel Prize for Literature;* he decided to go to Stockholm to receive the award in December, and not return to Princeton.

In London, as may be imagined, the news of Eliot's Nobel Prize award caused considerable preening and purring at 19 Carlyle Mansions. Christopher Sykes, a close friend of Eliot's and John Hayward's, tells how the news was received by his housekeeper. Hayward "had the kindly thought of telling the severe lady of the honor which had come upon the house. She received the news with no trace of emotion but merely remarked that she had known a girl in the West Country who was given the Nobel Prize for watercolors. John said that he rather doubted whether a Nobel Prize was awarded for watercolors, and that the art prizes were in any case usually given in recognition of a lifetime's work and not as an encouragement to youth. The severe lady drew herself up. 'I've known the family for many years,' she declared in awful tones, 'and if you don't believe me you can make enquiries at their home in Paignton.' With this she swept out of the room and shut the door with a bang. Eliot's prize was not discussed further."

In Princeton, the Reverend John Butler, Rector of Trinity, congratulated Eliot one morning after Mass, and received the reply: "Thank you, Father. I hope this means that some of the things you and I believe in still win some acceptance." Dr. Butler, a shrewd but

*In 1948 worth £11,019, or $44,406.57.

generous man, took this not as a canting speech produced by embarrassment but as evidence of Eliot's humility. With an interviewer from the New York *Times* who asked him how it felt to be famous Eliot acquitted himself better. "One doesn't feel any different. It isn't that you get bigger to fit the world, the world gets smaller to fit you. You remain exactly the same." To some graduate students at the University of Iowa who sent him a phonograph record, "You've Come a Long Way from St. Louis," Eliot replied that he particularly liked the last line: "But, baby, you've still got a long way to go!"

Eliot usually avoided the eleven o'clock service, where, said Dr. Butler, "he would have had to put up with a sermon, but he did come one Sunday unexpectedly, and I was quoting from his poem, *The Rock*.

> 'Here were decent godless people:
> Their only monument the asphalt road
> And a thousand lost golf balls.'

At the door of the church he greeted me with a puckish smile and said, 'I think it came off very well.' "

When Dr. Butler went to tea with Eliot and heard sections of the play-in-progress, and was then asked what he thought of it, he found this too an example of humility, rather than the tiger in the tiger pit avid to sample a member of the audience.

While Eliot was in Princeton he saw a Harvard-Princeton football game, and when asked to comment rose somewhat fishily to the occasion. "Football in America," he said, "has developed to such a point that I would imagine the players find their studies a relaxation. It is a more interesting game now, but it is also a more mystifying one."*

From Princeton Eliot made a trip to Washington, where he went to see his old friend Ezra Pound, now in the third year of his incarceration in St. Elizabeths Hospital.† He also lectured at the Library of

---

*Never having seen a game of rugby, Eliot was once persuaded by his friend Hugh Sykes Davies to go with him to the university match (Oxford versus Cambridge) at Twickenham, which that year turned out to be a classic. Whether or not Eliot really understood the subtleties he was witnessing, he pleased his host by saying afterwards "that the game seemed much more suitable to be played by university men than American football."

†It was Eliot's third visit. He had gone to see Pound at the hospital in 1946 and 1947.

Congress ("From Poe to Valéry"), and addressed an audience of church members in St. Thomas's parish house on the present state of the Church of England. An unsympathetic reporter described him as "tall, gaunt, of pallid hue, and tensely withdrawn from anything reminiscent of the flesh. . . . On the subject of dry rot Mr. Eliot (perhaps to no one's surprise) grew eloquent and emphatic. . . ."

At Bryn Mawr one of the students asked him if he didn't feel like Sweeney among the nightingales, with so many girls at his feet. No, said Eliot, not among the nightingales but among the mockingbirds. A man-of-the-worldly Episcopalian priest, who suggested to Eliot that *The Cocktail Party* was covertly all about the Mass, was told, "I really wanted to write a damn good play, and I hope I did." He revisited his old school, Milton Academy, where he addressed the students on "Leadership and Letters"; and he went to Andover to see Emily Hale. At Abbot, the girl's school where she was teaching, he was persuaded to read some of his poems to the adoring girls.

2

On a spring day in 1949, Ezra Pound's daughter Mary was in London and went to call on Eliot for news of her father.* She was "awed and yet sorry for him. . . . The room and his words felt chilly. . . ." She did not mention seeing Hayward. It was not a very satisfactory meeting. But when she left she felt that she had "met a great man and Loneliness." It might have been interesting to have her impressions of Eliot's "landlord."

Friendships are as often based on common interests as on reciprocal liking. Eliot's and Hayward's friendship was founded on a mutual concern with grammar, syntax, and etymology, and Eliot acknowledged Hayward's superiority as a grammarian. John Hayward was not an altogether estimable character (who is?), but no one ever heard him complain about his lot. Perhaps the closest he came to that sort of grumbling was to say, "Life would be a very displeasing business if it were not for the enchantment of friendship, bibliophily,

*She mistakenly says it was 1948, and gives his block of flats the wrong name (Tennyson Mansions instead of Carlyle).

and the view from my window." He had both a sharp eye and a sharp tongue; these, and the pent-up spite which was the sour residue of his confining and inhibiting illness, helped to make him, according to those well qualified to judge, the most malicious gossip in London.

He got out to parties and dinners as often as he could, and on Saturdays, winter and summer, Eliot and Christopher Sykes would wheel him out to Battersea Park or the grounds of Chelsea Hospital; but for the daily round he had only the view from his window. This view included a stretch of the Embankment, and a bench on which nursemaids or stenographers, sometimes pretty, used to sit, affording Hayward the pleasure—especially if they had good legs—of their distant company. Occasionally, whole days would pass without the appearance of one girl worth looking at. In such doldrums Hayward was in the habit of telephoning to one of his friends, Oliver Low, who was privy to this pastime, to deplore the evil days. Occasionally Hayward was too depressed even to talk about it, whereupon Low would say, "Bench trouble, John?" and Hayward would sigh assent.

Once, in high dudgeon, he reported to Low that some vandal, nihilist, or foreign agent had *moved* the bench so that it was no longer in clear view. Low sprang to the rescue, shifted the bench back to its rightful place and, regardless of passers-by, wired it firmly to cement uprights. This deliverance so fired Hayward's fancy that he tried to persuade Low to climb an intervening tree (it would best be done at night, he suggested, because of the police) and lop off its top, which somewhat obstructed Hayward's view of the bench. But at this Low drew the line.

Hayward kept his friends in separate compartments. When she wanted to see him, his own sister had to make an appointment. He never invited any of his family to the flat when Eliot was to be there. In consequence his sister hardly knew Eliot, and was rather afraid of him until "one wonderful afternoon" when she and her husband went with Eliot to a garden party at Buckingham Palace, and found him the most charming and simple person they could imagine.

When, early in 1949, twenty-two-year-old Valerie Fletcher, a robust Yorkshire girl, fulfilled her lifetime's dream by becoming secretary to the famous T. S. Eliot, Hayward soon made his "lodger" aware that she was a conspicuous target and could expect nothing but puncturing hits from him. Did his invalid's intuition warn him that her presence in Eliot's office would eventually lure Eliot from their flat, and even from the enchantment of friendship? At any rate, he seldom missed a chance to poke rather nasty fun at Miss Fletcher, and in consequence (it was almost entirely his doing) the enmity between him and her grew to be solid and permanent. Eliot tried to ignore this unpleasantness as a present fact, but he could not be unaware of it as a future contingency.

Furthermore, Eliot was a compassionate man—a truth which tends to be overlooked by those who can only explain his "putting up with" John Hayward for nine years by imagining that he merely endured him as a hair shirt. And how could Eliot help being continuously aware of Hayward's frightful burden, which, were it not for the merciful ministrations of others, confined him to his solitary quarters; whereas Eliot not only had the daily refuge of his office but could get away on business trips and holidays, and increasingly did so? Even when he was at home Eliot spent the morning—and often the evening as well—at work in his Spartan room; so that he and Hayward met only occasionally at dinner, when they dined at home, or at tea on weekends. Eliot had most of his meals in his bedroom, on a tray on his knee.

Hayward's attitude toward Eliot was one of bantering possessiveness: the banter (really a kind of boasting: "You see how little impression the 'greatness' of this 'great man' makes on me!") was probably more conscious than the possessiveness, which must have had in it considerable anxiety: the need of being loved, the fear of being left. Privately, i.e., behind Eliot's back, Hayward might tell other friends that Yeats was certainly a greater poet than Eliot and would long outlast him. But his official attitude, however derisively expressed, was that Eliot, besides being his private property ("my lodger"), was also the First Citizen in the republic of letters ("the Bard").

Their flat in Cheyne Walk—at least, the part of it generally seen by visitors—had an air of suburban steam-heated comfort that seemed to some too padded and cozy, not in keeping with the dwelling of a poet. But Eliot's room, to which only intimates were admitted, was as bare and monastic as the Emperor Franz Joseph's at Bad Ischl, with the same meager sort and sparse amount of furniture; a crucifix hung over the narrow, monkish bed, and one electric light bulb.* The window looked out on a blank wall. Those who were invited to tea by Hayward sometimes got Eliot too, and a cat as well. On these occasions Hayward did most of the talking, as he liked to do. Eliot's benign, almost wordless presence seemed to have an encouraging effect on him, like the silent flame under a singing tea kettle.

An American visitor to London has described an evening in their company in 1950:

I was invited to dinner and was told that Eliot and his friend John Hayward would come in afterwards. Before they arrived our host, Tom Dozier, told me that Hayward was a cripple, confined to his wheel chair, which we should have to manhandle out of the taxi and up the stairs to the living room. This would need four men: the taxi driver, Eliot, Dozier and myself. And that's the way it was. Hayward gave the orders, like a hulking, overweight coxswain, and we heaved and pulled accordingly. On the half-landing he made us stop and rest. By the time we got him ensconced in the living room we were puffed, but he was talking sixteen to the dozen.

His face was heavy and oblong, the face of a cruel clown; his eyebrows nearly met, and behind his black-rimmed spectacles his eyes moved as watchfully as an auctioneer's. His lips were gross, almost swollen (an effect of his disease) and hung open, giving him a voluptuous look. His voice was harsh. He was adept at raising a laugh, usually at someone else's expense. It must be said to his great credit that he was without self-consciousness and apparently without self-pity; he had evidently come to terms with his fate, and with traditional British gallantry could now pretend to ignore it and enable others to ignore it as well, though neither they nor he could ever really forget that it was daily devouring him.

For some time Eliot sat silent, smiling benignantly, with an expression of vague good will. He and Hayward had evidently dined well; the result had been to make him as mum as Hayward was talkative. This didn't suit Hayward's book: he wanted to show Eliot off, to "produce" him, and he tried again and again to get Eliot started. At last Hayward drew him, on the subject of Sherlock Holmes. Hayward averred that Eliot knew these stories so well that he could recite whole paragraphs from memory; he urged Eliot to give us a sample.

And Eliot finally complied. In a soft voice, almost as if to himself, he quoted a passage from one of the Sherlock Holmes stories: "It was some time before the health of my friend, Mr. Sherlock Holmes, recovered from the

---

*Only 60 watts. When the money was rolling in from *The Cocktail Party*, Hayward said to Eliot, "Don't you think we should do something about the flat?" Eliot replied, "Well, perhaps I might have a better light in my room." So a 100-watt bulb was put in.

strain caused by his immense exertions in the spring of '87 . . . at a time when Europe was ringing with his name, and when his room was literally ankle-deep with congratulatory telegrams, I found him a prey to the blackest depression."

That broke the log-jam; Eliot went on to quote a passage from another Holmes story, *The Retired Colourman,* in which Watson describes the scene of a crime: "You know that particular quarter, the monotonous brick streets, the weary suburban highways. Right in the middle of them, a little island of ancient culture and comfort, lies this old home, surrounded by a high sun-baked wall mottled with lichens and topped with moss, the sort of wall . . ."

"Cut out the poetry, Watson," said Holmes severely. "I note that it was a high brick wall."

" 'Cut out the poetry,' Eliot murmured. 'That's what I've been trying to do all my life.' "*

Kind man that he was, devotedly, desperately kind, as if he knew that in this howling world only kindness could be of any use at all, Eliot was, shall we say, an awkward leave-taker. He broke the news to his wife that he had left her by writing her a letter, delivered by a lawyer; and after their separation, in spite of all her pleas he saw her only once again, and that was her doing, not his. When at the last minute he told John Hayward that he was leaving their flat because he was going to marry his secretary, Valerie Fletcher, there are a number of conflicting versions of how and when he let Hayward know.

The official version, vouched for by the present Mrs. Eliot, is that, two days before the wedding, Eliot and Hayward had a long talk in Hayward's room. While this talk was going on, Valerie Fletcher, unbeknownst to Hayward, was also in the flat, in another room. Hayward took the news that Eliot was about to leave "extremely well." Eliot left with him a letter saying that he would pay £300 a year of the £470 rent of the flat for the next four years, until the lease expired. And he performed this promise.

But Hayward put about other versions of Eliot's nuptial flight.

---

*Eliot put on record some hard sayings about poetry: "The poetry does not matter," and "poetry with nothing poetic about it, poetry standing naked in its bare bones." These dictums can be taken in two different ways: either as a method of reviving a dangerously comatose subject—a slap in the face and a good shaking—or as the kind of dismissive remark he and Pound often made in their younger days—that poetry should be as well written as prose (presumably because, if written well enough, prose and poetry are almost the same, or at any rate interchangeable). The practice of both Pound and Eliot bears out this second interpretation).

One has Eliot breaking the news in a letter which he hands to Hayward and then "hovers about" while Hayward reads it. When Hayward says, "Sit down, my dear Tom, and let's talk about it," Eliot replies, "Oh, no, no, I can't, the taxi is waiting."

Hayward told Moura Budberg that Eliot had been stealthily removing his belongings, piecemeal, for weeks before his actual departure, then telephoned to say that he had married Valerie and was not coming back. Hayward was so staggered that he hung up without saying a word. What particularly angered him: "Think of the treacherousness of a man taking all his shirts and all his ties, little by little!"

Hayward told his sister a somewhat different story the very day of Eliot's marriage, or perhaps the day after, but before there was any news of it in the press. She and Hayward were giving a children's party in the flat, and inquisitive reporters kept coming to the door and being turned away. Eliot, he said, had gone off supposedly on holiday but secretly planning to get married; the French housekeeper at the flat had wondered why he said *"Adieu"* to her instead of *"Au revoir."* He telephoned the news of his wedding to Hayward, who said, "I'm delighted to hear it but why didn't you tell me?"

"Because I thought you'd be so cross."

Hayward gave Christopher Sykes still another version. On the morning Eliot left, very early, he came into Hayward's room and gave him a letter, saying, "I've got to go away, and I want you to read this."

Hayward: "All right, I'll read the thing."

"Aren't you going to read it now?"

"Yes, but—"

"But you ought to read it now."

Hayward read it, then said, "Well, that's fine, but why didn't you tell me?"

"Oh, because I thought you might be angry."

"My dear old Tom, I couldn't be angry with you."

Then Eliot leaned forward, put his arm about him and kissed him, saying, "Oh, I knew I could always rely on you."

Hayward said later, with a resigned grin, "Since I am the most un-homosexual man in London, I found this a most offensive gesture."

Be all these uncanonical gospels as they may, and however and whenever Eliot actually quit the premises, he and Valerie Fletcher were married in St. Barnabas's Church, Chelsea, at six o'clock in the morning on January 10, 1957, and flew to Nice for their honeymoon.

Eliot's marriage opened a rift between the two men which Hayward did nothing to bridge and a good deal to widen. Graham Greene, who sympathized with Hayward, characterized Eliot's act as "the moral cowardice of a sensitive man," and said he was "glad to see John fight back, without self-pity, with his sharp weapon of ridicule."

But as Christopher Sykes says, "I think this was the only time in John's life that his affliction got the better of him in a psychological sense. . . . He developed delusions that Eliot had behaved very badly to him. This was untrue, and at the time of the marriage John recognized that Eliot had behaved strangely (as he often did) but generously and honorably . . . the episode gave rise to libels, which persist, on Eliot's character, and which I know to be nonsense . . . soon after Eliot's death . . . he spoke of him with love. I think he had at last acknowledged his terrible misjudgement." And we may hope that Hayward was not just putting a good face on it when Janet Adam Smith asked him if he weren't sad about Eliot's leaving: "How could anything that makes Tom happy make me sad?"

Eliot and Hayward were never completely reconciled, though they did meet again occasionally. They died in the same year, Hayward a few months later, with the largely one-sided quarrel still a barrier between them.

3

In those years in Cheyne Walk Eliot's life was very different from the treadmill of his early days in the City. He gave barely half his time to his publishing job at Faber & Faber: the rest was taken up with his own work and his own concerns. In London he followed a regular schedule. After breakfast (egg and bacon, toast and tea) he played a few hands of patience, then for two or three hours worked at his writing. He wrote mainly at a typewriter placed on a high stand, so that he stood up to write. Once, when he was queried about this rather odd habit, he replied, "It is a mystery to me how anyone can write poetry except on a typewriter." And no doubt he uttered this Possumesque dictum in his solemnest tones.

About midday he would put on his coat and hat, take his umbrella (specially made for him with an unmistakably large handle, to prevent its being carried off from a cloakroom by mistake), and set off for the office. He usually took a bus to Piccadilly Circus, then the underground to Russell Square. The return journey, in the late afternoon, he often made by taxi.

It was a life that may have appeared constricted, but in comparison with the lives of the overwhelming mass of his contemporaries —the blacks of Africa, Chinese peasants, or even intellectuals very like himself in Russia and other police-states—he had all the room in the world. His disastrous first marriage, which had forced him into the seeming prodigality of exile and a hireling's lot, drove him into a waste land of suffering which changed him from a minor to a major poet. The space he had in which to maneuver was contained in the hollow round of his skull and within the dry bones that caged his heart: enormous room, more than enough. For the rest, he was content to appear correct, conservative, and calm: a snow-covered volcano, as symmetrical as Fujiyama.

The year after he and Hayward joined forces he had gone to the Edinburgh Festival for the opening of *The Cocktail Party.* In Edinburgh he was tackled by a literary man, Harvey Woods, who demanded to know why he had announced, fifteen years before, that *Sophonisba* was John Marston's masterpiece. Eliot's disarming reply: "Oh, I expect it was the only play of Marston's I had read at the time." In the light of Eliot's essay on Marston, this disclaimer is hard to credit.

His meeting with Woods was the beginning of a warm friendship. The Woodses' small daughter Alison did not take to him at first, but when she discovered that he liked cats, and had heard some of his verses about them, she changed her mind, climbed on to his knee and demanded more. At lunch one day she and Eliot both reached at the same time for the last potato. Eliot smiled and suggested that they share it, a compromise that relaxed the tension. A man less set in self-intent bachelor ways might, one may suppose, have yielded the whole potato.

It must have seemed to Hayward that his lodger was always on the go. Shortly after the Edinburgh Festival he made a tour of Germany, and the following winter accompanied the Geoffrey Fabers on a six-week trip to South Africa. And he visited America frequently: nine times during the last eighteen years of his life. And wherever he went, he always sent a postcard to Miss Swan, the receptionist at Faber & Faber.

In Cape Town he was entertained by Mr. Justice Millin and his wife, Sarah Gertrude Millin, the novelist and biographer, whose books were published by Eliot's firm. On his first evening he put his worst foot forward and lived up to his advance reputation of exhausting every subject that came up: on this occasion it was rock lobster, sea temperature, rats. Mrs. Millin complained about the rats that had begun to infest their house in Johannesburg. "How big are the rats?" asked Eliot.

"As big as kittens."

"But what sort of kittens? There are kittens and kittens."

Mrs. Millin gave him a look and said, "Well, just kittens."

That night before going to bed Mrs. Millin was brushing up her acquaintance with Eliot's verse (or perhaps running down a dimly remembered reference to rats) when her eye fell on *Burbank with a Baedeker: Bleistein with a Cigar*, and particularly these lines:

> The rats are underneath the piles.
> The jew is underneath the lot.

Mrs. Millin was a Jew. She went and rapped on Eliot's door, asked him whether he acknowledged these lines (he did) and then asked him to leave her house next morning. The only observable result was that in later editions of the poem *jew* was spelled with a capital J.

Strangers meeting Eliot for the first time found it impossible to connect this quiet person with the tigerish flickerings and atomic violence of his poetry. The sensible and sensitive made no attempt, though sometimes they wanted to:

My husband and I made our first trip to England in 1955 aboard the *Queen Elizabeth*, June 15–21. We were travelling First Class and were seated at a table of eight in the Dining Saloon, I next to an elderly gentleman who said his name was Eliot. . . . Two days later I was told I was sitting next to *T. S.* Eliot and I almost died wondering what drivel I had been speaking but when I saw him at the next meal I relaxed as he was indescribably courteous and kindly. I never asked him about the inner meanings of his writings (I'd have liked to) and this I think he appreciated. . . . He was *very* unassuming and shy. When the inevitable dining saloon picture of our table was taken he moved his chair behind mine so that he could hardly be seen in it. I have the picture. . . . He told us that he had been in the U.S. on business. He was then living in a flat in London. His housekeeper kept lizards which ran all over and he had to be careful not to step on them. When I asked if he was writing anything he said no but he hoped he'd "think of something in the fall."

I consider it a privilege to have known him during the crossing and I shed some tears when he died.

Eliot was by now a public figure, a chief *arbiter elegantiarum* of English letters; if laurels can indeed be rested upon, he had enough to ensure his repose. He did not particularly enjoy literary society but he did his careful duty by it. David Garnett tells of a cocktail party that Jonathan Cape, the publisher, gave in London for Robert Frost. The guest of honor showed up wearing very hairy tweeds and noticeably hirsute himself: hair coming out of his ears, hair coming out of his nose—"looking like last year's potato." Eliot was there too, on his way to some other function, with patent-leather hair and white tie and tails, the Order of Merit on a ribbon round his neck. Garnett wished that Max Beerbohm might have been there to make a cartoon of the American poet who came abroad and the American poet who stayed at home.

When Geoffrey Faber was knighted, the directors of Faber & Faber gave him a dinner and a presentation glass goblet engraved with these mock-heroic couplets by Eliot:

> AMAZ'D astronomers did late descry
> A new great luminary in the sky.
> Straight to the Queen the prompt petition came:
> Would She be pleased to give this Star a name?
> "SIR GEOFFREY let it be." Her Word benign
> The Heav'ns approved, and all the Muses Nine.

In October and November of 1950 Eliot was once again in America, lecturing at the University of Chicago and at Harvard, where he gave the first memorial lecture in honor of his late friend Theodore Spencer, of the Harvard English faculty. In Chicago Dr. Robert Hutchins, Chancellor of the University, came to a reception for Eliot, who asked him to explain something Hutchins had written recently that puzzled him: he had said that Eliot was a democrat and that Edmund Burke was not. "Our times considered," said Eliot, "I suppose that Burke was more of a democrat in his age than I am in ours." Dr. Hutchins made no answer and walked away. The lectures in Chicago were not a success. Eliot's droning delivery and subfusc humor had not the same appeal to Chicagoans as to the nasal mentality of New England, and the Chicago lectures were less and less well attended. This was exceptional in Eliot's experience: although he could not be considered a popular lecturer he was generally in greater and greater demand and, especially in America, attracted large audiences.

At the University of Minnesota, in 1956, where he was paid $2,000, the highest fee then on record for a literary lecture, his audience numbered more than thirteen thousand and had to be accommodated in the football stadium. On this trip, he was invited to stop off at Marquette University in Milwaukee. His cabled reply became locally famous: REGRET IMPOSSIBLE STOP WRITING. As academic jokes go, it was passable, but in fact it applied less to Eliot than to almost any writer in history. The sum of Eliot's published poems totals less than four thousand lines (Hardy's *Dynasts* alone has more than twenty-seven thousand, Browning's *The Ring and the Book* some twenty-two thousand), and in the last twenty-three years of his life he published only two pieces of verse: *The Cultivation of Christmas Trees* (1954), for which there is nothing much to be said, and *A Dedication to My Wife* (1959), of which the less said the better. When we think of the unstoppable garrulity of other aging poets— e.g., Wordsworth and Frost, or even Robert Graves—helplessly pouring out more and more highly polished imitations of themselves, we must thank God and T. S. Eliot for such wisdom and self-control, amounting to the humility of common sense, a rare attribute in a poet.

In the late winter of 1956 he gained a private victory: at the age of sixty-eight he gave up cigarettes. To accomplish this triumph, he told Allen Tate, one must first have a thorough fright about the consequences of smoking; second, be ordered to bed for several weeks; and third, allow oneself a cigar a day after dinner. (Later he cut his allowance to one cigar a week.)

At Austin in 1958, where he spoke at the University of Texas, he drew an audience of more than seven thousand. The lecture was given in a field house where basketball was played. The novelist Paul Horgan, who was there, described the evening: ". . . the most roaring central Texas thunderstorm I've ever heard. Hail clattering on the galvanized iron roof. Thunder and lightning crashing away. Without cease the downpour continues. Mr. Eliot had a very, very deliberate delivery, very quiet. . . . It was as powerful and dramatic as anything you've ever seen in the theater or the opera! And the incredible response of the audience! The ovation was overwhelming!"

4

Old man as he thought himself at sixty, Eliot believed that old men ought to be explorers; and the Northwest Passage he set himself to find or rediscover was the unmapped channel between poetry and drama. Many an English poet, from Shelley to Yeats, had tried before him; but channels change, and this one, which the Elizabethans had navigated so successfully, was hidden or clogged by the silt of centuries, by ice floes—some said, even by the shifting of the earth's skin.

Eliot had always been a dramatic poet. His early "lyrics" were like monologues, and *The Waste Land* was a variety show, with blackouts, quick scene changes, and a large cast of characters. The poetic parts of *Four Quartets* contain dramatic scenes, dramatic pictures. He had always been a spasmodic poet, with long periods—as much as three years—when he wrote no poetry and thought he would never again write any. He believed in writing as little as possible (three cheers for him!) and in not only abandoning a failed experiment but in not repeating a successful one. And more and more he came to think that "the ideal medium for poetry . . . is the theater."

But the theater does not pick its audience; the audience picks its theater. Eliot was not ready to accept that cultural fact; when poets are stagestruck it changes their stance as a poet. Hitherto, like most serious writers, Eliot had abominated the idea of deliberately wooing a large audience: he did not want to be a best seller but simply to attract more and more listeners. He thought wishfully he might find them in the theater. "I believe that the poet naturally prefers to write for as large and miscellaneous an audience as possible, and that it is the half-educated and ill-educated, rather than the uneducated, who stand in his way: I myself should like an audience which could neither read nor write. . . ."

He had already written two plays in verse *(Murder in the Cathedral* and *The Family Reunion)* and two fragments (the choruses from *The Rock* and *Sweeney Agonistes),* but all of these had been too specialized or too arty to please a large public. *The Rock* and *Murder in the Cathedral* had been written to ecclesiastical order. The next two were written to please himself. He abandoned the unfinished *Sweeney* as a failed experiment, and himself declared *The Family Reunion* a botched play—though it may well come to be regarded as the best of his not-so-bad bargains, and he later said of it, "I think *The Family Reunion* is still the best of my plays in the way of poetry, although it's not very well constructed."

Now, his *nolo episcopari* sounding ever more faintly, he set out to learn how to write a successful play, which by definition *must* be a best seller. This master of subtlety in conveying the shades of human feeling became the humblest of neophytes when it came to such practical problems as getting his characters on and off the stage. At the same time he undertook to infuse and transfigure a Broadway hit by putting it completely into verse—of which the audience should only unconsciously be aware. A tall order. He came closest to fulfilling it in his first attempt, *The Cocktail Party.*

The play was a fashionable hit, both in London and in New York. The critics mainly gave it a good hand. *Time* (Louis Kronenberger) said: ". . . not a complete success as a play. But it is a major event in the theater . . . no recent play combines so much polish with so much weight, or expresses its insights with so much of the gaiety which Stendhal demanded of healthy art." Audiences applauded it, and kept coming, not primarily because its "verse" was as crisp and clear as good prose but because the play was an entertaining sermon that left them uneasy. Christopher Fry's *The Lady's Not for Burning,* resolutely rhetorical and purposefully poetic, was also playing to full houses in New York at the same time. Fry's simple meaning could be cheerfully swallowed whole, whereas Eliot's dark hints stuck in the gullet like a bone. Fry's audiences left the theater grinning happily and looking at each other with an eye to kissing strangers—especially pretty girls; Eliot's chastened congregation felt that they should be stumping up the aisle on their knees, thumping their breasts and muttering *"Mea maxima culpa!"*

Nine years later, when Eliot was in Edinburgh for the opening of his last play, *The Elder Statesman*, he was asked whether he thought his writing had influenced Christopher Fry and other dramatists. After reflection he said, "While modesty makes me reject any such claim, vanity makes me hope that it might be true."

The West End impresario who produced *The Cocktail Party* and all of Eliot's subsequent plays was Henry Sherek, a crude, shrewd Gargantua of a man who made an odd pair with the rarefied poet. After the first night of *The Confidential Clerk* at the Edinburgh Festival, the two were opening telegrams in Sherek's room at the Caledonian Hotel. Sherek speaking: "When I had read half a dozen, I said: 'Really Tom, the ego of some people! Every wire I have read up to now is signed simply with the sender's Christian name. How on earth do they expect me to know who they are? I suppose it's because they think they are so famous. Anybody who does that sort of thing is a conceited nincompoop.' At the precise moment that I finished my tirade, Tom Eliot had just finished reading the first wire he had opened. He peered at me over his spectacles, and said slowly, with an absolutely impassive expression: 'I say, Henry, I wonder who this telegram is from? It's simply signed "Henry"!'"

All three of Eliot's commercial plays were comedies (though each had a Greek tragedy as its ancestor); the two later plays, *The Confidential Clerk* and *The Elder Statesman*, show a steady diminution in intensity, a perceptible loss in the crispness and clarity of the prosaic "verse." Neither play approached the success of *The Cocktail Party*. *The Elder Statesman*, his last play, was produced only in London. Though far from being his best play, it has a last scene as beautiful, calm, and moving as a good death—which it portrays, in the Greek manner, offstage. And in this final public statement Eliot allowed himself, although with perfect propriety and no risk of being unmasked, a few lines which, if not from the heart, are assuredly from the memory:

> Has there been nothing in your life . . .
> Which you wish to forget? Which you wish to keep unknown? . . .

I've spent my life
In trying to identify myself with the part
I had chosen to play . . .

And so we lived, with a deep silence between us,
And she died silently.

Eliot's plays were not the kind of success he wanted them to be
(they would never have brought him, or have helped to bring him,
the Nobel Prize) but they did make money, *The Cocktail Party* especially. In New York a run of 325 performances took in $7,000 a day.
Time estimated that the play grossed a million dollars. Eliot's own
profit was about £29,000, of which taxes, he complained, took
£25,000. But for a man of letters he was not doing badly. Two years
before, he had banked £11,000 from the Nobel Prize, and in 1950 his
annual income was around £4,000: Faber & Faber paid him £1,500
and his royalties from books and plays were approximately £2,500 a
year.

And the Northwest Passage? Did he rediscover the forgotten
secret? Alas, he did not. It is for his poetry, not his plays, that he will
be remembered.

5

A man on his deathbed will know better, if he can then know
anything at all ("living first in the silence after the viaticum"), but
while he has some health and even an eyeblink of future, fame or the
hope of it can still make him sweat. In 1957, although his deathbed
was still seven years away, Eliot was definitely an old man, and fame
and he were by now familiar. Nevertheless he had not finished his
latest exploration, and he still had hopes of its success. There was still
time to write one more play.

It may be quite true, and not simply Eliot's sharp way of speaking,
that old men ought to be explorers—that they should give up their
seat in the chimney corner and sally out to seek the last adversary.
It is certain that age explores old men. Dying, like being born, is a
long process; who can say when it really begins? The slow growth in
the womb from seed to fetus is balanced by the slow decline of old

age into senescence. We speak of death from "natural causes," but under the enormous aegis of nature what other kind is there? Is violent death not "natural"? The "cause of death," the terminal disease that appears on the death certificate, is only the finishing touch.

Yes, age explores old men. As we approach the time and the place of our death the world begins to break up around us, and we find ourselves accompanied by strangers with whom it is increasingly difficult to communicate. The appearance of our best-known friends undergoes an alarming change, their features thicken and blur into feeble caricatures of the faces we have known. Their voices, their thoughts, their talk coarsen and thicken in the same way, until we tell ourselves that these are dismal aliens whom we never knew. It is only occasionally, fleetingly, and with a horror that demands disbelief that we can see they are not strangers but mirrors of ourselves. We mock ourselves, without intending a parody. In like manner, every place we know and thought we loved has changed out of all knowledge, or has become stale and unbearable. We see that when our time comes there will be nowhere left for us to go, or that we shall have lost our bearings, like birds in a storm of snow.

Age explores old men, finally, as

> the cat which flattens itself in the gutter,
> Slips out its tongue
> And devours a morsel of rancid butter.

And how can we tell the results of this exploration—if there are any? The butter disappears into the cat, and we shall have to look sharp if we want to see it again. Old men disappear, if not so suddenly, into the maw of time. The expressionless face gives no indication of what they tasted like. Old men who have been poets, like Eliot, may try to leave us some word—a hint of what they have found, or think they were on the way to finding. What was it that Eliot tried to tell us? That it's all right, really—or that it *will* be all right, when the fire and the rose are one? That there *is* a Northwest Passage, and that it connects more important matters than poetry and plays?

> And the end of all our exploring
> Will be to arrive where we started
> And know the place for the first time.

NINE

—

Dust in the Air Suspended

(1 9 5 8 – 1 9 6 5)

1

ELIOT'S SECOND MARRIAGE, as many people could bear witness, was as happy as his first had been miserable. Although a septuagenarian, his behavior with his wife in the drawing rooms of friends and in public places was a spectacle—pathetic, endearing, or embarrassing, according to the eye of the beholder. They held hands and gazed tenderly at one another, while Eliot had his arm around her or patted her ample shoulder. He acted like a man who had been starved all his life of physical affection, and could not get enough of it.

Although they were rarely separated during the eight years of their marriage, he always wrote to her once a week. When in the winter of 1962 he was in the Brompton Hospital for five weeks with a bad attack of emphysema, his letters to her were written on lavatory paper. While he was confined to his bed she used to shave him, and he liked this so much that he asked her to keep on doing it. "Sometimes," she said, "it was hazardous," because he sang music-hall ditties: "The Man Who Broke the Bank at Monte Carlo," "A Bicycle Built for Two," and "Too many gins give the ladies double chins" were among his favorites. He sang in a dry, creaking tenor with a quaint parsonical timbre.

The songs of his American youth repeated again and again a trinity of simple rhymes: *June, moon,* and *spoon.* "Spoon" meant to cuddle, hold hands, gaze loonily into one another's eyes. Like the

171

turkey trot and the bunny hug, spooning had once been all the go. It was still all the go with the Eliots, who quite disregarded the discomfiture, delight, or disdain of onlookers. They were a blissfully happy if somewhat out-of-date couple. Aldous Huxley reported that "Tom Eliot is now curiously dull—as a result, perhaps, of being, at last, happy in his second marriage."

Valerie seemed to like bossing him, and he seemed to like being bossed by her. At tea at Prince Caetani's in Italy, Eliot dropped a canapé on the floor, picked it up and was about to eat it when she lightly slapped his hand and said, *"Tommy,* not off the floor!" When they went for a walk in Kensington Gardens she would nanny him across the grass, urging him to brisker efforts. In the evening they preferred to stay home and read aloud: Boswell, Coleridge's letters, poetry, Kipling's *Kim*—an old favorite of Eliot's—and P. G. Wodehouse, in whose works he was as well versed as he was in the tales of Sherlock Holmes.

Robert Craft tells of Stravinsky having dinner with the Eliots, the year after their marriage, in their dowdy, brownish, typically Kensington ground-floor flat. "The name does not appear on the roster of tenants, but they are waiting for us in the hall when we arrive, and holding hands. Their walls are bare except for bookshelves, and these are mainly in the dining room, 'which is where arguments come up,' Eliot says, 'and the reason that dictionaries and reference books should be kept there.' . . . The life in him [Eliot] is not in his voice but in his clear, piercingly intelligent gray eyes. He breathes heavily and harrumphs a great deal: 'Hm, hmm, hmmm,' deepening the significance, it seems, with each lengthening 'm.' His long, fidgety fingers fold and unfold, too, or touch tip to tip. . . ." Stravinsky remarked of him afterward: "He is not the most exuberant man I have ever known, but he is one of the purest."

At a later meeting in the same place, "the walls were graced with drawings of cats by Eliot's father . . . a watercolor by Henry Moore; a watercolor by Ruskin in the manner of Turner, which Eliot aptly described as 'gradely' (suitable, handsome);* an Edward Lear landscape; some Wyndham Lewis drawings; Jacob Epstein's head of Eliot; several towers of books standing on the end tables like modern sculptures. . . .

*A Yorkshire term which Eliot may well have learned from his wife.

". . . [Eliot] boasted of not having read any serious prose fiction since 1927. 'I think the last novel was *Middlemarch* . . . no, I am forgetting *The Heart of Midlothian*, which I enjoyed in hospital a few years ago. I confess I never finished *War and Peace*. But one shouldn't say so, I suppose. Remarks like that cut the critics' cake in half.'

"Eliot said that he was bitten once by Ferrarese fleas. . . ."*

At last, after a succession of harrowing years, Eliot was relaxing. In this mellow mood, when (as it were) he was enjoying the first cigarette after a very good dinner, he sometimes permitted himself phrases that sounded more like a bank manager than a poet. He once answered a question about "cutting out the poetry" thus, "My aim has been the maximum emotional effect with the minimum verbal decoration."

Eliot and his wife made three trips to the United States, two of them en route to a winter holiday in the Caribbean. Although Valerie was a poor sailor and was often seasick, she gallantly insisted on going by ship whenever they could, as she knew he preferred it. He took her to all his old haunts in America, and she and his family hit it off immediately. When he was seventy-five, in the last year of his life, he and Valerie had dinner one night in a New York restaurant with the Stravinskys. At the end of dinner Eliot asked Stravinsky to drink a toast "To another ten years for both of us." Stravinsky, who was then eighty-one (but who was to outlive Eliot by six years), thought the chances "so improbable that the clink of our glasses rang hollow, and the words sounded more like a farewell." As they left the restaurant "we could not help overhearing the *maître d'hôtel* say to the *vestiaire* that 'There you see the greatest living poet and the greatest living composer together.' But my wife saved the day by saying in just the right tone, 'Well, they do their best.' "

2

In these sunset days, no longer plagued by the need to write poetry or driven by the itch to lay down the critical law, full of honors

---

*. . . *De quatre jambes molles tout gonflées de morsures.*
On relève le drap pour mieux égratigner . . .
                                          —*Lune de Miel* (1919).

and crowded by respectful admirers,* he was constantly being questioned about the form and content of his canonical books. When poets are interviewed nowadays they seem to delight in answering the most searching questions about themselves, and as for their writing, they speak of it with reverence and with awe. Eliot was not like that. He managed to talk about his own work with a sense of its proper worth but without being obsessed by its importance or his own.

About his earlier criticism, especially, he was ruefully frank: "There are statements the meaning of which I no longer understand. There may be areas in which my knowledge has increased; there are areas in which my knowledge has evaporated . . . there are errors of tone: the occasional note of arrogance, of vehemence, of cocksureness or rudeness, the braggadocio of the mild-mannered man safely entrenched behind his typewriter. . . ." Questioned about his poetry, he was, if not altogether frank, equally blunt: "In *The Waste Land*, I wasn't even bothering whether I understood what I was saying." In his younger days he had once written with unguarded self-pity about a poet's lot: "There is no way out. There never is. The compensations for being a poet are grossly exaggerated; and they dwindle as one becomes older, and the shadows lengthen and the solitude becomes harder to endure." Thus Eliot in 1933. Twenty-six years later he put it more acceptably: "As things are . . . poetry is not a career, but a mug's game. No honest poet can ever feel quite sure of the permanent value of what he has written: he may have wasted his time and messed up his life for nothing."

At the same time, he never lost sight of the poet's duty to purify the dialect of the tribe. The poet, he said, bears the responsibility of preserving, developing, and revitalizing his native language. Poetry

*Honorary doctor's degrees from sixteen universities, the Dante Gold Medal of Florence, the title of Deputy Sheriff of Dallas County, the U.S. Medal of Freedom, etc., etc. As Sir Rupert Hart-Davis said in his memorial address at East Coker, Eliot came to be "almost as much sought after as a Beatle. He had to keep his address secret, remove his telephone number from the book, and set up an elaborate system of defenses against the army of admirers, journalists, professors and students, who, if he had allowed them to, would have occupied every minute of his days. When he gave readings or lectures in America he and his wife often had to be smuggled out of the back door to escape the crowds."

affects the language in which it is written to a much greater extent than readers suppose. People who murder their mother tongue cannot be considered civilized. The poet's duty is to keep the language from becoming barbarous—and for that reason more poetry is always needed.

Such praiseworthy sentiments were not always borne out in Eliot's practice. He was not one of those writers that turn naturally toward the Anglo-Saxon sun. Without the Latin-derived or Greek-rooted word he would have drooped, he would not have been himself, he might even have been tonguetied. He suffered from the intellectual's besetting sin of favoring fancy words. When he saw signs that the language was being corrupted or cheapened, as in the new translation of the Bible in 1961, he spoke out with the bite and scorn of a tribal high priest. A commission composed, as this one was, of the most distinguished scholars of the day might have been expected to produce a work of some dignity, even if it did not rise above the mediocre. But this translation failed to attain even that low eminence. It is so cheap, fatuous, and stilted that we ask ourselves in dismay, "Where is the English language going?"

On the other hand, if we assemble only a partial list of the indulgences he allowed himself, we might ask in equal alarm the same question of Eliot: *tergiversations, subsume, instauration, askesis, epigoni, analphabetism, banausic, pococurantism, fovea, encheiridion, recension, latifundian, endogamy, maieutic, mansuetude, hermeneutics, aporia, entelechy, sordor, debile, autotelic, cenobite, inspissation, obnubilation, progenerate, noetic.* And these, from his poems: *appetency, grimpen, chthonic, behovely, periphrastic, hebetude, defunctive, anfractuous, maculate, laquearia, mactations, impetrations, cavies, eructation.*

These five words are from *one* poem *(Mr. Eliot's Sunday Morning Service): polyphiloprogenitive,* superfetation, mensual, piaculative, polymath.* In only two lines of *The Family Reunion*, these three words appear: *batrachian, aphyllous, ophidian.*

---

*This Eliot later confessed had been a somewhat dubious coinage of his own, not meant to be legal tender, and he hoped that no one would pick it up and use it as such.

3

Perhaps the best thing Eliot did in his last years was to help rescue his old friend and fellow poet, Ezra Pound. Until the two met at St. Elizabeths Hospital in Washington, D.C., in 1946, they had not seen each other for many years. A few months before the war began, in the spring of 1939, Pound had sailed from Genoa to New York, to set America straight about Europe, particularly on the subject of his admired Mussolini. Pound traveled on the Italian liner *Rex,* which carried so few passengers that he was given a first-class suite to himself, though he had only a second-class ticket. It had been twenty-eight years since he had seen his native country. In New York he stayed with E. E. Cummings, which was pleasant, but he had no success anywhere.

For some reason (no doubt curiosity) he wanted to see the Stork Club, a garish and expensive nightclub run by the notorious ex-bootlegger Sherman Billingsley, where the gossip-columnist Walter Winchell held court every night, and from which rowdy drunks, Harold Ross, editor of the *New Yorker,* and other foes of Billingsley's, were rigorously excluded. Ezra Pound was turned back at the plush-covered rope across the entrance because of his clothes. He wore no tie (the equivalent of full frontal nakedness in the New York of those days) and an open-neck shirt with broad purple stripes. But his old college, Hamilton, gave him an honorary degree, and he read his poems to a somewhat startled circle at Harvard: "He read sitting down, held his breath for an incredible time before drawing another for the next few lines of poetry, and yet the voice was too soft to be heard, unless, as he did unexpectedly, he yelled."

For the rest, the trip accomplished nothing. Next year "the phony war" turned real, and everyone settled down to live with it as best they could. Pound went back to Italy, where he became a propagandist for Fascism (and the uglier, antisemitic side of Social Credit), broadcasting treasonable utterances from an enemy country at war with his own. In 1945 he was arrested by Italian *partigiani* and turned over to the American Army. He was imprisoned for some months in an open-air cage at Pisa (where, when he was at last allowed pencil and paper, he wrote the *Pisan Cantos*) and then sent back to the United States to stand trial.

Pound almost certainly never understood why he was accused of treason. He acknowledged that he had made hundreds of broadcasts from an enemy country during wartime denouncing the actions of his own country, but from his point of view he was simply trying to extricate the United States from an unjust and disastrous war, to point out to his countrymen the error of their economic and political ways, and to unmask the real traitor, Roosevelt—against whom he was certainly no more rabid or more treasonable than the thousands of right-wing Republicans all over the United States who shared and outdid his hatred for "that man in the White House" whom they (and he) called Rosenfeld.

Nevertheless, Pound was regarded by many of his fellow Americans as a traitor who had escaped the gallows only by shamming insanity. A panel of doctors had ruled him mentally unfit to stand trial, and in 1945 he had been committed for an indefinite period to St. Elizabeths Hospital for the Criminally Insane in Washington, D.C. After thirteen years of negotiation, argument, pulling strings, and waiting, Pound's friends (among them Archibald MacLeish, Robert Frost, Wyndham Lewis, and Eliot) succeeded at last in persuading the American government to drop the indictment and release Pound. He was himself a complication. As Eliot said, if Pound had been altogether mad or altogether sane, the situation would have been simpler. And the people he tended to accept as friends and helpers were not the kind who act sensibly either.*

As soon as Pound was released he went straight back to Italy, where he settled in Venice with Olga Rudge, the mother of his daughter, Mary. The once loquacious and ebullient Ezra was now dark and silent, rarely speaking, even to answer questions. His spirits were at a low ebb. He wrote to Eliot in almost despairing vein, suggesting that for him poetry had indeed been a mug's game, that he had botched his lifework, *The Cantos,* and messed up his life for

---

*Eliot would not go so far as to say that Pound was mad, but he did not regard him as wholly sane. A few years before Pound was released Eliot told Allen Tate his reasons for thinking so. First, Pound's complete lack of a sense of humor; second, his inability to understand or like his fellow men; third, his growing megalomania. This was a cool private view, in contrast to the warmth of Pound's public summary of Eliot.

nothing. Eliot's reply was characteristically compassionate. He did not make Pound wait for a letter but sent him a long telegram, assuring him that his anxieties were groundless and that he was a true poet who had written great poetry, some of which would certainly endure.

These two old comrades never met again, though they planned to; but they came close at the end. Pound, at the age of seventy-nine, flew from Venice to attend the memorial service for Eliot at Westminster Abbey, and later made this statement: "His was the true Dantescan voice—not honored enough, and deserving more than I ever gave him. . . . Who is there now for me to share a joke with? . . . Let him rest in peace. I can only repeat, but with the urgency of fifty years ago: READ HIM." And when, three years later, Valerie Eliot got her first look at the "lost manuscript" of the original *Waste Land* in New York, this indomitable old man surprised her by turning up there to see if he could be of any help in deciphering the scrawls in the margins. He could not always remember what they had meant, but Mrs. Eliot reported that he now felt "anguish" at having ventured to criticize Eliot at all, and said to her, "He should have ignored me. Why didn't he restore some of the canceled passages when Liveright wanted more pages?"

4

Hypochondria ("exaggerated or obsessive anxiety about one's health; mistaken belief that one is ill"), a state of mind to which most of us are more or less subject, especially when we don't feel well, grows on us with advancing age. For eventually, inevitably, our fears come true. The fact that after a death the doctor in the case is very rarely charged with murder is an indication of the feebleness of our faith in medicine, our realization of how flimsy a shield it must be against death's Parthian shot. We cannot exaggerate the deadliness of our final illness, nor deny that there will be one, unless accident prevents it. The fear of death does indeed perturb the old, though perhaps in not quite the way nor to quite the same extent that their juniors suppose. Fear of death and a reluctance to leave life are not exactly the same.

Eliot's hypochondria had a constant basis in fact (chronic hernia, tachycardia, emphysema).* But for one who came so late to happiness, his desire to hang on, his unwillingness to relinquish the joys and pleasures unknown to him for most of his life, is surely quite understandable. And since death crushes and obliterates all we know, all we have done, all we are, he must have dreaded that erasure.

For a hypochondriac who never took regular exercise and smoked immoderately, Eliot lasted for quite a long time: seventy-six years. In his youth his outdoor activities had been confined to sailing, an occasional game of Ping-Pong (which, according to Conrad Aiken, he enlivened by an angular crouch and by making "maniacal faces"), and what might be called social walking. This last was the only form of exercise he took with him into later life. But his habits were abstemious; he was of a naturally spare frame, and put on little weight over the years.

Women were the people who counted most in Eliot's life. His Unitarian grandfather, William Greenleaf Eliot, whom he never saw but whom he strongly resembled and many of whose characteristics he shared, was his lifelong rival. In his immediate family his favorites were his mother, his sister Marian, and his sister-in-law, Mrs. Henry Eliot, Jr. For most of his life Emily Hale was his loyal follower, friend, and almost-fiancée. Mary Hutchinson, his near contemporary, and Mary Trevelyan, much younger, were his close friends. Vivienne, his hopelessly loved and helplessly unloved first wife, overwhelmed his middle years as much as Valerie, his secretary and then for the same length of time his wife, lightened the end of his life.

The men whom he counted as friends were fewer: Conrad Aiken, his confidant and butt; Ezra Pound, his early guide and helper; Bertrand Russell, thwarted Mephistopheles to his youthful Faust; Wyndham Lewis and John Hayward, two unendurable companions whom he managed to endure. The list is not very long. In spite of the claims of many others to have been close to him and to have known him "better than anybody," these few were apparently closest to him. He

---

*When Eliot returned from South Africa in 1954, both John Hayward and Christopher Sykes noticed a slight slurring in his speech, and thought he might have suffered something like a stroke.

felt most at home with women, and he was at his warmest and most winning when he wrote to them. In some of his letters to them (which cannot be quoted) he lets himself go, in all kinds of ways. If it can be believed, he cavorts, kicks up his heels, *prattles.* One of these favorite correspondents brought out a side of him that was rarely suspected and which, most of the time, he rigorously suppressed: the master of nonsense, the Edward Lear.

Eliot was not easy as a "great man"; whether or not he actually disliked the role, he could not play it with the assurance and evident pleasure of such men as Churchill, Beaverbrook, or Franklin Roosevelt—all of them obviously his intellectual inferiors. If a stranger recognized him on a bus and spoke to him by name, he would get off at the next stop. But when a London taxi driver (in those days still a famously considerate breed) said to him as he got into the cab, "You're T. S. Eliot," he was rather pleased, and asked the man how he knew. "Ah," said the taxi driver, "I've got an eye for a celebrity. Only the other evening I picked up Bertrand Russell, and I said to him 'Well, Lord Russell, what's it all about?' and, do you know, he couldn't tell me."

His life, said Eliot, had been a Dostoevsky novel written by Middleton Murry. The jungle and the tea party: he was always bringing one into the other. While he was a poet, Eliot suffered, as a countryside suffers when it is overrun and ravaged by war. When he subsided into playwriting and giving interviews, the struggle that caused and accompanied his poems had ceased. The invasions of civil war were over, peace had come at last. There had been an unconditional surrender; but who had surrendered to whom? That the struggle was over was evident to everyone who saw him. Had he abandoned the fight because further resistance was useless? We may be permitted to think or at least hope that Eliot was not merely resigned, he was happy. The intolerable shirt of flame was now only a flannel vest; the consuming fire had moderated to a warming glow.

Since the cough-ridden country of England was thought to be deleterious in winter to lungs like Eliot's, as long as he was able to travel he and Valerie went to the Caribbean for part of each winter. But in 1962 illness intervened, and instead of a holiday in the tropical sun he spent five weeks in hospital. Two winters later he was too weak to go anywhere; for several months he faded away, and on January 4, 1965, he died.

The day after Eliot's death the *Times* printed a two-column obituary, headed "The Most Influential English Poet of His Time." The obituary, written by Cecil Day Lewis, afterward Poet Laureate, spoke of "a long-drawn-out private tragedy which darkened his middle years, left deep impressions on his verse: the rawness, the shuddering distaste, the sense of contagion, the dry despair which emerge from certain passages of *Ash-Wednesday,* for instance, and *The Family Reunion,* are traces of it. But for this emotional wound, so long unhealed, his poetry might well have been more genial, less ascetic; but equally, it might have been less intense. . . . The quality of his writing was inseparable, to those who knew him, from the integrity of his character."

Eliot had directed that his body be cremated and the ashes buried at East Coker. Before the small casket was taken down to Somerset it reposed for a short time on the altar of one of the chapels in St. Stephen's, Gloucester Road. One morning shortly after his funeral the server and a priest, Father Craib, were preparing to say early Mass there. Father Craib nodded toward the casket and whispered reverently, *"That* is T. S. Eliot."

Besides the private family funeral (Christopher Sykes and his wife Camilla were the only others there) there were two memorial services. The first, a month after his death, filled Westminster Abbey with famous names: the Queen and the Prime Minister sent representatives. Sir Alec Guinness read five passages from Eliot's poems. The choir sang an anthem by Stravinsky whose words comprised Part IV of *Little Gidding:* "The dove descending breaks the air." The second memorial service was at St. Michael's Church, East Coker, the following September. A memorial plaque, set into the wall above Eliot's ashes, was unveiled, and Sir Rupert Hart-Davis gave an address. The oval plaque had this inscription:

"in my beginning is my end"
OF YOUR CHARITY
PRAY FOR THE REPOSE
OF THE SOUL OF
THOMAS STEARNS ELIOT
POET
26TH SEPTEMBER 1888—4TH JANUARY 1965
"in my end is my beginning"

East Coker, in Somerset, a few miles south of Yeovil, is every American's idea of what an English village ought to be: approached by

> the deep lane
> Shuttered with branches, dark in the afternoon,
> Where you lean against a bank while a van passes,
> And the deep lane insists on the direction
> Into the village, in the electric heat
> Hypnotised . . .

The stone cottages have thatched roofs and gabled caps over the doorways; around them cling masses of roses, hydrangeas, valerian, dahlias, honeysuckle. The church, small and musty-smelling, on the hillside above the village, is not so old-fashioned as to display the Tables of Consanguinity* in its porch, but there is an admonitory notice, in antique typeface:

> Hints to Those who Worship God in this Church
> 1. Be in Time.
> 2. Go straight into Church.
> 3. Kneel down on your Knees.
> 4. Do not look round every time the door opens . . .
> 7. Do not whisper to your neighbour.
> 8. Keep your thoughts fixed . . .

Two other memorials were erected to Eliot's memory. A plaque on the south wall of St. Stephen's, Gloucester Road, topped by the cross of the Order of Merit, and reading

> Of your charity
> Pray for the repose of the soul of
> Thomas Stearns Eliot O.M.
> Born St. Louis Missouri
> 26th September 1888
> Died London 4th January 1965
> A churchwarden of
> this parish for 25 years
> He worshipped here until his death

---

*Listing those family connections between whom marriage is forbidden—most notably the "deceased wife's sister."

"We must be still and still moving
Into another intensity
For a further union a deeper communion"

The crowning memorial was a stone set in the floor of Poets' Corner in Westminster Abbey, and inscribed:

THOMAS
STEARNS
ELIOT
O.M.
Born 26 September 1888
Died 4 January 1965
"the communication
Of the dead is tongued with fire beyond
the language of the living."

This was dedicated on January 4, 1967.

Meantime the *Times* had reported, on June 12, that Eliot had left an estate valued at £105,272, which death duties had whittled down to £78,095. Everything was left to his widow.

5

Few men during their lifetime can have been the object of so much scrutiny as Eliot, so much speculation about the meaning of every word they have written; or have been discussed, on the whole, with so much respect and admiration. And yet few men have been so resented. The reaction against him and all his works set in long before his death. Some of it was caused by professional jealousy, the occupational hazard to which poets are prone. Robert Frost, whose hand was against every fellow poet, sneered at him as "a tricky poet and a mealymouthed snob." William Carlos Williams, between whom and Eliot there was a mutual aversion, and who was driven to incoherent bellows at the mere thought of him, once replied to Ezra Pound's announcement that Eliot was coming to America: "I'll kick him in the balls, provided he has any."

Van Wyck Brooks, fellow Harvard man and fellow member of the Fox Club, hated Eliot so extravagantly that he thought him not only a deserter from his own country but an "evil influence," a Christian with "small faith, less hope, no charity at all. . . . Eliot's characteristic note was a sneer suggesting the cold east winds at the tip of Nahant." When he heard once that Eliot was very ill, he said, "I hope he dies in agony!" To Max Eastman, Eliot was "dragging a generation behind the energetic brains of his time" (e.g., Bernard Shaw, Bertrand Russell). Since his death, a latent animosity against Eliot—which may be partly anti-American feeling, an irreducible constant in England since the eighteenth century—has manifested itself. The division between his earlier and later poetry is insisted upon, to an extent that relegates his later poems to insipidity or phonyness. *The Waste Land*, his best-known and most famous poem, has not escaped whipping: Angus Calder, for example, has called it "the muddled, morbid nonsense of a sick man." F. R. Leavis, who has been one of Eliot's champions, nevertheless now finds his attempts to render "low" speech embarrassing.

Richard Aldington was one of the few of Eliot's admiring friends who turned jealous enemy and tried to nail him to the barn door: ". . . Eliot is an intellectual snob appealing to an intellectually snobbish audience, in the sure and certain hope that if the poems were endorsed by the influential pundits nobody would dare to point out their essential sterility, their often trifling content, and above all that abuse of the unacknowledged quotation whereby Eliot became credited with that which was not his. . . . We might almost say that what is original in his poetry is not good, and what is good is not original."

It is true that in Eliot's poems no great bells sound, only their echoes, mocking or sinister. But these layered echoes sometimes reverberate so resonantly that the Eliot line usurps the place of the original. Take the famous simile from *Rhapsody on a Windy Night:*

> As a madman shakes a dead geranium

Two of its possible sources have been traced, one to Oscar Wilde's

> But each man's heart beat thick and quick
> Like a madman on a drum

and one to John Heywood's play, *A Woman Killed with Kindness:*

> Astonishment,
> Fear, and amazement play against my heart
> Even as a madman beats upon a drum

As Eliot said: "Good poets make [what they borrow] into something better, or at least something different." One of Eliot's most famous lines, "Not with a bang but a whimper," was lifted partly from a phrase in a lecture of George Santayana's, partly from a word in Kipling's *Danny Deever* (" 'What's that that whimpers over'ead?' said Files-on-Parade"). And so it goes, as Kurt Vonnegut correctly but unhelpfully remarks.

Names and phrases from Eliot's poems echoed (and still echo) throughout the Western world: in newspaper headlines, as titles of novels and of ballets, in Christmas catalogues, in speeches in the U.S. Senate,* in television serials, in humorists' newspaper columns. Even those who misspelled his name or who quoted him not quite correctly bore evidence to the wideness of his fame. Some of his loudest admirers were also his notable misquoters.†

The death of a writer, more often than not, erases him and his works from public memory, at least for a time, but eight years after Eliot's death one could hardly pick up a weekly paper without finding a reference to him or a quotation from him, sometimes unattributed. He had become a landmark of such massiveness that, like Venice, he sank only imperceptibly from view. Just as the industrial fumes of Mestre and the burrowing for fresh water under the lagoon are not the only causes of Venice's gradual foundering, neither can the exhalations from the thousand chimneys of the cottage industry that present-day poetry has become be held responsible for the slow wasting away of T. S. Eliot. Was there not something fatally hubristic in Venice's entrusting its weight to such oozy underpinnings, as there is something intrinsically topheavy in the very nature of poetry?

Eliot was aware of this topheaviness, at least as far as his own poetry was concerned. He knew his own merit; of the worth of his

---

*Where, on January 4, 1971, Senator Hugh Scott of Pennsylvania thus referred to the end of the 91st Congress: "If I may paraphrase H. G. Wells, we have indeed ended 'not with a bang but a whimper.' "

†A few examples—noteworthy because they show either a misapprehension of Eliot, a dull eye, a thick ear, or possibly all three—Djuna Barnes ("I'll show you fear in a handful of dust"); Sir John Betjeman ("And a clatter and a chatter from within/ where fishermen lounge at noon. . . . And the wind shall say: 'Here were godless people' "); Valerie Eliot ("riding seawards on the waves/ Combing the white hair of the waves blown back/ Where the wind blows the water white and black"); Wyndham Lewis ("I am growing old, I am growing old, I shall wear the bottoms of my trousers rolled"); Angus Calder ("the torment of love satisfied/the greater torment of love unsatisfied"); Stephen Spender ("Why should the agéd eagle stretch his wings?"); Anthony Burgess ("Old men should be voyagers").

writing he was not so sure. The fading of the emotional connotations of Eliot's "objective correlatives" would desiccate his poetry into bones too bare to stand up. And sooner or later such emotional radioactivity is almost bound to fade away. What will be left of Eliot then? Satire, wit, some lucid lines whose sharpness has been dulled by use—a case of the dry grins? Perhaps something on that order. But then the emotion, in time, might come seeping back!

6

What sort of person was Eliot? Can we trust his friends to tell us? Can we trust his friends?

Eliot's "official" friends generally had a somewhat repellent aspect: chilling, epicene, selfishly rude or fake-hearty. But some, who would admit to being on less than intimate terms, like the late W. H. Auden, had heart-lifting things to say about him: "So long as one was in Eliot's presence, one felt it was impossible to say or do anything base." Eliot himself could hardly be described as warm or open-hearted. What he did have was a languid charm, an air of disarming, deferential kindliness. Although you could not help seeing how tired he was, you felt that he wanted to help you, and would try, if the effort were not too great for his strength and the limited time at his disposal.

Hatred and love were lifelong contenders for the mastery in T. S. Eliot. The hatred did not often show itself—and then usually as contempt, "amusement," fear or revulsion—but it was there, under the timid and agonizing love. As he knew, better than most men, mutual forbearance is not a generous gesture, an extra dividend, or a bonus, but an absolute necessity, like our daily bread.

On the surface that he showed to the world he was charming, modest, likable; at a deeper level he was arrogant, contemptuous, sometimes cruel; at a deeper level still, a sinner and a would-be saint. And so on, down or in. When you start peeling the onion, where do you end? The conflicting testimony of his "friends," especially of those who "knew him better than anybody," may be at least partly explained by the illusion that we (some of us, at least) can get to the bottom of a human being, and without shutting our eyes or holding our noses. The fact is, we usually know better than to try. As Eliot himself said, "No one can be understood: but between a great artist of the past and a contemporary whom one has known as a friend there is the difference between a mystery which baffles one and a mystery which is accepted." Except for the dwindling few who knew him well, accepted him and were sure of him, Eliot must remain a mystery of the baffling sort.

Like many Americans, he was *un voyageur sur la terre*, a kind of nomad; as he said of himself, "a New Englander in the Southwest and a Southwesterner in New England"; as he did not need to say, an American abroad, forever wandering from here to there, *de Damas jusqu'à Omaha*. His New England ancestors presided over his future and took charge of his Midwestern upbringing, just as his formative years in St. Louis secured his life in Boston and London.

Was he a Christian? The word covers such a schismatic multitude of beliefs that it can mean almost anything or almost nothing. He was an Anglo-Catholic, trailing clouds of inherited gloom from his Unitarian, near-Calvinist forbears. One of the noble army of Eliot scholars, H. Z. Maccoby, thinks that "the average churchgoer . . . would be most disconcerted by a real glimpse into Eliot's mind. There is a savagery in that mind. . . . 'Christ the tiger,' 'the horror and the boredom.' " Eliot's God had many attributes, but in one of them he was a jealous God who visits the sins of the fathers upon the children, unto the third and fourth generation of them that hate him. Listening to the Epistle (St. Paul) for the fourth Sunday after Epiphany, this son and grandson of dour Protestantism must have felt very much at home: "Let every soul be subject unto the higher powers. . . . Render therefore to all their dues: tribute to whom tribute is due; custom to whom custom; fear to whom fear; honour to whom honour."

For most of us—except, of course, the saints—Christianity is a threadbare covering, the dogged repetition of a desperate creed. But Eliot loved the Anglican Church and all its traditions and trappings; he loved the seventeenth-century language of the Book of Common Prayer and the Bible, a language which has taken on over the years an incantatory magic. The collects in the Prayer Book, those ancient, anonymous, pithy prayers, particularly pleased him. Why then did he not follow the example of his admired Dr. Johnson, who wrote a whole book of such prayers, or of John Henry Newman, who added his famous petition to the Prayer Book? If Eliot ever did write any prayers, they were not published in his lifetime.

He was a forbidding rather than a welcoming Christian. An undergraduate at King's College, London, had admired Eliot from afar, and one Sunday morning went to early Mass at St. Stephen's, hoping to meet or at least to see him. After the Mass he plucked up the courage to speak to Eliot and told him how much he admired his poetry. Eliot, with a stern look, said, "I hope, young man, that you have not attended Mass this morning just to see me."

When we form an opinion of someone (and the real worth of a human being, in the eyes of his peers, is a matter of their opinion) are we in fact indulging in a euphemism for *judging*, against which, on good authority, we have been warned? No, it is a question of making up our minds. Various people may hold quite different opinions of the same person; from time to time our own opinion of a man may vary; but in most cases we end by casting our vote, yes or no, and sticking to it. And when we try to justify our dislike of someone, we criticize him for his imperfections—for being *imperfect!* Who do we think we are? With what measure do we measure ourselves—and with what measure do we measure him? It is not with any conscious idea of perfection that we compare him but with what we most like and secretly most admire: our own *idea* of ourselves. In an anti-Nixon joke in the *New Yorker* one horrible-looking tycoon says to another: "All right, so he isn't a lovable man. Am I a lovable man? Are you a lovable man?"

One of our innumerable fears is that there is an unalterable pecking order among human beings: that because A is more intelligent, B more learned, and C more saintly than we, we can never really meet A, B, or C on anything like equal ground or common terms. Our meekness before the mysteries of Eliot can be carried too far; the reaction may then take us too much the other way, so that we stamp angrily out of his rose garden, muttering that he is nothing but a pack of cards. We should take him more calmly, as a human being in many ways very like ourselves. He was one of us. He was terribly clever. He wanted to be good. He was unhappy, most of his life. He sometimes made people laugh. He made people anxious—or put their anxieties into magical and memorable lines. But who *was* he?

A mystery partly accepted, partly baffling. When a man dies, we can stop thinking about him—and do, to all intents and purposes. There are too many people to think about as it is. In an odd way, however, the dead man's attention does not seem to have been wholly withdrawn from us. Little by little we become aware that we are the objects of contemplation, as if we were alone in a forest, overlooked by great trees, or high on a mountain, naked to enormous distances.

> And what the dead had no speech for, when living,
> They can tell you, being dead.

7

Possum is also Latin for "I can." It would be impossible to write off Eliot's accomplishment as a sly trick, a bit of stealthy sleight-of-hand, as some of his extreme detractors seem to demand. Because we are used to him (his image is gathering dust in the pantheon, and his poetry is fifty years old) we tend to forget what an original Eliot was, what a shocker. *Prufrock* caused much the same sort of alarming sensation in literary circles as Stravinsky's *Firebird* had done, ten years before, in the music world; the effect of *The Waste Land* was comparable to that of *Le Sacre du Printemps.* Loud boos were heard from solid citizens in the stalls and from Vanity Fair in the boxes; but the galleries' applause raised the roof.

Nothing quite like Eliot's tone of voice had been known (in English, at any rate) since Alexander Pope: a tone of smooth and balanced paradox, dryness and intensity, gravity and wit, compact of phrases lucid and memorable as a slogan, dark as an unfamiliar proverb, enigmatic, intricate, unaccountably stirring. (Did Pound create Eliot? Does the midwife create the baby?)

Gradually, as his poems became better known, it was apparent that their originality consisted not merely in such devices as the pasting together of abrupt and unlikely contrasts, but in the revival of such a traditional artifice as lifting lines of poetry from other poets (or from himself), often in other languages, adapting them to his own uses, remodeling them to suit his purpose. Dante did it. And Marlowe used the trick to great effect in *Doctor Faustus: O lente, lente currite, noctis equi!,* a line pilfered from Ovid, the sigh of an insatiable lover transformed into the agonized cry of a man praying for his last night on earth to go more slowly.

Eliot's obscurity is sometimes triumphant, when his effect of chiaroscuro, the distribution and contrast of light and shade, is successful; he can also be blindingly dark. As Edmund Wilson has pointed out, Eliot is a difficult poet who is at the same time most effective. "He succeeds in conveying his meaning, in communicating his emotion, in spite of all his learned or mysterious allusions, and whether we understand them or not." Eliot himself (or was it Possum?) once observed that he often found other people's poems very obscure, but that his own seemed to him quite clear and simple. Does this illuminating radiance of Eliot's survive translation in other languages? It is devoutly to be hoped so, for if not, confusion is being spread across the world in thirty-nine different tongues, a modern rival to the Tower of Babel.

Eliot's use—or, rather, nonuse—of punctuation (e.g., in "Eyes that last I saw in tears") results sometimes in the same sort of ambiguous puzzle that Gertrude Stein liked to set. When you heard Gertrude Stein read aloud one of her punctuationless passages, the puzzle was usually resolved: the emphasis she gave to certain words supplied the missing punctuation and made the meaning clear. Was her ambiguity intentional? Eliot's almost certainly was. To hint, not to say, so that his readers must guess and not be sure. He defended this somewhat paradoxical position by asserting, in effect, that although a poet and his poem are not soon parted, when they are, they are as separate as a table and a carpenter. This assertion fails to explain why some tables are valued more highly than others.

Certain poets (e.g., Coleridge and Housman) have reminded us that poetry need not and should not be too exactly translatable into prose; that a few poems, at any rate, must be let alone to work on us in their own way, however dark and only partly comprehensible they may be. In some combinations of rhythm and meter there *is* a quality of magic. To realize that, it is not necessary to "understand" a poem or to fathom its "meaning." Look at such a piece of rhymed nonsense as *Jabberwocky,* which is undeniably poetry yet whose made-up words only suggest a meaning—a matter that does not bother us at all!

Eliot's poems are *violent*. And in every poem there is also something unclear, ambiguous, uncertain, not known. But we remember them; we are haunted by images and lines of poetry which we cannot or do not attempt to translate into our own words, and whose meaning we shall never clearly know. Nor can we ever forget the flashes of lightning. Though Joyce's *Ulysses* cannot usefully be compared with *The Waste Land*, the two are sometimes mentioned together, as the greatest novel and the greatest poem of the twentieth century. They have one phenomenon in common, the occasional triumphs of sudden illumination: Joyce's epiphanies, Eliot's pentecosts.

That there is small joy and only cold comfort to be found in Eliot's poetry is often cited against him as a nearly damning fact, enough in itself to confine him to the ranks of parochial, minor poets. But narrowness can be profound, like the wound Mercutio got from Tybalt: "Not so deep as a well, nor so wide as a church door; but 'tis enough, 'twill serve." If to terrify and comfort is what poetry is for, then Eliot's surely qualifies. "Comforting" does not have to be cozy. "Hear what comfortable words our Saviour Christ saith unto all who truly turn to him." And to criticize Eliot's poetry as lacking in warmth, in human feeling, is like finding the color blue unsatisfactory because it does not taste of chocolate nor cascade with bells. If T. S. Eliot is parochial, what a cathedral town his parish is!

How much of himself did he put into his poetry? Not less than everything. But he hid behind paraphernalia more elaborate than the contrivances of the Wizard of Oz. Only rarely is it possible to recognize the relation of any particular poem to his own life. The suppressed *Ode*, which apparently hymns the horrors of his wedding night, is one such instance.* In *Burnt Norton* Eliot complains so feelingly about the imprecision and the slipperiness of words that we realize it must have happened to him, and often: to be blurred and lose his balance.

Eliot himself was not a scholar, as scholars understand the term, and as his erstwhile friend, John Hayward, among others, did not fail

---

*It is possible to see the origin of another, *Macavity, the Mystery Cat*, in a rarely fortunate day at the dentist's —*Macavity's not there!*

to point out. He was, however, widely read and learned, a suit of armor perhaps no less useful to a man of letters. Though the tendency of his present editors (as in the *New Oxford Book of English Verse*) is to omit them, Eliot's practice was to preface his poems with one or more epigraphs—quotations, often from foreign or classical authors, which serve as a kind of text or gloss on the poem that follows. Their relevance to the poem is sometimes obscure. Eliot's use of these epigraphs seems to have been characteristically equivocal: partly to cover up his tracks, partly to beckon on the hunt. He wanted to be at least partly understood; he did not want to be found out. The epigraph of *Marina*, for example, is two lines of Latin verse from a play of Seneca's: Hercules is speaking; he is in a daze, just coming to himself after killing his children in a fit of madness. What has this to do with *Marina*? Eliot, so far as we know, was never a father. Did he intend a guarded reference to his own unborn children, the children that he and Vivienne, for their own guarded reasons, would not conceive?

Eliot made a distinction between "pure" and "applied" poetry (the verse in his plays). He thought his pure poetry was finished after *The Hollow Men*. Then Faber began publishing a series of *Ariel* poems, a kind of glorified Christmas card with verses by a well-known poet, and Eliot promised to write one. That promise produced *Journey of the Magi, A Song for Simeon, Animula, Marina, Triumphal March,* and led on to *Ash-Wednesday*. Kipling used to say, of a piece of writing he had done at the top of his bent, that his *daimon* had been with him. Eliot might have said—of his poetry, at least, that unless his *daimon* was with him he could not write.

How often was his tongue in his cheek, how many solemn utterances did he make while his fingers were crossed behind his back? Did he *really* think of himself as a minor poet—a romantic one at that—on a level with Cyril Tourneur? He once said as much to Paul Elmer More but whether in pique, humility, a flash of insight (a will-o'-the-wisp?), or a fusion of all three, how can we be sure?

The recently published *Oxford Book of Twentieth Century English Verse*, edited by Philip Larkin, raised a williwaw among the critics, as such official anthologies are bound to do, not only because of the poems they include but also on account of those they leave out. To the surprise of many and the delight of a few, the poet who was given the most space was Thomas Hardy, who began writing poetry in 1865 and who was sixty years old when the twentieth century began. One reviewer gave them the order of precedence according to the number of pages allotted to each poet: Hardy, Eliot, Auden, Kipling, Yeats, Betjeman. He also commented: "There has never been a time when poets were more in agreement as to Hardy's pre-eminence: he has runners-up now, but no rivals."

A list that includes the present Poet Laureate in the top six, and puts Kipling in front of Yeats, would be hard to defend seriously, except on the grounds of popular appeal rather than excellence; but, as they say in Hollywood, it's a point of view. It is not a point of view that would have appealed either to Eliot or to Yeats. Eliot thought very little of Hardy's verse, which he characterized as the kind of poetry a novelist writes. But the fact that Eliot badly underrated Hardy, who was, on the whole, more of a poet than Tennyson and almost as good as Browning, cannot be a sufficient excuse for under-rating Eliot.

When Yeats wrote

> There is not a fool can call me friend,
> And I may dine at journey's end
> With Landor and with Donne

he was claiming his right to high company but also in all mock-modesty suggesting that he would deserve a place even farther above the salt. Similarly, when T. S. Eliot seemed to put himself on a level with Yeats and Valéry, he too may have been awaiting the summons: "Friend, go up higher." And so he shall; even so soon after his death he can be written down as the most influential American writer since Walt Whitman, a critic of the stature of Matthew Arnold, and the finest poet of his kind since Alexander Pope.

Many gaps in Eliot's life story remain to be filled in—gaps to which this biography of sorts, these notes toward his definition, have sometimes called attention, sometimes passed over. But before we bring this necessarily incomplete book to an end, it seems fitting to address T. S. Eliot himself, to offer his shade apologies, blessings, and thanks. Apologies are due him for digging, or attempting to dig, the dust enclosed in the south wall of the transept in St. Michael's Church at East Coker, and for all the future exhumations that will certainly be made; for presuming, on the mere basis of a similar upbringing, background, and heritage, to speculate about thoughts and feelings of which no one, some of them not even he himself, could ever be certain. He once said, or tried to say, in the heat of an undergraduate argument, that to understand him, you have to believe him first. We must accept this apparently tall order, even as we must ask to be forgiven for our trespasses. Belief in anyone entails forgiveness, which we all need every day of our lives.

We die in any case, as T. S. Eliot has, as the minnowy writers of the shoals of books about him all must. Meantime, whether or not we can pray for the repose of his soul, we owe him our blessings and thanks: blessings for the "comfortable words" he has left us; thanks for their odd and memorable beauty. For this writer particularly, to have spent three years in his company, if not in his confidence, has been an experience rewarding beyond all expectation.

APPENDIX

—

Parodies of Eliot

Only God is not mocked: everyone else can be. But there have been surprisingly few parodies of T. S. Eliot, and even fewer good ones; they may be counted on the fingers of one hand. By far the best is *The Sweeniad*, by Myra Buttle (Victor Purcell).* Excerpts:

Sunday is the dullest day, treating
Laughter as a profane sound, mixing
Worship and despair, killing
New thought with dead forms.
Weekdays give us hope, tempering
Work with reviving play, promising
A future life within this one.
Thirst overtook us, conjured up by Budweisserbrau
On a neon sign: we counted our dollar bills.
Then out into the night air, into Maloney's Bar,
And drank whiskey, and yarned by the hour.
Das Herz ist gestorben, swell dame, echt Bronx,
And when we were out on bail, staying with the Dalai Lama,
My uncle, he gave me a ride on a yak,
And I was speechless. He said, Mamie,
Mamie, grasp his ears. And off we went
Beyond Yonkers, then I felt safe.
I drink most of the year and then I have a Vichy.
. . .
Because I do not want to think again
Because I do not want

*(New York, Sagamore Press, 1957.)

195

Because I do not want to think
Desiring the blessed fame and saintly crown
I no longer want to want what you want me to want
(Why should the baptized infant want the font?)

Perhaps the next best is Henry Reed's *Chard Whitlow*:*

(Mr. Eliot's Sunday Evening Postscript):

As we get older we do not get any younger.
Seasons return, and today I am fifty-five,
And this time last year I was fifty-four,
And this time next year I shall be sixty-two.
And I cannot say I should care (to speak for myself)
To see my time over again—if you can call it time,
Fidgeting uneasily under a draughty stair,
Or counting sleepless nights in the crowded Tube.
There are certain precautions—though none of them very reliable—
Against the blast from bombs, or the flying splinter,
But not against the blast from Heaven, *vento dei venti*,
The wind within a wind, unable to speak for wind;
And the frigid burnings of purgatory will not be touched
By any emollient.

        I think you will find this put,
Far better than I could ever hope to express it,
In the words of Kharma: 'It is, we believe,
Idle to hope that the simple stirrup-pump
Can extinguish hell.'

        Oh, listeners,
And you especially who have switched off the wireless,
And sit in Stoke or Basingstoke, listening appreciatively to
    the silence
(Which is also the silence of hell), pray not for yourselves
    but your souls.
And pray for me also under the draughty stair.
As we get older we do not get any younger.
And pray for Kharma under the holy mountain.

An Old Rhyme Re-Rhymed by Edgell Rickwood:†

        Those who are much obsessed by death
        and see the skull beneath the skin,

*(London, Jonathan Cape, 1946.)
†From *Collected Poems* (London, The Bodley Head, 1947.)

may cheat their fear of wanting breath
with dry philosophy or gin;
or with the ardours of the birch
or lure of buxom female form,
but whose lot creeps into the Church
to keep its inhibitions warm?

James Joyce tried his hand at parodying *The Waste Land:**

Rouen is the rainiest place getting
Inside all impermeables, wetting
Damp marrow in drenched bones.
Midwinter soused us coming over Le Mans
Our inn at Niort was the Grape of Burgundy
But the winepress of the Lord thundered over that grape of Burgundy
And we left it in a hurgundy.
(Hurry up, Joyce, it's time!)

A lively prose parody, too long to quote here, was written by Charles Kaplan ("Eliot Among the Nightingales: Fair and Foul") and published in an anthology of parodies, *The Overwrought Urn* (Pegasus, New York, 1969).

*In *Dear Miss Weaver,* Jane Lidderdale and Mary Nicholson, eds. (New York, Viking Press 1970, London, Faber & Faber, 1970.)

Notes

Numbers refer to pages in the text. Publication information for major sources will be found in the Selected Bibliography.

Foreword

Page

xvi "I do not suggest that the personality": T. S. Eliot, "The Frontiers of Criticism," in *On Poetry and Poets* (Farrar, Straus & Cudahy, New York, 1957).

xvii "Hints and guesses": *The Dry Salvages.*

xvii "Biographies will continue": *The New York Review of Books,* June 17, 1971.

ONE
"A Strong Brown God" (1888–1904)
[The Dry Salvages]

2 "The first time I saw": Theodore Dreiser, *A Book About Myself* (Boni and Liveright, New York, 1922).

3 "Short of stature and delicate of frame. . . . 'If I could have had Dr. Eliot for a partner . . .'": C. C. Eliot, *William Greenleaf Eliot.*

3 ". . . On one occasion being present": *ibid.*

4 "Mr. Eliot and she went from Washington": *ibid.*

5 "The mere fact of a minister's continued residence": *ibid.*

5 "I am sorry to be again at this work": *ibid.*

6 " 'But,' said Dr. Eliot, 'on this condition' ": *ibid.*

6 "The office of President of the United States": *ibid.*

6 "Fain would I breathe that gracious word": *ibid.*

12 "When the long, sultry, summer days": J. A. Dacus and James W.

Page

Buel, *A Tour of St. Louis* (Western Publishing Company, St. Louis, 1878).

13 "The river with its cargo": *The Dry Salvages*.

13 "In the rank ailanthus": *ibid.*

13n "T. S. Eliot later lamented": Horace Gregory, *The House on Jefferson Street* (Holt, Rinehart & Winston, New York, 1971), p. 54.

14 "A boy's will is the wind's will": Henry Wadsworth Longfellow, *My Lost Youth*.

15 "The word within a word": *Gerontion*.

16 "A number of very gloomy": Interview in *Paris Review*, Spring/Summer, 1959.

TWO

"Shall I Part My Hair Behind?" (1905–1914)
[The Love Song of J. Alfred Prufrock]

21 "Then he knew that he had been a fish": *The Death of St. Narcissus, The Complete Poems and Plays of T. S. Eliot*.

23 "The sleek Brazilian jaguar": *Whispers of Immortality*.

23 "Is it perfume from a dress": *The Love Song of J. Alfred Prufrock*.

23 "The smell of hyacinths across the garden": *Portrait of a Lady*.

23 "With smell of steaks in passageways": *Preludes I*.

23 "That smells of dust and eau de Cologne": *Rhapsody on a Windy Night*.

23 "And female smells in shuttered rooms": *ibid.*

23 "La sueur aestivale, et une forte odeur de chienne": *Lune de Miel*.

25 "Everyone threw his poems into a basket": H. W. A. Powel, Jr., "Notes on the Life of T. S. Eliot." (M.A. dissertation, Brown University, 1954.)

26 "Sunday afternoon was the time": Samuel Eliot Morison; *One Boy's Boston* (Houghton Mifflin, Boston, 1962).

26 ". . . that woman": *Rhapsody on a Windy Night*.

29 "Genuine poetry can communicate": T. S. Eliot, *Dante* (Faber & Faber, London, 1966).

29 "Heaven knows what it would have sounded like": T. S. Eliot, "What Dante Means to Me," *To Criticize the Critic*.

31 "A writer is great, not only by what he says": Irving Babbitt, *Literature and the American College*.

31 "It is well to open one's mind": Irving Babbitt, *Democracy and Leadership*.

31 "[In Rousseau's notion]": *ibid.*

31 "The purpose of the college": Irving Babbitt, *Literature and the American College*.

31 "[The Terror] lends color": Babbitt, *Democracy and Leadership*.

Page
31 "The notion that wisdom resides": *ibid.*
31 "It may be said some day of us": *ibid.*
35 "I will show you fear in a handful of dust": *The Waste Land.*
35 "I thought this remark so good": *The Autobiography of Bertrand Russell, 1872–1914* (Atlantic Monthly Press, Boston, 1968).
37 "that airy fairy hairy 'un": Conrad Aiken, "King Bolo and Others," in *T. S. Eliot: A Symposium*, ed. by Richard March and Tambimuttu.

THREE
"They Called Me the Hyacinth Girl" (1914–1920)
[The Waste Land]

39 "The best poem I have yet had or seen": Letter from Ezra Pound to Harriet Monroe, September 30, 1914; *The Letters of Ezra Pound 1907–1941.*
39 "Passed one of the most delightful afternoons": Letter from Eliot to Pound, February 2, 1915, in Noel Stock, *Ezra Pound: Perspectives* (Henry Regnery, Chicago, 1965).
39 "Come, let us desert our wives": Conrad Aiken, "King Bolo and Others," in *T. S. Eliot: A Symposium*, ed. by Richard March and Tambimuttu.
44 "By Richmond I raised my knees": *The Waste Land.*
46 "Friday evening I dined": Letter to Lady Ottoline Morrell, July 1915, in *The Autobiography of Bertrand Russell, 1914–1944* (Atlantic Monthly Press, Boston, 1968).
46 "It is quite funny": *ibid.*
47 "Mrs. Eliot was ill": *ibid.*
48 "My nerves are bad tonight": *The Waste Land.*
48 "Hope Mirrlees said of her": *The Listener*, January 14, 1971.
49 "But I am having a wonderful time": Introduction to *The Waste Land: A Facsimile and Transcript*, ed. by Valerie Eliot.
50 "Unlike most poets": Richard Aldington, *Ezra Pound and T. S. Eliot.*
52 "It's such a pity, Tom": Elizabeth Bowen, *Recollections of Virginia Woolf*, ed. by Joan Russell Noble (Peter Owen, London, 1972).
52 "But from such assaults": Quentin Bell, *Virginia Woolf: A Biography* (Harcourt Brace Jovanovich, New York, 1972).
53 "He should never . . . discuss"; Conrad Aiken, *Ushant.*
54 "Nearly every important innovation": G. S. Fraser, *Vision and Rhetoric* (Faber & Faber, London, 1959).
56 "Basil Bunting said of him": *The Observer*, November 12, 1972.
56 "He was as much concerned": Noel Stock, *The Life of Ezra Pound.*
57 "Here is some of the evidence": *ibid.*
58 "Apart from [Pound's] exotic appearance": *ibid.*
59 "A great operation": Robert Craft and Igor Stravinsky, *Dialogues*

Page

    and a Diary (Faber & Faber, London, 1959).

60 "An American poet": Graham Martin (ed.), *Eliot in Perspective: A Symposium.*

60 "The two great American writers": *New York Times,* November 30, 1952.

61 "In my earlier years": T. S. Eliot, *The Classics and the Man of Letters* (Oxford University Press, London, 1942).

61 "Had I been the house": Arnold Bennett, December 12, 1917, entry, *The Journal of Arnold Bennett* (Viking Press, New York, 1933).

62 "I have read Eliot's little book": B. L. Reid, *The Man from New York.*

62 "I remember how": Letter from T. S. Eliot, *Times Literary Supplement,* January 17, 1958.

63 "A crowd flowed": *The Waste Land.*

65 "Definitely placed their author": F. O. Matthiessen, *The Achievement of T. S. Eliot.*

65 "If you see our young friend": I. A. Richards, "On T.S.E.," in *T. S. Eliot: The Man and His Work,* ed. by Allen Tate.

FOUR

Life Is Very Long (1921–1925)
[The Hollow Men]

67 "Emotionally deranged": Letter from Eliot to Richard Aldington, in Introduction to *The Waste Land: A Facsimile and Transcript,* ed. by Valerie Eliot.

68 "Pale, marmoreal Eliot": Leonard Woolf, *Beginning Again.*

70 "On Margate Sands": *The Waste Land.*

71 "Some forms of ill health": T. S. Eliot, *The Use of Poetry and the Use of Criticism* (Faber & Faber, London, 1967).

71 "All that's stopping him": Conrad Aiken, "An Anatomy of Melancholy," in *T. S. Eliot: The Man and His Work,* ed. by Allen Tate.

73 "The water-dripping song": Letter from Eliot to Ford Madox Ford, August 14, 1923, quoted in Editorial Notes, *The Waste Land: A Facsimile and Transcript,* ed. by Valerie Eliot.

74 "In the manuscript": Introduction, *Ibid.*

74 "You will find": B. L. Reid, *The Man from New York.*

76 "My God man there's bears on it": *The Waste Land: A Facsimile and Transcript,* ed. by Valerie Eliot.

77 "Kingfisher weather": *Ibid.*

77 "Pope has done this so well": T. S. Eliot, Introduction to *Ezra Pound: Selected Poems.*

79 "Have to retire": T. S. Eliot, *The Sacred Wood.*

80 "The most intelligent man": *Egoist,* January 1918.

80 "What Othello seems to me": T. S. Eliot, *Selected Essays.*

Page

80 "We should be thankful": T. S. Eliot, *The Use of Poetry and the Use of Criticism* (Faber & Faber, London, 1933).

80 "Eliot's opinions, so cool": Edmund Wilson, *A Literary Chronicle: 1920–1950.*

81 "That there was a family of Tourneurs": T. S. Eliot, *Elizabethan Dramatists* (Faber & Faber, London, 1968).

81 "In preparation a trilogy": T. S. Eliot, *For Lancelot Andrewes* (Faber & Gwyer, London, 1928 and Doubleday, New York, 1929).

82 "These books were never written": Edmund Wilson, *The Bit Between My Teeth.*

82 "His criticism urged": Leonard Unger, *T. S. Eliot: Moments and Patterns.*

83 "I am worn out": B. L. Reid, *The Man from New York.*

83 Fanny Marlow (pseud. of Vivienne Eliot), "Fête Galante," *Criterion,* July 1925.

85 "Apart from the fact": Letter to Quinn, quoted in Donald Gallup, "T. S. Eliot and Ezra Pound, Collaborators in Letters," *Atlantic,* January 1970.

86 "He was a gentleman": F. V. Morley, "T. S. Eliot as a Publisher," in *T. S. Eliot: A Symposium,* ed. by Richard March and Tambimuttu.

FIVE

You Don't See Them, But I See Them (1926–1932)
[Sweeney Agonistes—epigraph]

87 "I always felt": Herbert Read, in *T. S. Eliot: The Man and His Work,* ed. by Allen Tate.

88 "To kneel/Where prayer has been valid": *Little Gidding.*

90 "The forces of deterioration": "Observations," *Egoist,* May 1918.

90 "I am amazed": T. S. Eliot, *Selected Essays.*

93 ("Why should the agéd eagle"): *Ash-Wednesday.*

93 "Then fools' approval": *Little Gidding.*

93 "Infinitely gentle": *Preludes IV.*

93 "Christ the tiger": *Gerontion.*

94 "Reflected from my golden eye": *Lines for an Old Man.*

94 "Perpetual angelus": *The Dry Salvages.*

95 "As the years passed": Herbert Read, in *T. S. Eliot: The Man and His Work,* ed. by Allen Tate.

96 "Nor dread nor hope": W. B. Yeats, *Death.*

97 "Do I dare": *The Love Song of J. Alfred Prufrock.*

97 "The tiger springs": *Gerontion.*

97 "Not all of us": *T. S. Eliot: The Man and His Work,* ed. by Allen Tate.

97 "In the present ubiquity of ignorance": T. S. Eliot, *The Idea of a Christian Society* (Faber & Faber, London, 1939).

SIX

Teach Us to Care and Not to Care (1933–1947)
[Ash-Wednesday]

Page
127 "The poetry does not matter": *East Coker*.
128 "I should either": TSE quote on *Family Reunion*, in T. S. Eliot, *On Poetry and Poets* (Farrar, Straus & Cudahy, New York, 1957).
128 "An old charwoman came": Igor Stravinsky and Robert Craft, *Themes and Conclusions* (Faber & Faber, London, 1972).
129 "When he was in England": W. H. Auden, "Tribute," broadcast, January 5, 1965. Published in *Homage to T. S. Eliot*, a program of poetry, drama, and music presented at the Globe Theatre, London, June 13, 1965.
130 "Almost impenetrably obscure": Helen Gardener, *The Art of T. S. Eliot*.
131n "Burnt Norton might have": John Lehmann interview with Eliot.
133 "The common word": *Little Gidding*.
134 "It seems, as one becomes older": *The Dry Salvages*.

SEVEN

Meeting Is for Strangers (1908–1957)
[The Family Reunion]

149 "Do not let me hear": *East Coker*.

EIGHT

Old Men Ought to Be Explorers (1948–1957)
[East Coker]

152 "But I do not go out": T. S. Eliot, *A Sermon* (Cambridge University Press, Cambridge, 1948).
161 "I think this was the only time": Christopher Sykes, "Some Memories," *The Book Collector*, Winter, 1965.
170 "The cat which flattens": *Rhapsody on a Windy Night*.
170 "And the end of all our exploring": *Little Gidding*.

NINE

Dust in the Air Suspended (1958–1965)
[Little Gidding]

172 "The name does not appear": "The World of Stravinsky," *The Observer*, July 9, 1972.
174 "In *The Waste Land*": T. S. Eliot, *To Criticize the Critic*.
174 "There is no way out": Harold Monroe, *Collected Poems*, Foreword by T. S. Eliot (Cobden-Sanderson, London, 1933).
174 "As things are": Interview, *Paris Review*, Spring/Summer, 1959. Also T. S. Eliot, *The Use of Poetry and The Use of Criticism* (Faber & Faber, London, 1964).
176 "He read sitting down": Charles Norman, *Ezra Pound* (Macmillan, New York, 1960).

Page
184 "Eliot is an intellectual snob": Richard Aldington, *Ezra Pound and T. S. Eliot.*

185 "Good poets make": T. S. Eliot, *The Sacred Wood.*

185n "Riding seawards": Editorial Notes, *The Waste Land: A Facsimile and Transcript,* ed. by Valerie Eliot.

187 "No one can be understood": Joan Russell Noble, *Recollections of Virginia Woolf* (Peter Owen, London, 1972).

189 "And what the dead had no speech for": *Little Gidding.*

190 "He succeeds in conveying": Edmund Wilson, *Axel's Castle,*

193 "There is not a fool": W. B. Yeats, *To a Young Beauty.*

Selected Bibliography

AIKEN, CONRAD. *Ushant.* New York, 1952, London, 1963.

ALDINGTON, RICHARD. *Ezra Pound and T. S. Eliot.* London, 1954.

BABBITT, IRVING. *Democracy and Leadership.* Boston and London, 1924.

———. *Literature and the American College.* Boston, 1908.

BERGONZI, BERNARD. *T. S. Eliot.* New York, 1972.

BRAYBROOKE, NEVILLE. *T. S. Eliot: A Symposium.* London, 1970.

BROOKS, CLEANTH. *Modern Poetry and the Tradition.* Chapel Hill, 1939, London, 1948.

BROOKS, VAN WYCK. *The Wine of the Puritans.* New York, 1909, London, 1908.

BROWNE, E. MARTIN. *The Making of T. S. Eliot's Plays.* Cambridge, 1969.

CHIARI, JOSEPH. *T. S. Eliot, Poet and Dramatist.* London, 1972.

DE RACHEWILTZ, MARY. *Discretions.* Boston, 1971.

DREW, ELIZABETH. *T. S. Eliot: The Design of His Poetry.* New York, 1949, London, 1950.

ELIOT, C. C. *William Greenleaf Eliot.* Boston, 1904.

ELIOT, T. S. *After Strange Gods.* New York and London, 1934.

———. *Ara Vos Prec.* London, 1920.

———. *The Complete Poems and Plays of T. S. Eliot.* New York and London, 1969.

———. *The Sacred Wood,* New York, 1921, London, 1920.

———. *Selected Essays.* New York, 1932, 1950, London, 1932.

———. *Thoughts After Lambeth.* London, 1931.

———. *To Criticize the Critic.* New York and London, 1965.

ELIOT, VALERIE (ed.). *The Waste Land: A Facsimile and Transcript of the Original Drafts.* New York, 1971.

ELIOT, WILLIAM GREENLEAF. *The Discipline of Sorrow.* Boston, 1855.

GALLUP, DONALD. *T. S. Eliot: A Bibliography.* New York and London, 1969.

GARDNER, HELEN. *The Art of T. S. Eliot.* London, 1968.

207

GROSS, JOHN. *The Rise and Fall of the Man of Letters.* New York and London, 1969.

HARRISON, JOHN R. *The Reactionaries.* New York, 1967, London, 1966.

HOWARTH, HERBERT. *Notes on Some Figures Behind T. S. Eliot.* Boston, 1964, London, 1965.

JONES, GENESIUS. *Approach to the Purpose.* New York, 1965, London, 1964.

KENNER, HUGH. *The Invisible Poet: T. S. Eliot.* New York, 1959, 1964, London, 1960, 1965.

_____ (ed.). *T. S. Eliot: A Collection of Critical Essays.* New York, 1962.

KIRK, RUSSELL. *Eliot and His Age.* New York, 1972.

LEVIN, HARRY. *The Waste Land from Ur to Echt.* New York, 1972.

LIDDERDALE, JANE, AND NICHOLSON, MARY. *Dear Miss Weaver.* New York and London, 1970.

MAIRET, PHILIP. *A. R. Orage.* New York, 1966, London, 1936, 1966.

MARCH, RICHARD, AND TAMBIMUTTU. *T. S. Eliot: A Symposium.* New York, 1949, London, 1948.

MARTIN, GRAHAM (ED.). *Eliot in Perspective: A Symposium.* New York and London, 1970.

MARX, GROUCHO. *The Groucho Letters.* New York and London, 1967.

MATTHIESSEN, F. O. *The Achievement of T. S. Eliot.* New York, 1958, 1969.

MUSGROVE, S. *T. S. Eliot and Walt Whitman.* Cambridge, 1954.

MCALMON, ROBERT, AND BOYLE, KAY. *Being Geniuses Together.* New York, 1968.

POUND, EZRA. *The Cantos of Ezra Pound.* New York, 1948, London, 1964.

_____. *Indiscretions.* Paris, 1923.

_____. *The Letters of Ezra Pound 1907–1941.* New York, 1950, London, 1951.

_____. *Literary Essays.* New York, 1968.

_____. *Selected Poems.* London, 1928.

_____. *Sophocles' Women of Trachis.* New York, 1957, London, 1956.

REID, B. L. *The Man from New York.* New York, 1968.

ROBBINS, RUSSELL. *The T. S. Eliot Myth.* New York, 1951.

SENCOURT, ROBERT. *T. S. Eliot, a Memoir.* New York, 1971.

SMIDT, KRISTIAN. *Poetry and Belief in the Work of T. S. Eliot.* New York and London, 1961.

SMITH, GROVER. *T. S. Eliot's Poetry and Plays.* Chicago, 1956.

SOUTHAM, B. C. *A Student's Guide to the Selected Poems of T. S. Eliot.* New York, 1969, London, 1968.

STEFFENS, LINCOLN. *The Shame of the Cities.* New York and London, 1904.

STOCK, NOEL. *The Life of Ezra Pound.* New York and London, 1970.

STRAVINSKY, IGOR, AND CRAFT, ROBERT. *Themes and Episodes.* New York, 1972.

SYMONS, ARTHUR. *The Symbolist Movement in Literature.* New York, 1919, London, 1899.

TATE, ALLEN. (ED.). *T. S. Eliot: The Man and His Work.* New York, 1966, London, 1967.

UNGER, LEONARD (ED.). *T. S. Eliot: A Selected Critique.* New York, 1948.

_____. *T. S. Eliot, Moments and Patterns.* Minneapolis, 1966.

WASSERSTROM, WILLIAM. *The Time of the Dial.* Syracuse, 1963.

WILLIAMSON, GEORGE. *A Reader's Guide to T. S. Eliot.* New York, 1953, London, 1955.

_____. *The Talent of T. S. Eliot.* Seattle, 1929.

WILLIAMSON, HUGH ROSS. *The Poetry of T. S. Eliot.* New York and London, 1932.

WILSON, EDMUND. *Axel's Castle.* New York and London, 1929.

_____. *The Bit Between My Teeth.* New York, 1965.

_____. *A Literary Chronicle: 1920–1950.* New York, 1956.

_____. *The Shock of Recognition.* New York, 1943.

WINTERS, YVOR. *In Defense of Reason.* Denver, 1947, 1959, London, 1960.

WOOLF, LEONARD. *Beginning Again.* New York and London, 1964.

Index

211